TOTTENHAM HOTSPUR

PLAYER BY PLAYER

IVAN PONTING

TOTTENHAM HOTSPUR

PLAYER BY PLAYER

GUINNESS PUBLISHING

ACKNOWLEDGEMENTS

The author would like to thank the following: Pat, Rosie and Joe Ponting, Steve Small, Charles Richards, Steve Perryman, Les Gold, Dave Mackay, Pat Jennings, Cliff Jones, Alan Mullery, Peter Taylor, Nigel Dando, Geoff Simms, Ken Jones, Alan Rosenthal, John Alsford, Morris Keston, Richard Mitchell, Glyn Church, Gavin Hadland, Barry Hugman, Laurie Gray, Alf D'Arcy, Simon Duncan, Tony Williams, Amanda Broughton, and never forgetting that indefatigable sleuth (and photographer!), Andy Cowie of Colorsport.

The author is also grateful for permission to reproduce photographs.
The vast majority are from the comprehensive library of Colorsport, whose willingness to go above and beyond the call of duty in the quest for pictures has been a crucial factor in the compilation of this book.

Efforts have been made to trace copyright holders of all photographs.
We apologise for any omissions, which are unintentional, and would be pleased to include appropriate acknowledgement in any subsequent edition.

Pictured on the front cover are: Jimmy Greaves *(top left)*; Pat Jennings *(centre left)*; Paul Gascoigne *(centre)*; Glenn Hoddle *(top right)*; Steve Perryman *(bottom left)*; Danny Blanchflower *(bottom centre)*; and Gary Lineker *(bottom right)*.

On the back are: *(centre)* Ossie Ardiles, *(clockwise from top left)* Dave Mackay, Chris Waddle, Martin Chivers, Garth Crooks, Alan Gilzean, and Gary Mabbutt,

First published in 1993 by
GUINNESS PUBLISHING
33 London Road, Enfield
Middlesex, EN2 6DJ

Designed and typeset by Steve Small

Text copyright © 1993 by Ivan Ponting

Illustrations copyright © 1993 as credited

A catalogue record for this book is available
from the British Library

Printed and bound in Great Britain by The Bath Press

'Guinness' is a registered trademark
of Guinness Publishing Ltd

ISBN: 0-85112-717-7

INTRODUCTION

Though football is an unrelentingly serious business for those who make their living from it - indeed, there are many who regret the grimness and commercialism that has permeated the game, particularly at the top level - it remains essentially an entertainment for the only people who make that living possible. I refer, of course, to the supporters, who seek and deserve so much in exchange for their loyalty and hard-earned cash. They want to be thrilled, to be diverted from the everyday round, to have their dreams enacted in front of their eyes by young men who spice strength, athleticism and professionalism with imagination, verve and even - at the very best of times - a touch of beauty. And so to Tottenham Hotspur. While it would be patently absurd to suggest that all, or even most, of Spurs' footballers down the years have been purveyors of style and culture, it is true, nevertheless, that the club has sought always to espouse a skilful, smooth, exhilarating mode of play and in the process has paraded a scintillating array of magical performers.

Between these pages I have endeavoured to do justice, in words and pictures, to all the heroes since 1958, as well as the legion of lesser lights so crucial to the fabric of any club's history. My starting point has a double significance, one obvious, the other personal: most important, it signalled the beginning of Bill Nicholson's long and glorious managerial reign; but also it coincided with the birth of my own addiction to soccer, which consumed me in early boyhood and has never loosened its hold. Since then I have been an avid spectator at grounds all over the country, and the evidence of my own eyes has been a central pillar of *Tottenham Hotspur Player by Player*. However, I have drawn extensively on the reminiscences of many former Tottenham players, who have been exceedingly generous with their time - a special mention here for Steve Perryman, who was gracious enough to contribute the foreword - as have some of the most knowledgeable and opinionated fans it has been my pleasure to meet.

The book contains a photograph of every man to wear the famous cockerel on his chest in senior competition since 1958/59. In almost every case, this is accompanied with my assessment of the individual; where he has played so few games as to render this meaningless, only his career figures are included. All records, including service with other clubs, are complete to May 15, 1993. As a number of excellent statistical works on Spurs exist already, I have attempted to dwell on the essence of each performer, seeking to portray something of his footballing character as well as detail his achievements, though all the essential facts - games played (with substitute appearances in brackets), goals scored, previous clubs, caps won etc - are included. Spurs appearance and scoring records appended to each profile refer to all matches (a breakdown for each competition appears at the end of the book) but under the heading of 'Other clubs', the games and goals are in the League only. The dates in large type refer to the seasons in which each man appeared in Tottenham's first team, not when he joined or left the club. Under 'Honours' I have included only those won with Spurs, except in the case of caps, the figures for which cover complete careers to date. All transfer fees are those reported in the press at the time.

I have paved the way for the main part of the book with a brief glimpse at Tottenham's post-War scene, which was dominated by Arthur Rowe's revered practitioners of 'push-and-run'. Dearly would I have loved to give them the comprehensive coverage accorded to their successors but, alas, I never saw them play. However, having been privileged to follow the fortunes of so many magnificent footballers in the white and navy-blue, it ill becomes me to cavil on that score. Though it can be fascinating and instructive to look back - at least, I hope so! - the future is of paramount importance, and at the time of writing, a new crop of exceptional talent is already in place on the White Hart Lane production line. How well that augurs for all who glory in the soccer institution that is Tottenham Hotspur.

Ivan Ponting

CONTENTS

PUSHING AND RUNNING

The history of Tottenham Hotspur has encompassed a succession of sides who have played their football attractively and with distinction, creating a tradition for which the White Hart Lane club has become justly renowned. But taking the long view, there are two teams who have stood out above all others, and it is no coincidence that they are the only two Spurs combinations to lift the League title since the Second World War.

The men who made up the second of these - the great League and FA Cup double-winners of 1961 - are dealt with in detail elsewhere in this book. But while the meat of *Tottenham Hotspur Player by Player* dwells on the era which began with Bill Nicholson's accession to the management in 1958, it would be inappropriate not to set the scene with a reference to Spurs' first Champions. Arthur Rowe's visionary 'push-and-run' method - based on ceaseless, fluid movement and wonderful skills - earned him and his team an immortal place in soccer folklore. It was enough to win the Second Division Championship in 1950, then cap that achievement by claiming the major crown a year later. The side was skippered by dynamic Welsh left-half Ron Burgess, and featured outstanding contributors such as inside-forward Eddie Baily - later to serve Spurs nobly as a coach - full-back Alf Ramsey, goalkeeper Ted Ditchburn and Nicholson himself as a supremely practical right-half. Though they finished as League runners-up in 1952 and reached the FA Cup semi-final in 1953, the team was to decline in the mid-fifties. Arthur Rowe, who had served Tottenham magnificently as a centre-half before the War, resigned in 1955 through ill health, his former deputy Jimmy Anderson stepping into the breach for three years. Though some of Jimmy's signings were to prove inspired, results were moderate and in October 1958 he departed, another victim of the stress attendant on the occupation of football club manager. Bill Nicholson's time had come.

ARTHUR ROWE

TOTTENHAM HOTSPUR AFTER THE WAR

Back row *(left to right):*

CECIL POYNTON (trainer).

ALF RAMSEY (49/50-54/5, full-back, 250 games, 24 goals).

LEN DUQUEMIN (47/8-56/7, centre-forward, 307 games, 134 goals).

PETER MURPHY (50/1-51/2, inside-forward, 38 games, 14 goals).

TED DITCHBURN (46/7-58/9, goalkeeper, 452 games, 0 goals).

HARRY CLARKE (48/9-56/7, centre-half, 322 games, 4 goals).

LES BENNETT (46/7-54/5, inside-forward, 294 games, 118 goals).

CHARLIE WITHERS (47/8-55/6, full-back, 164 games, 2 goals).

Front row:

BILL NICHOLSON (38/9-54/5, wing-half, 342 games, 6 goals).

SONNY WALTERS (46/7-55/6, winger, 233 games, 71 goals).

ARTHUR WILLIS (45/6-53/4, full-back, 160 games, 1 goal).

RON BURGESS (38/9-53/4, wing-half, 325 games, 16 goals).

EDDIE BAILY (46/7-55/6, inside-forward, 325 games, 69 goals).

LES MEDLEY (45/6-52/3, winger, 164 games, 46 goals).

Insets *left to right:*

VIC BUCKINGHAM (35/6-48/9, wing-half/full-back, 231 games, 1 goal).

RON REYNOLDS (52/3-57/8, goalkeeper, 95 games, 0 goals).

SID TICKRIDGE (46/7-50/1, full-back, 101 games, 0 goals).

Opposite page:

ARTHUR ROWE (31/2-37/8, centre-half, 201 games, 0 goals; manager 49-55).

FOREWORD BY STEVE PERRYMAN

A playing career in professional football is a very deceptive thing. When it's happening and going well, it feels as though it will last forever. When it's over, you realise how it flew past. So for people like myself, who have enjoyed a wonderful life courtesy of our great game, books like *Tottenham Hotspur Player by Player* are vital - to recapture the feeling of days that weren't just wonderful with hindsight, they were marvellous at the time.

Naturally, I am particularly proud to have been asked to write the foreword for a book about the club where I spent 19 years - from a humble start as the youngest player on the staff, to being the most experienced man and club skipper, taking in just about everything in between! In that time I was lucky enough (and I mean that when you consider how many players' careers are foreshortened by injury) to make my way to the club's record appearance mark. When it happened, that felt special, but as I flicked through this book and pored over the careers of the great Spurs players of the last 35 years, my personal pride in that achievement was redoubled.

Pride is a very important word as far as Tottenham Hotspur Football Club is concerned. Indeed, at White Hart Lane it was, and is, a key word. I was made aware when I was signed as a schoolboy by Bill Nicholson in 1967 that the club had certain standards on and off the field. Everyone was expected to aspire to those standards - and then adhere to them. They were standards that applied win or lose, in training or on match-days. I like to feel I honoured them.

Of course, in my time at Tottenham there were highs and lows. They're summed up for me by two games against the same club, Manchester City. They were our opponents under my captaincy when we lost 5-0 at Maine Road in May 1977 to be relegated to what was then Division Two - and they also faced us one May night in 1981 when, after a replay, I lifted the FA Cup, still as skipper. That's 12 years ago now and more achievements for the club have followed, as well as more individual highs and lows - that's the way it will always be.

But the constant factor at White Hart Lane remains pride. The symbolic jutting chest of the world-famous cockerel sums up what every player in this book will have felt each time he pulled on that pristine lilywhite shirt. I, for one, am grateful to have had that opportunity.

TED DITCHBURN

There must have been moments when the name of Ted Ditchburn made those who followed him between the Tottenham posts feel heartily sick. Even Ted's respected long-term successor, the Scottish star Bill Brown, and - astounding though it may seem in retrospect - the ultimately majestic Pat Jennings in his early, rather faltering days at White Hart Lane, were not immune to unflattering comparisons with the towering Kentish custodian. For 15 years and more after his retirement, if a cross was dropped or a shot fumbled, there would be dark mutterings - not only from the terraces but also from Spurs insiders - that such a calamity would never have happened in Ditchburn's day.
Of course, Ted made mistakes, but they were precious few and to see him line up behind the North Londoners' defence, all lithe muscle and imposing presence, it was difficult, at times, to doubt his omnipotence.

Certainly, this son of a professional boxer - as a youngster he had contemplated a career in the ring - possessed a range of goalkeeping qualities that was well-nigh complete. A magnificent catcher of crosses, breathtakingly agile on his line and endowed with fierce concentration, Ted was peerless in dealing with close-range threats, descending like some vast, grasping blanket to smother the ball at the feet of incoming forwards.
His reflexes, like his all-round fitness, were honed to a point where seemingly impossible saves became commonplace, a level of performance which owed much to a personally devised training routine in which he would combat point-blank shots in a non-stop sequence of dive, save, throw and dive again. Kicking was not the most impressive aspect of his game, but he made up for it by a fruitful understanding with Alf Ramsey, often launching attacks by throwing the ball to his thoughtful right-back, a method of distribution not often used at that time.

Ted's other huge asset was his quite staggering consistency. After joining Tottenham in 1939 and losing his early prime to the war, he missed just two League games in the seven post-war seasons - including an unbroken sequence of 247 outings between April 1948 and March 1954 - and many shrewd contemporary judges maintain he was the most important figure in Arthur Rowe's famous push-and-run side that won the Second and First Division titles in successive seasons. Those same observers aver, also, that Ted was the finest *club* 'keeper in the land, the qualification being necessary because of some unfathomably indifferent performances in an England jersey, his six caps being spread over eight years. Somehow, when representing his country, the confidence and boldness so familiar to Spurs fans appeared to desert him and, in an era of outstanding custodians, he lost out frequently to Bert Williams of Wolves in the contest to succeed the great Frank Swift. As the fifties wore on, Ted lost his Tottenham place periodically to Ron Reynolds, but always he buckled down uncomplainingly to spells in the reserves and every time he won back the senior role. His top-flight days ended with a broken finger at Chelsea in August 1958, and eight months later - by now the only survivor from the 1951 Championship team - he became player-boss of non-League Romford.

A forthright character on and off the field - fire and aggression were no handicaps to a 'keeper in the days when centre-forwards were allowed to make vigorous bodily contact - Ted left Spurs as one of the most beloved figures in the history of a club not exactly short of heroes. A tribute to his enduring reputation is that many experts cannot choose between Ditchburn and Jennings as the greatest custodian the Lane has known. More telling yet, others - including one Terry Venables - disdain equivocation by naming Ted as the top man. Persuasive advocacy, indeed.

BORN: Gillingham, Kent, 24.10.21.
GAMES: 452. GOALS: 0.
HONOURS: League Championship 50/1;
Second Division Championship 49/50.
6 England caps (48-56).

1946/47 - 1958/59

GEORGE ROBB

England amateur international star George Robb had already impressed in guest outings on the Tottenham left wing when Arthur Rowe signed the dashing, dark-haired teacher as a part-time professional from non-League Finchley in June 1953. On his debut, on Christmas Day 1951, he had scored in a 3-0 victory over Charlton Athletic and subsequent appearances had confirmed his talent. Understandably, George never quite matched the deeds of Les Medley, his brilliant predecessor, but when he left the club in 1958 he could look back on his stay at White Hart Lane with considerable pride. Playing under three managers in a period of under-achievement by Spurs, he had provided service that was at times exhilarating and never less than staunch, and he had won a full England cap into the bargain.

George was a strong-running, hard-shooting raider who made up in vigour and aggression what he lacked in Medley-style finesse. In 1953/54, his first full term, he netted 16 times in 37 matches and, following a concerted campaign by the London press, was called up by his country. Unfortunately for George the opponents were the majestic Hungarian side who, at least for those with eyes to see, nailed emphatically and enduringly the myth of eternal English superiority.

Though never capped again - the nearest he got was a trio of 'B' internationals - George continued to perform reliably at club level, and enjoyed a particularly active FA Cup campaign in 1956. After scoring three times in the early rounds, he was about to push the ball into an empty net for a semi-final equaliser against Manchester City when German goalkeeper Bert Trautmann appeared to grab his legs. Amazingly, no penalty was given and Spurs were out, leaving George to reflect - when a combination of age, knee injuries and the arrival of Cliff Jones signalled his retirement and full-time return to the classroom in 1958 - on a career devoid of medals but certainly not without worth.

BORN: Finsbury Park, London, 1.6.26.
GAMES: 200. GOALS: 58.
HONOURS: 1 England cap (53).

1951/52 - 1958/59

ALFIE STOKES

Viewed purely in cold statistics, the Tottenham career of Alfie Stokes remains something of a mystery. Here was a marksman who could occupy any inside trio position and whose goals-to-games ratio was remarkable - in the region of one strike every match-and-a-half. In addition, he was strong and skilful with a fierce shot and adequate pace; why then, was Alfie rarely assured of a regular berth, and why was he allowed to depart for Fulham, ostensibly a giveaway at £10,000, having netted 33 times in his last 50 League appearances?

The fact was that the well-liked blond local boy, who had signed for Spurs from non-League Clapton in February 1953, was maybe a mite too easy-going to forge a career at the top level. Habitually, it seemed, Alfie's best form would be displayed in the early part of a game, his contribution tending to fade disappointingly as the second half grew old, a circumstance which raised questions concerning fitness and commitment.

There was, however, no doubting the Stokes goal-scoring pedigree, especially when he was prompted by the likes of Tommy Harmer and Danny Blanchflower. He hit the target on his debut at Bolton in his first spring as a Spur, netted twice in his only outing for England under-23 in 1955, and on one unforgettable evening at White Hart Lane in September 1957 he cracked five past Birmingham City's England goalkeeper Gil Merrick.

That season Alfie played for the Football League and England 'B' but made no further progress and, languishing increasingly in the shadow of Bobby Smith at Tottenham, he took his talents to Craven Cottage in the summer of 1959. His sojourn with Fulham was brief, however, and after sampling non-League football, the amiable Alfie completed an ultimately rather unsatisfying career with a short stint at Watford.

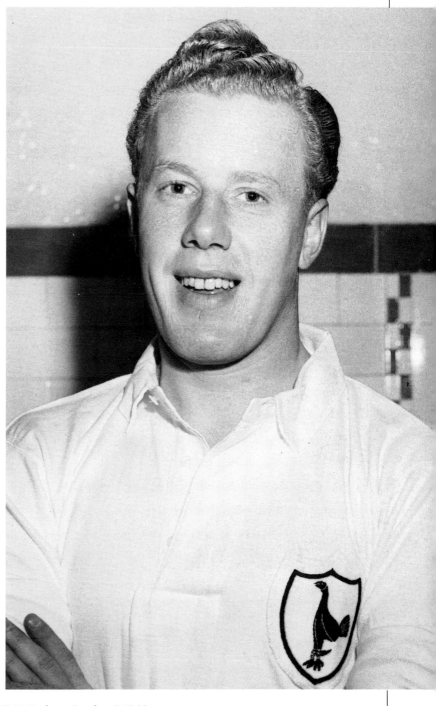

BORN: Hackney, London, 3.10.32.
GAMES: 69. GOALS: 42.
OTHER CLUBS: Fulham 59/60 (15, 6);
Cambridge City (non-League);
Watford 61/2 (14, 2).

1952/53 - 1958/59

DAVE DUNMORE

Dave Dunmore was a dashing centre-forward who flattered to deceive during six years at White Hart Lane. The unassuming north-easterner cost £10,500 from York City a few days before his 20th birthday in February 1954, and was given an early chance to show his mettle. Replacing the faithful Len Duquemin for the local derby at Highbury, he showed enough promise to earn an extended opportunity until season's end.

Building on this foundation, Dave started 1954/55 brightly, netting a home hat-trick against Wolves in the second game, and retained his place until 'The Duke' returned in January. Thereafter his progress was stunted both by National Service and the purchase of Bobby Smith, and never again did he quite convince as the Spurs' spearhead. Big, fast and with respectable control, Dave, who could also play on the right flank, was at his best running on to a ball played into space, and could climax his sprint with a dynamic shot. But too much of his most telling work was performed outside the box and he appeared to lose confidence at close range. This limited his effectiveness and in March 1960 he was exchanged for West Ham's John Smith. Later Dave enjoyed his most successful spell with Leyton Orient, top-scoring as the O's won promotion to the First Division in 1962.

BORN: Whitehaven, Cumberland, 8.2.34.
GAMES: 81. GOALS: 26.
OTHER CLUBS: Cliftonville, Northern Ireland;
York City 51/2-53/4 (48, 25);
West Ham United 59/60-60/1 (36, 16); Leyton Orient
60/1-64/5 (147, 55); York City 65/6-66/7 (63, 13).

1953/54 - 1959/60

JOHN RYDEN

John Ryden put his heart and soul into playing centre-half for Spurs, but in a time of transition for the North Londoners, he lacked the overall quality to make the position his own. The blond, angular Scot arrived from Accrington Stanley for £8,400 in November 1955 as one of Jimmy Anderson's first managerial signings. After waiting five months for his debut, he deputised for veteran Harry Clarke at Preston and made an immediate impression by scoring in a 3-3 draw. With Harry's career drawing to an end, John was given his first settled run in mid-1956/57 before making way for the younger and more mountainous Maurice Norman.

Nothing if not a trier - he was fearless in the tackle and combative, if not wholly dominant, in the air - he reclaimed the number-five shirt to kick off 1957/58 and became captain following the departure of Tony Marchi. That term John played his finest football, making 35 League appearances including a lengthy stint at left-half, as Tottenham finished third. But Maurice's game was improving while John's remained constant and a handful of appearances in 1958/59 proved to be his senior swansong. He remained at the Lane until June 1961, when he joined Watford before serving a succession of non-League clubs.

BORN: Dumbarton, Scotland, 18.2.31.
GAMES: 68. GOALS: 2.
OTHER CLUBS: Alloa Athletic 51/2-53/4;
Accrington Stanley 53/4-55/6 (80, 0);
Watford 61/2 (24, 1).

1955/56 - 1958/59

JOHNNY BROOKS

Through all their glory years, Spurs have boasted few more gifted footballers than one who never helped them to lift an honour.
In training Johnny Brooks displayed freely the most scintillating of skills: he was a brilliant dribbler who could lay defences to waste, he possessed superb touch with either foot, he was as clean and crisp a kicker of the ball as it is possible to imagine.
Yet so often, when it came to applying his abundant talent to the practical business of winning games, the curly-haired inside-forward failed to deliver. Some crucial ingredient - call it devil, determination or whatever - was missing from the Brooks make-up, and without it he was never going to fulfil that vast potential.

Not that Johnny's career was a flop; far from it. After arriving from Reading, his hometown club, in February 1953, he did much to convince Arthur Rowe of his fitness for a key role as that most thoughtful of managers set about major surgery to his beloved 'push-and-run' title-winners. Johnny, who could scheme and score with equal facility, gave some memorable displays in the mid-fifties but there was always an underlying, worrying lack of consistency. This was never illustrated more aptly than when in the winter of 1956, during which he was helping Spurs achieve an eventual runners-up slot in the First Division, he was picked for England, then dropped by his club within a month.

Thus Johnny's frustrating progress continued until December 1959 when Chelsea recruited him for their relegation battle, exchanging his services for those of Les Allen. Having helped to stave off the drop, he didn't linger at Stamford Bridge, seeing out his career in the lower divisions.
He will go down as a player with special abilities but one who, perhaps, never relished life among the muck and bullets. Johnny, whose son Shaun was to enjoy a long League career, retained his appetite for the game and his fitness long after retirement and was playing local football beyond his 60th birthday.

BORN: Reading, Berkshire, 23.12.31.
GAMES: 179. GOALS: 51.
HONOURS: 3 England caps (56).
OTHER CLUBS: Reading 49/50-52/3 (46, 5);
Chelsea 59/60-60/1 (46, 6); Brentford 61/2-63/4 (83, 36);
Crystal Palace 63/4 (7, 0).

1952/53 - 1959/60

DANNY BLANCHFLOWER

Twentieth-century soccer has produced no more inspiring, challenging and downright fascinating personality than Danny Blanchflower. A born leader who captained Spurs to their unforgettable triumphs of the early sixties, the charming but waspishly outspoken Ulsterman was a revolutionary free thinker, an incurable romantic and perhaps the most beguiling talker the game has known. But though he held forth so eloquently, Danny was no mere blarney merchant. Anyone fortunate enough to have caught him at the zenith of his playing powers, between 1957 and 1962, would speak of a magnificently creative right-half who could dictate the tempo of a game like few footballers before or since.

Wirily slim, though minimally endowed with power and pace, Danny possessed the priceless knack of losing his marker at crucial moments. Having thus seized centre stage, he imposed his presence emphatically, dispensing shrewd first-time passes, both long and short, that could paralyse at a stroke the most meticulously marshalled defence. Always he wanted the ball and would demand it vociferously; then his poise and grace would be seen at their most vivid, often wherever the combat raged fiercest and no matter how dire the physical danger.

Such rare qualities had impressed Tottenham manager Arthur Rowe who, in December 1954, outbid Arsenal to sign the artistic 28-year-old from Aston Villa for £30,000, then a British record for a half-back. Having bemused the staid Villa Park regime by suggesting tactical experiments, the Irishman was captivated by Spurs' intricate passing style. What might have matured into a visionary partnership was fractured when ill health forced Arthur's retirement, but Danny progressed to the captaincy under Jimmy Anderson, only to be deprived of it in April 1956 after his bold bid to reverse the tide in an FA Cup semi-final against Manchester City by making positional changes had ended in defeat. Ironically, similar enterprise had paid off in earlier matches.

Despite this hiccup, the Blanchflower influence continued to grow and in 1957/58 he completed what many contemporaries assert was his finest individual season, then led his valiant countrymen to the quarter-finals of the World Cup. Even then, however, the path to glory was not to be unremittingly smooth. New boss Bill Nicholson, from whom Danny had inherited Spurs' number-four shirt, dropped him the following winter, declaring the Irishman to be invaluable in a good side but a luxury in a poor one, and citing the need for more defensive input. A transfer request was refused before the 33-year-old was reinstalled as captain in March 1959, immediately displaying the majestic form that he was to maintain through the League and FA Cup double campaign and beyond.

Defying the evidence of his birth certificate, Danny was voted Footballer of the Year in 1961 - as he had been in 1958 - and continued to plot his opponents' downfall, both as Britain's canniest midfield general and by taking an increasingly dominant role in training, until suffering severe knee damage against Rangers at Ibrox in December 1962. Even then he carried on, his distribution destroying OFK Belgrade in the Cup Winners' Cup semi-final and, having been injected with painkillers, he performed nobly in the final thrashing of Atletico Madrid. Come 1964, aged 38 and in considerable discomfort, he could no longer stave off the inevitable: the great footballing intellectual, perfectionist and wit, a coaxer of lesser lights, champion of players' rights and mortal foe of self-righteous authority, had played his last game.

Later Danny, who was Bill Nicholson's choice to succeed him at the White Hart Lane helm - the board were less keen on such an independent spirit - excelled as a journalist and dabbled elsewhere in management before falling tragic prey to a debilitating illness in his sixties. Nothing, though, could erase the name of Danny Blanchflower from any list of the sporting elite; he was the ultimate in soccer culture.

BORN: Belfast, 10.2.26. GAMES: 382. GOALS: 21.
HONOURS: European Cup Winners' Cup 62/3; League Championship 60/1;
FA Cup 60/1, 61/2.
56 Northern Ireland caps (49-62).
OTHER CLUBS: Glentoran, Northern Ireland, 45/6-48/9;
Barnsley 48/9-50/1 (68, 2);
Aston Villa 50/1-54/5 (148, 10).
MANAGER: Chelsea (78-79); Northern Ireland (79).

1954/55 - 1963/64

JOHNNY HILLS

In the late fifties, Peter Baker stood between Johnny Hills and a regular berth in the Tottenham first team. Unfortunately for Johnny, like many a wingman of the era he was unable to find a way around the stalwart and more experienced right-back. Recruited from non-League Gravesend by Arthur Rowe in August 1953, Johnny waited four years for his senior debut, ousting Peter on merit for the second half of the 1957/58 term, in which Spurs recovered from a disappointing start to finish a creditable third. During this period of grace, the powerful, stockily-built Hills let no one down, tackling hard, keeping his game simple and offering a potent attacking option with his long throw-ins. But there was a question-mark over both his positional play and speed of recovery and, quite simply, he lacked the overall class of his rival.

Thereafter Peter returned, and although Johnny remained at the Lane until 1960/61, he didn't get a game as the League and Cup double was won, having fallen behind Ken Barton in the pecking order of deputies. That summer he joined Bristol Rovers but, sadly, injury brought a premature end to the Eastville career of this cheerful Kentishman, an all-round sportsman who wielded a cricket bat with memorable verve.

BORN: Northfleet, Kent, 24.2.34.
GAMES: 32. GOALS: 0.
OTHER CLUBS: Bristol Rovers 61/2 (7, 0).

1957/58 - 1959/60

JIM ILEY

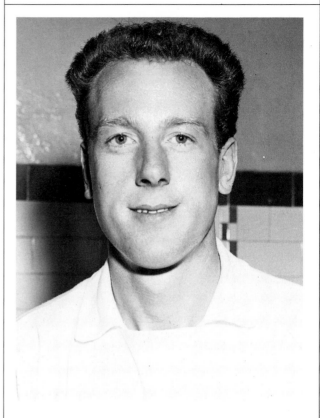

Mention the name of Jim Iley to most football fans and they will conjure up an image of Newcastle United's bold, bald midfield driving-force in the middle and late sixties. But Tottenham aficionados of the previous decade will recall a fellow with a little more hair who was bought from Sheffield United by manager Jimmy Anderson in August 1957 to replace the temporarily departed Tony Marchi.

In fact, Jim was a splendidly creative wing-half who might have carved a long-term niche at White Hart Lane had he not been paired with Danny Blanchflower. The two smooth-passing prompters offered contributions that were too similar, and they had a disconcerting habit of sallying forward together, thus leaving yawning gaps behind them. Though there were a few occasions when the Yorkshireman was preferred to Danny, there could be no doubt - with no slight intended to an admirable and popular performer - that the Irishman was the better player, and it was no surprise in August 1959 when Bill Nicholson allowed Jim to join Nottingham Forest. But it was as a Magpie that his all-round ability and leadership qualities were seen to best advantage, before he embarked on a solid managerial career in the lower divisions.

BORN: South Kirkby, Yorkshire, 15.12.35.
GAMES: 57. GOALS: 1.
OTHER CLUBS: Sheffield United 54/5-57/8 (99, 7); Nottingham Forest 59/60-62/3 (92, 3); Newcastle United 62/3-68/9 (232, 15); Peterborough United 68/9-72/3 (68, 4).
MANAGER: Peterborough United (69-72); Barnsley (73-78); Blackburn Rovers (78); Bury (80-84); Exeter City (84-85).

1957/58 - 1958/59

MEL HOPKINS

A sickening accident on international duty robbed Mel Hopkins of his Tottenham place as Bill Nicholson's side were on the threshold of greatness. The Welshman's nose was smashed horrifically in a collision with Scotland's Ian St John at Hampden Park in November 1959, leaving Ron Henry to slip into Spurs' left-back berth. Until then Ron had been no more than an understudy and there had been no question of Mel standing down; but the Englishman took his chance so well that he wore the number-three shirt through the 1960/61 League and FA Cup double campaign and half a decade beyond.

It was a cruel cut for Mel, who certainly would not have disgraced that great team. While his loping, spidery gait made him seem awkward, that was a deceptive impression of an accomplished all-rounder. Aerially combative and quick, he passed smoothly and those long legs were adept at last-minute saving tackles, even if he didn't exude *quite* the same aura of impregnability as his successor. He enjoyed getting forward, too, though the nearest he came to the scoresheet was hitting the bar in his only European encounter, at home to Slovan Bratislava in March 1963.

Mel, who grew up in a Rhondda rugby stronghold and as a boy had to form his own team to get a game of soccer, was highly rated by Spurs boss Arthur Rowe, who blooded him as a 17-year-old at Derby in October 1952. With Arthur Willis and Charlie Withers ageing, he claimed a regular place in 1954/55 and retained it ably until that fateful day at Hampden. His international career flourished, too, the highlight being the 1958 World Cup, Wales bucking the odds to reach the quarter-final in which the left-back gave a faultless display against the revered Garrincha.

After five years in the White Hart Lane shadows, Mel followed Bobby Smith to Brighton in October 1964, playing a sterling part in that season's Fourth Division Championship triumph. That medal was the least he deserved.

BORN: Ystrad, South Wales, 7.11.34.
GAMES: 240. GOALS: 0.
HONOURS: 34 Wales caps (56-63).
OTHER CLUBS: Brighton 64/5-66/7 (58, 2);
Ballymena, Northern Ireland;
Bradford Park Avenue 68/9-69/70 (30, 0).

1952/53 - 1963/64

TOMMY HARMER

Tommy Harmer was born too late to be a soccer superstar. Perhaps in the first half of the century, before the clarion calls for strength, speed and stamina were so stridently insistent, this frail but wondrously gifted Tom Thumb of an inside-forward would have been feted as an entertainer supreme. Lamentably for those who delight in sleight of foot, revering artistry while remaining unmoved by mere athleticism, he was granted a comparatively brief tenure as Spurs' premier play-maker.

For sheer wizardry on the ball, Tommy was unrivalled. Shy and nervous in the dressing room - half a calming cigarette before a game, with the rest saved for half-time, became a Harmer ritual - he was capable of an astonishing transformation if the Muse was with him when he walked on to the pitch. There he became impudent, even insolent at times, tempting the lungers and scythers into his orbit before swaying his puny frame and dancing away with the ball at his feet. Yet beguiling though his dribbling undoubtedly was, it was matched inspirationally by a passing technique that bordered on the sublime. Tommy was a master of backspin, swerve and every variation of trajectory, and, moreover, could produce his devilish manipulations in the heat of battle.

So with such prodigious ability, why did the gaunt-featured 5ft 6in Eastender not claim a regular first-team slot until he was 28? The answer is not merely his lack of physical stature - which years of special beef-steak diets failed dismally to improve - although certainly that was a major factor, causing him to be relatively ineffective in a significant percentage of matches. But he was handicapped, too, by turning professional in 1948, at a time when Spurs were developing their distinctive push-and-run style. Manager Arthur Rowe, while recognising Tommy's rare talent, reckoned that he interrupted the flow of his fluid combination, consequently not offering the schemer a senior debut until he was 23 and limiting his opportunities thereafter.

Policy changed drastically when Jimmy Anderson succeeded Arthur in mid-decade, and for two seasons Tommy flourished in a delightfully creative midfield partnership with Danny Blanchflower which helped Tottenham finish as First Division runners-up in 1956/57 - during which Tommy answered criticism about his lightweight contribution by netting 17 League goals - and come third the following term. As the decade drew towards its close with Bill Nicholson now at the helm, Tommy remained a near-regular, occasionally appearing as a deep-lying outside-right.

The beginning of the end for the little Londoner was the arrival in October 1959 of John White, though at first they played together as twin inside-forwards, then in tandem on the right flank. But the balance was wrong and, understandably in view of his 32 years, Tommy made way. A £6,000 fee took him to Watford in October 1960 - reluctance to stray far from his home city led him to reject approaches from higher-ranking but more distant clubs - and later he lent his experience to Tommy Docherty's young braves at Chelsea, scoring the goal that won promotion to the top flight in 1963, before coaching at Stamford Bridge.

At White Hart Lane, where he was held in high affection, fans still recount tales of his uplifting performances, none more remarkable than in the 10-4 annihilation of Everton in 1958, in which legend has it he made nine goals and scored one! Movingly described by Danny Blanchflower as a beloved outcast, he was arguably the right man at the wrong time for Spurs, missing out on the League and FA Cup double and contenting himself philosophically with an England 'B' cap as his sole representative honour. Born too late? Maybe, but those who watched him play should guard the memory jealously. The like of Tommy Harmer will not be seen again.

BORN: Hackney, London, 2.2.28.
GAMES: 222. GOALS: 51.
OTHER CLUBS: Watford 60/1-61/2 (63, 6);
Chelsea 62/3-63/4 (8, 1).

1951/52 - 1959/60

PETER BAKER

In terms of popular public acclaim, Peter Baker was the poor relation in Tottenham Hotspur's greatest side. Of the other so-called journeymen in the 1960/61 League and FA Cup-winning combination, even his similarly unsung full-back partner and close pal Ron Henry went on to earn the kudos of an England cap, while the only other non-internationals, Les Allen and Terry Dyson, inevitably grabbed more of the limelight as members of a free-scoring forward line. Yet the slightest suggestion that Peter was fortunate to find a place in such star-studded company was rejected emphatically by the only authorities who mattered, his team-mates and manager at White Hart Lane.

In fact, the blond, squarely-built number-two was a consummate professional who performed a crucial and highly specialised function - albeit of the unspectacular variety - in the double-winning side. No verdict on Peter's contribution is valid without due consideration of the telling circumstance that the right-half in front of him was a certain Danny Blanchflower, and though it was undeniably a privilege to be in the presence of such an immense talent, life behind the Irish rover was not always easy. When his adventurous skipper disappeared on his habitual attacking sorties, Peter found himself frequently with two men to mark, and occasionally with an unholy mess that was not of his own making to clear up.

The loyal Londoner was perfectly equipped for the demanding role. Fast and intelligent, composed and reliable, he was not prone to commit himself to rash challenges, electing instead to jockey opponents away from the danger area until cover arrived. When the need arose, however, he could be remorselessly hard in the tackle and was brave too, as he showed when heading the ball off Albert Cheesebrough's boot to deny the Leicester winger an almost certain goal in the 1961 FA Cup Final. Although not prone to over-elaboration on the ball - Peter's preferred option was the simple push to Blanchflower - occasionally he would catch opponents unawares, unleashing a sudden, penetrating through-pass after appearing to dally tranquilly in possession. Add to that his powers of motivation - he was voluble both on and off the field - and the picture of a splendidly capable competitor is complete.

Indeed there was a time in the early fifties, after he had arrived at the Lane from local amateurs Enfield, that the youth international inspired predictions of a long-term England career. Then, having made his League debut alongside the veteran Bill Nicholson in April 1953, he settled as understudy to no less a personage than Alf Ramsey, from whom he learned voraciously. However, possibly the weight of expectation was detrimental and his rate of progress slowed so much that when the future England boss departed in 1955, Peter found himself losing out to Charlie Withers and Maurice Norman in the contest for the right-back berth. He persevered, though, winning a regular place in 1956/57, surviving a challenge from Johnny Hills the following term, and emerging to play a full part in Tottenham's early-sixties triumphs.

One of the older members of that wonderful side - as the irreverent Jimmy Greaves, who as a boy had hunted the Baker autograph, never tired of reminding him - Peter nevertheless continued to offer stalwart service until mid-decade, seeing off one stern challenge from Mel Hopkins before the young Cyril Knowles arrived to take his place. Still supremely fit - probably the best all-round sportsman at the club - Peter emigrated to South Africa in 1965, becoming player-boss of Durban City before embarking on a successful business career in that country. He could depart happily and honourably, knowing that only a very fine player could have satisfied that ultimate perfectionist, Bill Nicholson, for so long.

BORN: Hampstead, London, 10.12.31.
GAMES: 342. GOALS: 3.
HONOURS: European Cup Winners' Cup 62/3;
League Championship 60/1;
FA Cup 60/1, 61/2.

1952/53 - 1964/65

BOBBY SMITH

Bobby Smith was an immense individual - in terms of physique, personality and, yes, footballing talent. Down the years there were always elitists who decried the bulky, bustling buccaneer of a centre-forward as crude and uncomely, the type who might have his uses as a battering ram but who lacked the necessary class for Spurs and England. Yet while the broad-shouldered son of a Yorkshire miner could be awesomely aggressive - indeed, he put the fear of God into faint-hearted opponents and was not above heightening the effect with the kind of menacing mien beloved of boxers before a fight - it was, and is, scandalously unjust to write him off as a mere slugger.

The record books offer eloquent testimony, but more of that later; first, let the memory reveal the extent of Bobby's skills. Most easily recalled, perhaps, are his rather similar goals against Leicester and Burnley in the FA Cup Finals of 1961 and 1962. In both cases he controlled the ball with one sure touch, wrongfooted his marker by sheer guile, then netted unstoppably. Equally exhilarating was his strike as Spurs clinched the title at home to Sheffield Wednesday in April 1961: in a glorious blur of action he flicked the ball over one of his England colleagues, Peter Swan, then strode on to crash a first-time half-volley past another, Ron Springett. But for sheer artistry - yes, we *are* still talking about Bobby Smith - that was nothing compared to his perfectly-judged chip over Spain's goalkeeper at Wembley in 1960, a moment that graced the international stage he was to occupy so fleetingly.

Now for those statistics. In his first five years at White Hart Lane, Bobby became the highest scorer in Tottenham history; he exceeded 30 League and Cup goals in each of the four seasons between 1957/58, in which he notched 38 in 40 outings, and 1960/61, the year of the double; and for his country he hit the target 13 times in 15 games before being discarded.
All that must have seemed unthinkable to the fans who jeered him as a carthorse following his £18,000 purchase from Chelsea, then champions, in December 1955. At Stamford Bridge, Bobby had languished in the shadow of Roy Bentley and the apparent absence of tactical acumen in his early Spurs appearances appeared to indicate why. But before long the goals flowed in profusion, manager Jimmy Anderson's judgement was vindicated and Tottenham's intensely demanding terrace critics took the burly marksman to their hearts. At this time there were many Smith performances to savour, but especially satisfying was an Old Trafford hat-trick in November 1957 that lifted the North Londoners to victory over the pre-Munich Busby Babes and spawned talk of silverware.

In fact, it would be several years before space was needed in the White Hart Lane trophy cabinet, but Bobby's eminence grew rapidly and he was even tried as club captain. A happy-go-lucky soul who enjoyed himself ebulliently and could hardly be described as a stickler for training, he was not an ideal choice as skipper and his reign was short. But with Danny Blanchflower in charge, both Bobby and Spurs prospered royally, and it was not until 1962/63, when he was dropped temporarily in favour of Les Allen, that his star began to fall. In the past he had seemed impervious to pain, sometimes taking the pitch with severely swollen ankles, but now, perhaps, the years of taking punishment as well as dispensing it were beginning to have an effect.

Thus in May 1964, with pace if not power diminished, Bobby joined Brighton for a paltry £5,000 and scored freely to help the Seagulls take the Fourth Division title. Thereafter he entered non-League football, his weight ballooned and he experienced hard times. But no amount of personal misfortune could deprive Bobby Smith of his place among Spurs' all-time greats. Whatever the snipers said, that was his by right.

BORN: Lingdale, Yorkshire, 22.2.33.
GAMES: 317. GOALS: 208.
HONOURS: European Cup Winners' Cup 62/3; League Championship 60/1;
FA Cup 60/1, 61/2.
15 England caps (60-63).
OTHER CLUBS: Chelsea 50/1-55/6 (74, 23);
Brighton 64/5 (31, 18).

1955/56 - 1963/64

TERRY MEDWIN

Terry Medwin was a blond-thatched, fleet-footed attacker whose exhilarating right-flank dashes and goal-scoring menace took the eye throughout the late fifties and early sixties. Sadly for the Welsh international, the one season in which he was comprehensively eclipsed by constant rival Terry Dyson was 1960/61, when Spurs won the double.

An £18,000 recruit from his hometown club of Swansea in May 1956, Terry made a telling early impact in the number-seven shirt, helping Tottenham finish as League runners-up in his first term. He crossed the ball precisely, boasted a powerful shot in either foot and was sufficiently adept in the air to merit infrequent stints at centre-forward, the role in which he struck four times in the 6-0 home thrashing of Leicester in April 1959. That day he capitalised implacably on the service of Danny Blanchflower, with whom he enjoyed a fruitful understanding - occasionally the two would stage-manage a bogus argument over a throw-in to catch opponents off guard.

However, it must be said that ruthlessness was not a prime characteristic of the Medwin game. Considerably more gifted than Dyson, he lacked some of the smaller man's spirit and aggression, leaving Bill Nicholson with a perpetually difficult choice. In favour of the former Swan was his strike-rate - he netted 14 League goals in each of his first three Spurs campaigns - though ironically when he regained his place periodically in the post-double years he was less prolific.

To the satisfaction of the many who championed his cause, the genial Terry played just enough games - deputising on either flank for Dyson and Cliff Jones - to earn a Championship medal in 1961, and made up for that year's Wembley absence by helping to beat Burnley in the 1962 final. A broken leg on the 1963 summer tour of South Africa brought premature retirement, though later he returned to the professional game by coaching at Fulham, then serving Swansea as assistant manager to John Toshack.

BORN: Swansea, 25.9.32.
GAMES: 215. GOALS: 72.
HONOURS: League Championship 60/1; FA Cup 61/2.
30 Wales caps (53-62).
OTHER CLUBS: Swansea Town 51/2-55/6 (148, 59).

1956/57 - 1962/63

TONY MARCHI

Rarely can a newspaper tag have been more unwelcome than the one foisted on Tony Marchi in 1960/61. The tall, elegant utility man was dubbed the best reserve in British football, a compliment of a kind but hardly ideal for a talented performer in his prime who could only kick his heels in frustration as his team-mates won the League and FA Cup double.

Tony was, it should be stressed, a Spurs man heart and soul. London-born of an Italian father, he had been an ardent fan as a boy whose uncle, George Dorling, had once played for the club. So it was that he turned down Arsenal to sign for Arthur Rowe and made his debut as a teenage deputy for left-half Ron Burgess in the 1949/50 Division Two Championship side. Thereafter chances were few until the mid-fifties, when he inherited Ron's shirt and became an influential team member.

The Marchi game consisted of skill and vision combined with a reassuringly solid presence. He was a composed, intelligent reader of play who exuded a certain arrogance, but as he strode confidently around the pitch there were times when he appeared to lack urgency. This impression, heightened by his meagre pace, fuelled the case of those who maintained he would never reach the highest class.

Nevertheless Tony was an England 'B' international and much-respected club captain when he joined Lanerossi for £42,000 in 1957. Two years later a £20,000 fee brought him back as the eventual replacement, or so the pundits thought, for Danny Blanchflower. But the Irishman didn't see it like that and with Dave Mackay immovable in the other wing-half slot, Tony was on the margin. However, as Spurs suffered injury problems after 1962, he was often in the side and his Italian experience was crucial in his role as an extra defender in European campaigns. His reward was to replace the sidelined Mackay in the 1963 Cup Winners' Cup Final, and the biggest tribute to Tony is that Dave was barely missed. In 1965, he left to manage non-League Cambridge City, then held the reins at Northampton Town.

BORN: Edmonton, London, 21.1.33.
GAMES: 260. GOALS: 7.
HONOURS: European Cup Winners' Cup 62/3.
OTHER CLUBS: Lanerossi, Torino and Juventus, (all Italy).
MANAGER: Northampton Town (67-68).

1949/50 - 1956/57 & 1959/60 - 1964/65

MAURICE NORMAN

Nature intended Maurice Norman to be a centre-half. To begin with, there was an awesomely powerful physique which would have served him splendidly had he made his living farming the fields of his native Norfolk; then, if 6ft 1in of muscular athleticism was not enough to make opposing marksmen quail, the effect of towering dominance was heightened by the shock of wavy black hair that stood out several inches from the crown of his head. Not that Maurice - irreverently but affectionately dubbed 'Swede' by Jimmy Greaves, in reference to his bucolic background - conformed conveniently to the strong-but-limited stopper stereo-type. Indeed, the Norman game was infused with highly distinctive character, never more evi-dent than when he sallied out of defence, cantering down the centre of the pitch with neck outstretched and long limbs extended in unexpected directions, like some fantastic cross between runaway giraffe and quickstepping spider.

Maurice's enduring fame is assured by his presence as pivot in the League and FA Cup double-winning side of 1961, yet when he arrived at White Hart Lane from Norwich City in November 1955 - in exchange for £18,000 and winger Johnny Gavin - he was a right-back. Indeed, the quietly-spoken newcomer won England under-23 honours in both full-back berths and had to wait behind the less effective John Ryden before emerging as the long-term successor to Harry Clarke. It was not until the autumn of 1957 that he could call the central position his own, and even then there were occasions when he appeared nervy and lacking in confidence. But experience brought true authority and by the turn of the decade, Maurice was exhibiting the attributes that made him a crucial cornerstone of Bill Nicholson's team. Of paramount impact, of course, was his aerial ability at both ends of the pitch; he was one of the first centre-halves to make a habit of attacking excursions - none more productive than his important headed goal in an Eastertime encounter with Chelsea at Stamford Bridge in 1961 - and while his personal tally was hardly startling, the mere fact of his attendance was often enough to unsettle opponents into making costly mistakes.

As a tackler, he was usually firm though occasionally awkward, as if he couldn't decide with which foot to meet the ball, and he gave the impression of preferring interceptions, at which he was magnificently adept. So often the ball appeared sure to bypass Maurice when a leg would shoot out to claim possession, sometimes with its owner seeming to perform contortions in mid-air. His enviable sense of anticipation was underpinned by speed unusual in such a big man, enabling him to fill gaps left by more creative colleagues, to recover quickly if beaten and, not least, to compensate for a certain ponderousness on the turn. This latter weakness could make Maurice vulnerable to quick, skilful centre-forwards who were given space to run at him, as Arsenal's David Herd demonstrated devastatingly with a two-goal display at Highbury in 1958.

Overall, though, he was a formidable contributor to Tottenham's success, and his two years of regular England service in the early sixties were well deserved. Come 1965, by then in his thirties and operating once more at right-back, Maurice suffered an horrific accident in a home friendly with a Hungarian Select XI, his leg being broken in five places. Despite a two-year fitness fight, during which his shinbone had to be reset, he was forced to retire, and Spurs had lost not only a marvellous player but also an impeccable ambassador for the game. Testimony to both his attitude and his popularity came when local fans formed a team and christened it Norman FC. His reaction was to offer sincere encouragement and become club president. That said it all about Maurice Norman.

BORN: Mulbarton, Norfolk, 8.5.34.
GAMES: 411. GOALS: 19.
HONOURS: European Cup Winners' Cup 62/3;
League Championship 60/1;
FA Cup 60/1, 61/2.
23 England caps (62-64).
OTHER CLUBS: Norwich City 54/5-55/6 (35, 0).

1955/56 - 1965/66

RON HENRY

It was the biggest day in the history of Tottenham Hotspur; the gaze of the sporting world was riveted on Bill Nicholson's wondrous assembly of artists as they lined up against Leicester City at Wembley as white-hot favourites to complete the much-coveted League and FA Cup double. But which of Spurs' extravagant firmament of stars would dazzle on the grand stage? Inevitably, the names of Blanchflower and Mackay, Jones and White, were on the pundits' lips; Smith, too, was mentioned as a possible key man. But when it came to this last, nerve-twanging obstacle between Spurs and eternal soccer glory, the popular heroes were, in general, less than scintillating - and the performer who took the eye most vividly was the unfussy, untrumpeted but utterly efficient left-back Ron Henry.

That afternoon the neat, compact Londoner, whose upright, correct carriage was strikingly reminiscent of Alf Ramsey, gave a well-nigh perfect display of positioning and tackling, interception and distribution, shackling the dangerous Howard Riley and barring all Leicester progress down the Tottenham left flank. Ron's all-round excellence was encapsulated in one dextrous manoeuvre that thwarted Albert Cheesebrough as he hared for the byline. It seemed that the winger had broken through, with Ron and his fellow defenders trailing, when the Henry leg snaked out to trap the ball and avert a potential crisis. After the match many critics declared that the classy number-three was a natural for England, but with Ray Wilson and Mick McNeil then vying for a place in a successful national side, Ron had to wait two more years for his call-up. When it came - in Ramsey's first game as manager - England lost 5-1 to France and the Spurs man paid the penalty, never getting another chance at the top level.

To be consigned so summarily to the international scrapheap seemed rough justice on a splendidly consistent all-rounder who was renowned for his perfectly timed sliding tackles but whose subtle skill in ushering opponents into unprofitable avenues was perhaps even more valuable. Though Ron could appear ponderous on the turn, it was rare that a winger got past him, and critics of his heavy left-sided bias could not claim that it prevented him linking sweetly in the flowing passing movements for which Spurs became famous. There had been a time, however, when it seemed he might never rise from the reserve ranks in which he spent the mid-fifties. After being spotted as a teenage outside-left when stationed at Woolwich during his National Service, Ron was converted into a left-half and made his senior debut as a centre-half before becoming a left-back - only to be confronted by an apparently immovable obstacle to his first-team ambitions in the form of Mel Hopkins. But he refused to give up and in 1959 his patience was rewarded when the Welshman was sidelined by a serious injury. Even then, most observers judged that Ron would fill in only until Mel regained fitness, but they had reckoned without the deputy's determination. In the event, his form made it impossible for Bill Nicholson to drop him, he was ever-present throughout the 1960/61 double-winning campaign, and contributed nobly to subsequent triumphs.

Ron, who served briefly as skipper in the post-Blanchflower days, retained his place until knee trouble ended his senior tenure in the mid-sixties, but not before netting a belated first goal of his career in February 1965, his speculative 35-yarder against eventual champions Manchester United amazing and delighting a packed White Hart Lane. There followed doughty service for the reserves and 'A' team, combined with a coaching stint in which his honesty and directness proved of immeasurable benefit to the club's young hopefuls. Few men have given more to the cause of Tottenham Hotspur than Ron Henry.

BORN: Shoreditch, London, 17.8.34.
GAMES: 287. GOALS: 1.
HONOURS: European Cup Winners' Cup 62/3;
League Championship 60/1; FA Cup 60/1, 61/2.
1 England cap (63).

1954/55 - 1965/66

BILL BROWN

Bill Brown didn't conform to the popular notion of what a goalkeeper should look like. He was tall, sure enough, but where the majority of top custodians boasted immense, muscular frames suggestive of barrier-like impregnability, Bill was lean and stringy and seemingly insubstantial; every line of the Brown figure was angular, an effect heightened by his aquiline features. But - and this was all that mattered - throughout Spurs' most fruitful era, he did his job magnificently.

The point was that the Scottish international was ideally tailored to Tottenham's needs. If the one occasional weakness in his game was collecting crosses, that was hardly relevant with mountainous Maurice Norman in front of him, and in other respects Bill was impeccable. Agile but unshowy, he was a superb shot-stopper possessed of keen reflexes, perceptive positional sense and unparalleled powers of concentration. This last-mentioned quality was crucial in the days when Spurs were accustomed to dominate matches and he might remain isolated for long periods. It was reassuring for the fans - at least, those who could wrest their eyes momentarily from the attacking exploits of Blanchflower and company - to note their 'keeper half-crouching in an attitude of total involvement when all the action was taking place at the opposite end of the pitch. In his own mind, Bill kicked every ball and made every challenge, and often left the field looking drained after games in which he had been a virtual spectator.

Composure was another Brown attribute, particularly when the stakes were highest. He was never known to fail in a big match, performing immaculately in the FA Cup Finals of 1961 and 1962, in which he made a mockery of any supposed aerial fallibility. But it was during the triumphant Cup Winners' Cup campaign of 1963 that Bill was seen at his admirable best, rarely more so than in the quarter-final first leg defeat by Slovan in Bratislava. Playing with a plaster across his nose after taking a heavy knock, he defied the Czechs with a series of stirring saves, limiting their lead to two and paving the way for eventual victory. Then came two splendid semi-final displays against OFK Belgrade, but his *piece de resistance* was reserved for the final encounter with Atletico Madrid. By half-time Spurs were 2-0 up and apparently coasting, but then the Spaniards scored a penalty and for 15 minutes they peppered the Londoners' goal. As his fellow defenders reeled in the face of the onslaught, the 'keeper stood firm, coping heroically until the crisis had passed and three more Tottenham strikes secured the trophy.

It was the fourth major prize to come Bill's way since his £16,500 transfer from Dundee in June 1959. Although, at 27 and an established international, he had hardly represented a gamble in an age before Scottish net-minders became a prime source of material for English comedians, Spurs followers were relieved by his contribution after Ted Ditchburn's understudies had failed to make the grade . The green jersey became Bill's personal property until spring 1964, when injuries began to erode his position, and a callow Irishman named Pat Jennings arrived that summer. For two seasons, veteran and youngster vied for the job, playing an almost equal number of games, but in the end there could be only one winner and in October 1966 the older man left for Northampton.

Bill, who later emigrated to Canada, left behind many friends in North London. They speak fondly of a modest fellow who smoked incessantly and never put on weight despite indulging a voracious appetite; and professionally, while Messrs Ditchburn and Jennings must take precedence, Bill Brown proved beyond doubt that he was worth his place in any team.

BORN: Arbroath, Scotland, 8.10.31.
GAMES: 262. GOALS: 0.
HONOURS: European Cup Winners' Cup 62/3;
League Championship 60/1;
FA Cup 60/1, 61/2.
28 Scotland caps (58-65).
OTHER CLUBS: Dundee 49/50-58/9 (214, 0);
Northampton Town 66/7 (17, 0);
Toronto Falcons, Canada.

1959/60 - 1965/66

DAVE MACKAY

The stature of Dave Mackay in Tottenham folklore is vast and indisputable; indeed, to imagine Spurs' great sixties side without the vibrant Scot is to picture the Huns without Attila or the Alamo without Davy Crockett. Yet while it is right that so much is made of Dave's dynamic, warrior-like qualities - many have written that if Blanchflower was the brains of the team, Mackay was its heart - there is a danger of under-selling his sheer, unadulterated all-round talent. In fact, his control was second to none, he was the cleanest striker of a ball at the club and he passed with the utmost precision. And how the mighty left-half revelled in his skill; in training he would astonish team-mates by volleying continuously against a wall from ten or even 15 yards - anyone who doubts the difficulty of this trick should attempt it for themselves - and later, as Spurs captain, he would run on to the pitch, kick the ball high in the air, then catch it infallibly on his instep, a subtle form of intimidation that demanded of his opponents, 'Can you do that?'

All this is not to say, of course, that the traditional image of Dave Mackay is a myth. Despite standing just 5ft 8in, he exerted an awesome physical presence, muscular thighs and a barn-door of a chest topped by features that were positively piratical. The man tackled like a granite avalanche, exuding a passionate will to win and apparently consumed by a devilish, ruthless relish for his work. Colleagues leapt to do his bidding as he drove them on, invariably by stirring personal example, often by melodramatic gesture and abrasive Caledonian invective. Though lacking in outright pace, he bustled tirelessly between attack and defence, typically winning the ball, flicking a pass, then surging forward to receive the return. On reaching enemy territory, he could finish venomously - as he proved with a hat-trick against West Ham in 1962 - and another potent weapon was a prodigiously long throw.

Addicted as he was to winning at everything - Dave would pour his entire being into a casual game of snooker - it followed that he was devastated in defeat, a situation he strove so hard to avoid that in some 40 cup finals at all playing levels, he never finished on the losing side. Such unquenchable spirit was never more evident than in recovery from a twice-broken left leg - the first fracture came in a clash with Noel Cantwell in a European tie at Old Trafford in December 1963, the second nine months later on his comeback against Shrewsbury reserves. Such calamity would have ended the career of lesser men; in his case, it merely added to the aura of indestructibility that had enveloped him since his indomitable contribution to Tottenham's early-sixties triumphs. Yet, unthinkably now, the Scottish international might never have arrived at the Lane. In March 1959, Bill Nicholson had been making overtures to Swansea's Mel Charles, and had the Welshman not opted for Arsenal he would almost certainly have joined Tottenham instead of Dave. Later Bill maintained that it was Mackay he wanted all along, and was delighted to pay Hearts £32,000 for his signature.

Come the mid-sixties, Dave had taken over as skipper and, his mastery over ball and men undimmed, led Spurs to FA Cup Final victory in 1967. By then, he was operating in a mainly defensive role but the earlier years of midfield effort had exacted a toll and injuries became more frequent. Perhaps, too, he needed a new challenge and he found it at Derby, whom he joined for £5,000 (a reduced fee in recognition of his services) in July 1968. Under Brian Clough he played masterfully alongside centre-half Roy McFarland and in his first season helped the Rams lift the Second Division title, as well as sharing the Footballer of the Year award with Manchester City's Tony Book. Success in management followed, including a Championship at Derby, but it is to his fabulous achievements as a Spur that Dave owes his undying reputation. Nicholson called him his best signing, and he has been compared to the great Duncan Edwards. Nothing more need be said.

BORN: Edinburgh, 14.11.34.
GAMES: 318. GOALS: 51.
HONOURS: League Championship 60/1; FA Cup 60/1, 61/2, 66/7.
22 Scotland caps (57-65).
OTHER CLUBS: Hearts 53/4-58/9 (135, 25);
Derby County 68/9-70/1 (122, 5); Swindon Town 71/2 (26, 1).
MANAGER: Swindon Town (71-72); Nottingham Forest (72); Derby County (73-76);
Walsall (77-78); Kuwait as coach (78-87); Doncaster Rovers (87-89);
Birmingham City (89-91); Egypt as coach (91-).

1958/59 - 1967/68

CLIFF JONES

Like a hungry cheetah at full stretch on the trail of its hapless prey, Cliff Jones running towards goal was a spectacle to take the breath away. The Welsh dasher was that rare and glorious being, a speed merchant with ball control, and he was undoubtedly the most thrilling, eye-catching entertainer in Spurs' greatest team. Appearing to skim effortlessly over the ground, he would dart beyond his markers before they had the chance to make a fair tackle. When he was fouled - often the only way to hinder his headlong flight - Cliff would hurtle horizontally for yards after the impact, and it was tempting to look for scorchmarks on the turf.

Yet velocity and skill were not the only Jones qualities that became an integral part of the White Hart Lane success story in the early sixties. Mention Cliff's name to many who saw him at his peak and they speak in awe of his matchless courage; indeed, no less a warrior than Dave Mackay describes the wiry wingman as the most fearless player he has known. This bravery was most evident in aerial combat, into which Cliff threw himself body and soul. If there was the slightest sniff of a goal, the 5ft 7in dynamo would dive unhesitatingly among flailing feet - a fabulous full-length strike at home to Fulham in November 1960 comes to mind - or wrap himself around the woodwork in an effort to get a decisive touch. His timing was uncanny as he wormed into position to steal the ball from the foreheads of hulking opponents, though he took many sickening knocks and carries the scars to this day.

Naturally right-footed, Cliff could play on either wing - left when Terry Medwin was in the team, right to accommodate Terry Dyson - but was particularly potent cutting inside from the left before streaking for goal or freeing a team-mate in the touchline space he had just vacated. However, he was perhaps most menacing when roaming free, and one of his characteristic thrusts through centre field with a posse of petrified defenders retreating in front of him was a sight to savour.

Cliff's success as a Spur came as no surprise to supporters in his homeland, who were used to following the family's fortunes - his father, Ivor, and uncle, Bryn, were Welsh internationals and his brother, also Bryn, played for five League clubs - but were gratified by the handsome manner in which he upheld the tradition. Capped at 18, Cliff starred for Swansea before a £35,000 deal - then a record for a winger - took him to White Hart Lane in February 1958. However, the road to glory can be rocky, as he discovered on his debut at Arsenal, whom he had at one time looked certain to join. The game finished 4-4 but Cliff was disappointing, and as his form failed to improve over subsequent weeks, the Gunners fans gloated. The Jones fortunes appeared to dip still further when he broke his leg in a pre-season training collision with Peter Baker, but the enforced lay-off gave him breathing space. On his return to action that December he seemed less overawed by the size of his fee, and began to give value for money.

Thereafter Cliff matured into arguably the world's finest flankman, sharing in Spurs' headiest triumphs and prompting Juventus to offer a then-monumental £100,000 for his services in 1962. Bill Nicholson was too wise to be tempted and Cliff went on to complete ten years at the Lane, being the last member of the double-winning side to depart when he left for Fulham, aged 33, in October 1968. Though hampered since 1965 by injuries to hamstring, knee and shoulder, he never ceased to give maximum effort and a flash of the old Jones magic could never be ruled out. Throughout his career Cliff remained a friendly, positive character who brought a spirit of enjoyment as well as moments of sheer inspiration to the game he loved. His youthful charges in North London, where he now teaches PE, can count themselves lucky.

BORN: Swansea, 7.2.35.
GAMES: 370 (8). GOALS: 159.
HONOURS: European Cup Winners' Cup 62/3;
League Championship 60/1;
FA Cup 60/1, 61/2, 66/7 (non-playing sub).
59 Wales caps (54-69).
OTHER CLUBS: Swansea Town 52/3-57/8 (168, 46);
Fulham 68/9-69/70 (25, 2).

1957/58 - 1968/69

JOHN WHITE

No major footballing talent since the War has plied his trade more subtly than John White, the slender Scottish schemer whose influence at the hub of the majestic Spurs side of the early sixties can hardly be overstated. Rarely did he garner personal glory, often not catching the attention of supporters even in games dominated by his skills, but he was feted royally by fellow professionals, who recognised the scale of his contribution. In fact, it was the likes of Blanchflower and Mackay, with whom he had shared an international stage, who had urged Bill Nicholson to sign him; they saw his golden gift of making others play - indeed, never has the tag of 'play-maker' been more apt - and coveted it for the Tottenham cause.

This priceless quality was based on a nigh-uncanny positional sense which earned John the nickname of 'The Ghost', a tag made all the more appropriate by his slender figure and wan appearance. When Spurs went forward, he was an elusive, flickering wraith, flitting unobtrusively into space to ensure that attacks did not break down for the want of a passing option, then keeping the move flowing with an instant pass. Though not as overtly entertaining as the ball-juggling Tommy Harmer, whom he ultimately replaced, John was endowed with superb control and vision. Invariably his deliveries were dispatched with perfect weight, his tactical brain was sharp and he was the master of every technique, notably the chip - one that brought a goal at Nottingham Forest in October 1960 was an example to savour.

The key was that John integrated his skills more successfully than Tommy, mainly because of his superior mobility and a deceptive strength that seemed unlikely to be housed in so willowy a frame. Actually, as a teenager he had been turned away by both Rangers and Middlesbrough as being too slight, but Bill Nicholson, reluctant to reject an artist on the grounds of physique, was shrewd enough to investigate further and discovered that the teenage White had excelled as a cross-country runner, so stamina would be no problem. At a casual glance, he didn't offer the impression of being a workaholic, but closer examination revealed that he seldom stopped moving and thus was a nightmare to mark.

John - who had been offered to Charlton for £3,000 while at Alloa, his first club - arrived at White Hart Lane as a £20,000 capture from Falkirk in October 1959 while still doing his National Service. Stationed at Berwick, he was making regular 700-mile round trips to and from London, and the strain told as he faded towards the end of his early games. But he toiled to improve his fitness, his lack of self-confidence eased gradually - in those days he was a shy lad whose penchant for practical jokes was yet to become evident - and when he settled in the south, his performances mushroomed in stature. At first John operated in tandem with Harmer - sometimes as twin inside-forwards, occasionally with the Scot on the wing - but as it became apparent that they were duplicating each other's jobs, the older man made way.

All Spurs' triumphs over the next three seasons owed plenty to the quiet, unfussy White input, none more so than victory in the 1963 Cup Winners' Cup. In the first round at home to Rangers he nodded two goals - John's strike-rate is underrated, he managed double figures in three of his four full terms at the Lane - and in the final he tormented Atletico Madrid with his passes, adding a smart goal for good measure. By the summer of 1964, with Blanchflower newly retired, John was set to assume extra midfield responsibility; a new phase in his career was about to begin. But on July 21, while practising alone at Crews Hill golf course, Enfield, he was caught in a thunderstorm and sheltered under an oak tree. Lightning struck and, at 26, John White was dead. Just how good, or great, he might have become, no one will ever know.

BORN: Musselburgh, Midlothian, 28.4.37.
GAMES: 219. GOALS: 47.
HONOURS: European Cup Winners' Cup 62/3;
League Championship 60/1; FA Cup 60/1, 61/2.
22 Scotland caps (59-64).
OTHER CLUBS: Falkirk 58/9-59/60 (27, 6).

1959/60 - 1963/64

LES ALLEN

The Spurs career of Les Allen fell victim to genius. After scoring 27 goals and playing in every match as Bill Nicholson's awe-inspiring side completed the League and FA Cup double in 1960/61, the chunky marksman looked set for a long and bountiful White Hart Lane tenure. Indeed at 24, with both youth and experience in his favour and while learning eagerly from team-mates of the highest quality, Les seemed capable of sufficient improvement to add full international honours to the under-23 cap already garnered. But out of a clear sky, just seven months after Tottenham's twin triumph, there appeared a certain Jimmy Greaves. Now while folklore has it that Jimmy ousted Les and that was the end of the story, it was not quite that simple. In fact, the two men played in harness for the newcomer's first dozen games, with Les wearing the number-nine shirt until it was reclaimed by Bobby Smith. There followed a Smith-Allen battle for the role of spearhead throughout 1962/63 and it wasn't until after the arrival of Alan Gilzean in December 1964 that Les slipped irrevocably out of contention.

The next summer signalled a £21,000 switch to Third Division QPR, an anti-climactic departure in view of his early progress after arriving from Chelsea in exchange for Johnny Brooks in December 1959. Though Les - ironically a teenage amateur with Spurs before turning professional at Stamford Bridge - had lately been confined to the Pensioners' reserves, his manager Ted Drake had dubbed him the best young footballing centre-forward in the top flight and Bill Nicholson was ready to back a hunch that he would flourish away from the boo-boys who had tormented him at Chelsea. Pitched straight into the Tottenham first team, Les was not slow in justifying that faith. Come January he endeared himself to his new fans by scoring twice against Arsenal at an ice-bound White Hart Lane, then trespassed towards the realms of fantasy in February, notching five in the 13-2 FA Cup replay drubbing of Crewe Alexandra.

Yet despite the strike-rate - he finished that campaign with 15 goals in 19 outings - Les was not a confident character, his basic shyness perhaps emphasised, at least temporarily, by transferring to a team containing so many stars. On the pitch his features were clenched invariably in the tensest of expressions, though certainly he had no occasion to feel inferior. While his most commonly lauded attributes were strength on the ball, remarkable unselfishness and willingness to graft ceaselessly, Les was blessed also with excellent control, a savage shot and, perhaps most significantly, the intelligence to apply his gifts to maximum effect. Many of his goals were of the so-called bread-and-butter variety, the product of gliding unobtrusively into dangerous positions, but there were spectacular moments, none more so than the waist-high volley against Sheffield Wednesday that decided both match and Championship in April 1961. As a provider, too, Les could be devastating, as his dribble past four Sunderland defenders to set up a Terry Dyson strike in the FA Cup quarter-final replay at White Hart Lane that same spring demonstrated exhilaratingly. All he lacked - and there had to be something - was outright pace; with that one addition to his game, he might have risen to the giddiest heights.

On retirement as a player, Les sampled management, but even after he slipped out of the hot-seat at Swindon the family name was to return to prominence. His son, Clive, was destined to score freely for various clubs, but most notably for Spurs. Yet despite the prolific achievements of Allen junior, and the lavish praise that he earned, there are those who maintain that the gifted son was never *quite* the equal of his less acclaimed father.

BORN: Dagenham, Essex, 4.9.37.
GAMES: 137. GOALS: 61.
HONOURS: League Championship 60/1; FA Cup 60/1.
OTHER CLUBS: Chelsea 56/7-59/60 (44, 11);
Queen's Park Rangers 65/6-68/9 (128, 54).
MANAGER: Queen's Park Rangers (69-70);
Swindon Town (72-74).

1959/60 - 1964/65

TERRY DYSON

There is a school of churlish pundits who maintain, to this day, that Terry Dyson was an honest but essentially ordinary workman and was lucky to take his place in one of the greatest club sides of all time. They are, this writer would humbly submit, purveying hogwash.
What they ignore when advancing the claims of the more skilful Welshman, Terry Medwin, is that Tottenham's most significant triumphs - completing the League and FA Cup double in 1961 and taking Britain's first European trophy, the Cup Winners' Cup, two years later - were attained when the plucky Yorkshireman held sway in the constant struggle for supremacy between the two wingmen. With artistry hardly in short supply in a team of all talents, what was needed to achieve a successful blend was a hyperactive beaver who could contribute in all areas of the pitch and who would donate his dying breath to the common cause.
Bill Nicholson found him in Terry Dyson.

The son of leading northern jockey Ginger Dyson, sandy-haired Terry was, at 5ft 3in, the ideal size to take up the silk himself. Instead, after playing at non-League level for Scarborough, he signed for Spurs in 1954, the prelude to half a decade in the Football Combination relieved by only occasional senior outings. Indeed, Terry remained very much a reserve in status until the tail-end of 1959/60 when he won a place on merit, then cemented it by a series of sterling displays when Cliff Jones was injured at the start of the double campaign. Thereafter Medwin was dropped and his namesake prospered, linking effectively on the left flank with Dave Mackay but also roaming, now popping up alongside centre-forward Bobby Smith, then snapping at the heels of opponents in his own penalty area.

Admittedly the Dyson distribution was wild at times, and he was not always quick to spot the most profitable passing option, but he compensated amply by perpetual motion and bravery, and his finishing, too, could be lethal. The crowd loved him for his enthusiasm - when he found the net his face radiated pure joy as his body launched into an ecstatic war dance - and respected him for aerial efforts hardly commensurate with his 1961 position as the League's smallest player. In fact, two of the most telling moments of that memorable year came from Terry's headers, the first when he outjumped the hulking Don Megson to lay on a goal for Smith in the title-clinching clash with Sheffield Wednesday, the second when he nodded precisely to complete the scoring in the FA Cup Final against Leicester.

Understandably, Terry started 1961/62 in confident vein, scoring five goals in three August days - including a hat-trick at home to Arsenal - but Medwin was a formidable rival and that winter, as Spurs strove for a second double, the Welsh international regained his place. It was not in the Dyson nature to give up, however, and he fought back to take a crucial part in the 1963 Cup Winners' Cup campaign, scoring the winner in the semi-final first leg against OFK Belgrade before contributing the game of his life in the final 5-1 hammering of Atletico Madrid. After helping to create the second goal for John White, Terry made a vital saving tackle when Spurs were 2-1 up and floundering. Then he seized the initiative, increasing the lead with an admittedly flukey curler, laying on the fourth for Jimmy Greaves and adding the fifth himself with a venomous 25-yard shot after a slick exchange of passes with Tony Marchi. No wonder Bobby Smith was moved to quip that the wee fellow ought to retire there and then, as he could never play as well again! In the event, Terry went on to complete two more seasons in the first team, his irrepressible dressing-room presence a bonus to the morale of a side in the process of breaking up. Quite clearly, by the time he joined Fulham in June 1965, the case for Terry Dyson was open and shut.

BORN: Malton, Yorkshire, 29.11.34.
GAMES: 209. GOALS: 55.
HONOURS: European Cup Winners' Cup 62/3;
League Championship 60/1;
FA Cup 60/1.
OTHER CLUBS: Fulham 65/6 (22, 3);
Colchester United 68/9-69/70 (56, 4).

1954/55 - 1964/65

JOHN SMITH

It was through no shortfall of skill that wing-half cum inside-forward John Smith failed to make the grade as a Spur. Indeed when he left West Ham for White Hart Lane, swapped for front-runner David Dunmore in March 1960, there was wide-spread belief that his imaginative passing and instinctive feel for the ball guaranteed the recently-capped England under-23 international a glowing future. True, the sturdy Londoner was never the quickest mover, always having to watch his weight, but he was extremely fit and was seen by many as the long-term successor to Danny Blanchflower, already 34 at the time.

Unfortunately for John, the Irishman made a nonsense of his years, and Bill Nicholson achieved his magnificent midfield blend without the help of the talented newcomer. Thus he was relegated to the status of reserve, doing well enough as deputy for Danny, John White or Dave Mackay but never making his services indispensable. Come March 1964, the purchase of Alan Mullery made his position clear and he left for Coventry. The peak of his career came five years later when he helped Swindon deprive Arsenal of the League Cup in one of Wembley's most memorable upsets. John, who sampled management at Walsall, died in 1988.

BORN: Shoreditch, London, 4.1.39.
GAMES: 24. GOALS: 1.
OTHER CLUBS: West Ham United 56/7-59/60 (127, 20);
Coventry City 63/4-65/6 (35, 1); Leyton Orient 65/6-66/7 (39, 3); Torquay United 66/7-67/8 (68, 8);
Swindon Town 68/9-70/1 (84, 9); Walsall 71/2 (13, 1).
MANAGER: Walsall (72-73); Dundalk, Northern Ireland.

1959/60 - 1963/64

JOHN HOLLOWBREAD

John Hollowbread was the sort of goalkeeper needed by any club striving for top honours. Not quite accomplished enough to claim the first-team spot for himself, nevertheless he was a solid performer who could be relied on to deputise for Bill Brown without letting the side down. In addition, he was impeccably loyal to the cause of Tottenham Hotspur, emphatically not the type to clamour for a transfer in a bid to establish himself elsewhere.

Spurs signed John from non-League Enfield in 1952, and he demonstrated his patience by waiting six years for his senior debut. That came in August 1958, when he stepped in after Ted Ditchburn broke a finger and impressed sufficiently with his all-round competence - particularly his bravery in diving at feet - to retain his place for the rest of that term.

But the arrival of Brown in June 1959 made John's position clear and for the next five seasons he accepted the role of faithful understudy. Perhaps a spell in the limelight when the Scot was sidelined in the spring of 1964 heightened the Londoner's appetite for senior action, and come the summer, with the signing of Pat Jennings on the horizon, he joined Southampton for £2,000. John retired through injury in 1966.

BORN: Enfield, London, 2.1.34.
GAMES: 73. GOALS: 0.
OTHER CLUBS: Southampton 64/5-65/6 (36, 0).

1958/59 - 1963/64

EDDIE CLAYTON

Loyal and steady, Eddie Clayton was limited to a century of senior outings over 11 campaigns with Spurs. For all but one of those seasons, the amiable, dark-haired Londoner never rose above the rank of reserve, leaving unanswered the question of whether he might have excelled at a slightly lower station in the top flight. Certainly, an indication of the inside-forward cum wing-half's worth is that no less a judge than Alf Ramsey, then manager of Ipswich, expressed interest in signing him during the early sixties, though when Eddie actually asked for a transfer in 1964 only lowly Lincoln made an inquiry.

What is not in doubt is that the Clayton presence was a considerable asset to Bill Nicholson throughout his first ten years as a manager. Though Eddie was not always appreciated by fans who expected him, unrealistically, to emulate the stars for whom he deputised - Messrs Harmer and White, Greaves and Allen, Mackay and Venables - he could be relied upon to fit competently into a team method with which he had been imbued since stepping out of local football in December 1957. His service at half-back was sterling, but probably he was more accomplished in a forward role in which his capable passing and finishing skills - he had the important knack of keeping his shots low - were seen to best advantage.

Early in his career, naturally, Eddie had harboured aspirations of a regular first-team spot and four months after arriving he did his case no harm with a brace of goals on his top-flight debut, a 4-3 victory at Everton. However, so intense was the competition for places that he was to remain on the sidelines almost perpetually until 1965/66, when he made 41 senior starts. Thereafter he slipped out of contention once more, finally relinquishing ambitions of betterment when, in March 1968 and aged 30, he accepted a move to Southend United.

BORN: Bethnal Green, London, 7.5.37.
GAMES: 99 (4). GOALS: 20.
OTHER CLUBS: Southend United 67/8-69/70 (73, 16).

1957/58 - 1967/68

JIMMY GREAVES

Joe Mercer described him as 'a blinking little genius'; Dave Mackay recalls how he took pressure off his team by grabbing goals out of nothing; Pat Jennings reckons he was such a complete player that he was worth his place whether he found the net or not!
But however football folk choose to remember Jimmy Greaves, there is one point on which all are agreed: when it came to scoring goals, he was, simply, the best. What placed Jimmy apart from his peers, and from magnificent marksmen of other eras? Perhaps, if it is ever valid to make judgements that span the ages, it is that he was unique as a specialist finisher with outstanding *all-round* talent. What other full-time striker - a category that, of course, excludes the likes of Best, Law and Charlton - could pick the ball up in the centre circle and dribble past half a team before outwitting the 'keeper? And we're not talking about an isolated incident here - the man made a habit of it. There was the day at White Hart Lane in November 1962 when Leicester's Gordon Banks had the dubious honour of retrieving the ball; Manchester United were the victims in October 1965; then it was poor Leicester's turn again in October 1968, this time Peter Shilton tasting humiliation as Jimmy paused impudently before applying the *coup de grace*.

There were other such incidents, goals of equal audacity, but they did not form his staple diet. The majority of Jimmy's vast total - his career average of approximately three strikes every four matches is phenomenal - came from inside the box and were the product of a rarified combination of qualities. Wicked intelligence, instinctive anticipation, perfect balance, magnetic control, explosive pace, supreme confidence - it seems ridiculous, unfair even, but he had the lot. When the ball ran loose in half a yard of space, invariably he would be the first to move, and by the time a defender had latched on to his shirt-tails it would be too late. Small but wirily muscular, Jimmy could strike as firmly as the next man, but usually he opted for precision, passing the ball into the net, his customary accuracy giving 'keepers no chance.

This cornucopia of riches was expected to land in Tottenham's lap when the Greaves schooldays ended, but an eloquent Chelsea scout persuaded him to Stamford Bridge, whence he switched to AC Milan in summer 1961. Four miserable months later, Jimmy joined Spurs for £99,999 - Bill Nicholson refused to pay a six-figure fee! - and began by maintaining his tradition of scoring on debut at every level. Even by his standards, however, this time was special as he weighed in with a hat-trick at home to Blackpool, starting with a gravity-defying scissors-kick. Soon the baggy-shorted Eastender with the jaunty air of an eternal schoolboy was contributing a veritable deluge of goals that helped win the FA and Cup Winners' Cups, then did much to mask a gradual team decline. At times manager and colleagues alike despaired over his, shall we say, laid-back approach, and it's true that many blades of grass remained uncovered by the Greaves feet. But, as he might say himself, he did the business; and, as he would be too modest to add, there was no one who could match him. Nicholson, such a wise man, knew this and left well alone.

Jimmy excelled for England, too, overshadowing all other strike-rates with 44 goals in 57 matches; indeed, but for the strength-sapping jaundice that cost him four months of 1965/66, he would surely not have missed the final stages of the World Cup. Eventually, in March 1970, he left for West Ham, valued at £54,000 in the Martin Peters deal. His Upton Park sojourn was not the happiest, and ahead lay the well-documented drink problems that threatened his very existence. Rehabilitation was followed by new stardom as a TV pundit, a role in which he revels. But to all those who saw him play, the name of Jimmy Greaves will always conjure up images of the greatest of all goal-poachers. Not for the first time, Joe Mercer had the measure of his man.

BORN: East Ham, London, 20.2.40.
GAMES: 379. GOALS: 266.
HONOURS: European Cup Winners' Cup 62/3; FA Cup 61/2, 66/7.
57 England caps (59-67).
OTHER CLUBS: Chelsea 57/8-60/1 (157, 124);
AC Milan, Italy (14, 9);
West Ham United 69/70-70/1 (38, 13).

1961/62 - 1969/70

DEREK POSSEE

Derek Possee, like Keith Weller, was an accomplished young forward who grew disaffected with perpetual reserve team football at White Hart Lane and decided on a fresh start elsewhere. Accordingly, in the summer of 1967 when the opportunity arose to follow his friend to Millwall in a £25,000 deal, the 21-year-old accepted and Spurs bade farewell to another talented prospect they could ill afford to lose.

Small and compact, Derek was a quick, darting raider who could operate on either flank. Indeed, such was his speed that he won sprint titles as a youth and gave up the chance of an athletics career in favour of soccer. Though not quite of Weller's all-round quality, he was brave, with sure ball control and blessed with good timing in his aerial work.

Derek's senior debut, at home to Aston Villa in January 1964, was a personal triumph marked by a goal and a magazine award for the best sporting performance of the week. But he was not offered anything approaching a settled senior sequence until 1965/66, when he did well enough before being consigned to the stiffs for another term. Then followed his move to The Den, where he broke the Lions' League scoring record before returning briefly to the top flight with Crystal Palace.

BORN: Southwark, London, 14.2.46.
GAMES: 19. GOALS: 4.
OTHER CLUBS: Millwall 67/8-72/3 (223, 79);
Crystal Palace 72/3-73/4 (53, 12);
Orient 74/5-76/7 (80, 11).

1963/64 - 1965/66

KEITH WELLER

Keith Weller was the one that got away. In the mid-sixties, the young, ambitious North Londoner impressed mightily as an all-purpose forward whose talent was equalled only by his zest. But despite acquitting himself admirably whenever he deputised for one of the established stars, Keith was unable to claim a regular place. Demoralised to find himself in a tunnel at the end of which he could discern no pinprick of light, he accepted a £20,000 move to Millwall in June 1967, leaving for The Den burning with desire to prove Spurs wrong.

That he did so, going on to play for England as an attacking midfielder, is now a harrowing slice of Tottenham history, but in fairness to the management, they *were* reluctant to let him go.
Just 21 at the time, Keith was a lovely, flowing, natural footballer blessed with the skill and pace to go past defenders, smooth passing ability, a savage shot, enviable versatility and an apparently bottomless reservoir of stamina. He was never more outstanding than in Mexico on the club's 1966 summer tour, when his sheer dynamism in searing heat flabbergasted his toiling team-mates. Unluckily that was one trip Bill Nicholson did not make, and a potential White Hart Lane hero took his leave.

BORN: Islington, London, 11.6.46.
GAMES: 19 (2). GOALS: 1.
HONOURS: 4 England caps (74).
OTHER CLUBS: Millwall 67/8-69/70 (121, 38);
Chelsea 70/1-71/2 (38, 14);
Leicester City 71/2-78/9 (262, 37); New England Tea Men, USA;
Fort Lauderdale Strikers, USA.

1964/65 - 1966/67

FRANK SAUL

At 17, Frank Saul looked like hot property. Strong, eager and with no shortage of skill, the sandy-haired centre-forward played six games and scored three goals as deputy to Bobby Smith during Spurs' 1960/61 League and FA Cup double campaign. At 18, he confirmed the impression of limitless potential, netting twice in the away leg of the European Cup clash with Feyenoord and showing maturity beyond his years; the future could hardly have beckoned more promisingly. But at 24, he departed for Southampton, a £40,000 makeweight in the Martin Chivers deal.

Where had all that youthful impetus gone? Disappeared, perhaps, with the buoyancy of a team that had declined from its 1961 peak. Certainly Frank would not be the first man to shine in a great side, then lose his lustre in less rarified circumstances. The turning point came in 1964/65 when, with Bobby gone, he was given a substantial uninterrupted sequence as Jimmy Greaves' striking partner. Despite netting five times in the first four games, including a hat-trick at home to Burnley, Frank did not carry the consistent threat demanded of a Spurs spearhead. Accordingly, Alan Gilzean arrived in midwinter and thereafter the England youth international, who had shelved an ambition to join the Merchant Navy to turn professional, was edged towards the shadows.

But Frank, honest trier that he was, did not roll over and die at the first hint of competition. He showed his mettle and versatility by adapting to a wide position, while remaining an able substitute in the centre, and was rewarded with at least 20 senior outings in each of his last four seasons. Two high spots came in the 1967 FA Cup, with decisive and beautifully dispatched goals against Nottingham Forest in the semi-final and Chelsea at Wembley. Clearly Frank deserved better than the supporters' jibes which came his way when his progress did not match early predictions. When he left for The Dell in January 1968, he could do so with his head held high.

BORN: Canvey Island, Essex, 23.8.43.
GAMES: 125 (4). GOALS: 45.
HONOURS: FA Cup 66/7.
OTHER CLUBS: Southampton 67/8-69/70 (50, 2);
Queen's Park Rangers 70/1-71/2 (43, 4);
Millwall 71/2-75/6 (96, 4).

1960/61 - 1967/68

LAURIE BROWN

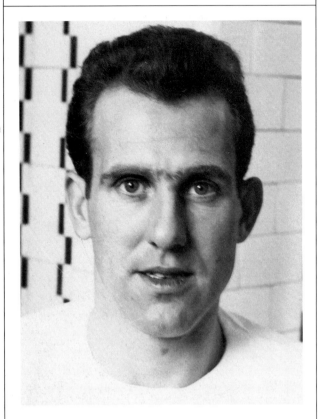

Laurie Brown was the life and soul of any dressing room, a bluff north-easterner whose constant wisecracking masked an unswervingly serious approach to the game. Unfortunately, the unquenchable enthusiasm of a memorably endearing character was never matched by his footballing ability. After winning England amateur international caps during early days with Bishop Auckland, Laurie experienced life in the lower divisions before joining Arsenal, then moving to Tottenham for £40,000 in February 1964.

Though primarily a central defender, he was pressed into immediate service as an emergency spearhead, proving rather blunt in his first match - against his former club - in which he was bested by Ian Ure. Though brimming over with self-belief, Laurie soon found himself out of the side, and he did not reclaim a regular place until reverting to centre-half in the spring of 1965. Thereafter he performed loyally for a season and a half, his awkwardness on the ball offset by his aerial strength, before being replaced by Mike England and joining Norwich in September 1966. Nobody tried harder than Laurie Brown, and at White Hart Lane he is remembered with affection.

BORN: Shildon, County Durham, 22.8.37.
GAMES: 65. GOALS: 3.
OTHER CLUBS: Darlington 58/9 (3, 0);
Northampton Town 60/1 (33, 21); Arsenal 61/2-63/4 (101, 2);
Norwich City 66/7-68/9 (81, 2);
Bradford Park Avenue 68/9-69/70 (36, 1).
MANAGER: Bradford Park Avenue (69).

1963/64 - 1965/66

NEIL JOHNSON

On a crisp autumn afternoon in 1965, Spurs fans thought they had discovered a new star. League champions Manchester United were the visitors to White Hart Lane and their defence was shredded, comprehensively and repeatedly, by a 19-year-old outside-right who gave polished Irish international left-back Tony Dunne a rare chasing. That day everything Neil Johnson attempted came off; he scored once and had a hand in two more goals as the Red Devils were eclipsed 5-1. Sadly for the young flankman, and for Tottenham, he would never again perform to such scintillating effect.

Neil's principal assets were speed and directness. Indeed, he tore into the game with such all-consuming enthusiasm that he seemed in danger of screwing himself into the ground. Unfortunately, he lacked any degree of subtlety, his control and passing ability were poor, and although his tackling and tenacity made him handy as a one-on-one marker - he once did a creditably limpet-like job on Manchester City's Colin Bell - much of the time he looked out of his depth at the top level. After only two substantial senior sequences - in 1965/66 and 1968/69 - Neil remained in the reserves, sometimes at right-back, until joining Torquay in 1971.

BORN: Grimsby, Lincolnshire, 3.12.46.
GAMES: 31 (7). GOALS: 6.
OTHER CLUBS: Charlton Athletic *on loan* 70/1 (1, 0);
Torquay United 71 /2 (6, 1).

1965/66 - 1970/71

JIMMY ROBERTSON

The White Hart Lane faithful were dumbfounded when international winger Jimmy Robertson was exchanged for Arsenal's unproven David Jenkins in October 1968. Their sense of grievance increased as poor David fared dismally, making memories of the popular Scot all the more poignant and high-lighting the uncharacteristic eccentricity of Bill Nicholson's most controversial deal.

Jimmy was dripping with potential when he arrived from St Mirren for £25,000 in March 1964. Sure enough, within six months he had won a full cap - destined to be his only one - and soon his searing pace had installed him as a terrace favourite. Rare was the full-back who could stay with the leggy 19-year-old flier if he was given the room to push the ball past and run, and though his control and crossing did not always match his velocity, the Robertson service offered a rich source of fodder for Jimmy Greaves and Alan Gilzean.

Capable of performing on either flank but more comfortable on the right, Jimmy was at his most effective when operating at speed and following his instinct. At full stretch his delivery was likely to be accurate, while time for deliberation, it seemed, gave rise to mistakes.

Though never a prolific scorer, he could strike with brutal force as Manchester United discovered at the Lane in October 1965. On an afternoon of magical entertainment, Jimmy advanced from the corner of the box to crash home an unstoppable rising shot and complete a 5-1 rout of the champions. More significant, of course, was his opener against Chelsea in the 1967 FA Cup Final - in which he excelled - when an Alan Mullery effort rebounded into his path and he netted from 15 yards.

After switching to Highbury, Jimmy was ousted summarily by Peter Marinello, and he left to shine at Ipswich and Stoke. That he could have done a valuable job for Spurs during their mid-seventies travail is beyond doubt.

BORN: Glasgow, 17.12.44.
GAMES: 177 (4). GOALS: 31.
HONOURS: FA Cup 66/7. 1 Scotland cap (64).
OTHER CLUBS: Cowdenbeath 61/2 (25, 7); St Mirren 62/3-63/4 (52, 18);
Arsenal 68/9-69/70 (46, 7); Ipswich Town 69/70-71/2 (87, 10);
Stoke City 72/3-76/7 (114, 12); Walsall 77/8 (16, 0);
Crewe Alexandra 78/9 (33, 0).

1963/64 - 1968/69

JEFF IRELAND

LEN WORLEY

KEN BARTON

RON PIPER

JEFF IRELAND 1957/58-1958/59

Outside-right. BORN: Paddington, London, 1.12.35.
GAMES: 3. GOALS: 0.
OTHER CLUBS: Shrewsbury Town 59/60 (38, 4).

BILLY DODGE 1958/59-1959/60

Wing-half. BORN: Hackney, London, 10.3.37.
GAMES: 10. GOALS: 0.
OTHER CLUBS: Crystal Palace 62/3 (3, 0).

FRED SHARPE 1958/59

Central defender. BORN: Greenwich, London, 11.11.37.
GAMES: 2. GOALS: 1.
OTHER CLUBS: Norwich City 63/4-68/9 (111, 0);
Reading 69/70-70/1 (64, 1).

LEN WORLEY 1959/60

Winger. BORN: Amersham, Buckinghamshire, 27.6.37.
GAMES: 1. GOALS: 0.
OTHER CLUBS: Charlton Athletic 56/7 (1, 0).

KEN BARTON 1960/61-1963/64

Full-back. BORN: Caernarfon, 20.9.37.
GAMES: 4. GOALS: 0.
OTHER CLUBS: Luton Town 64/5 (11, 0).

JIMMY COLLINS 1961/62

Inside-forward. BORN: Ayr, Scotland, 21.12.37.
GAMES: 2. GOALS: 0.
OTHER CLUBS: Brighton 62/3-66/7 (201, 44).

RON PIPER 1962/63

Inside-forward. BORN: Lowestoft, Suffolk, 16.3.43.
GAMES: 1. GOALS: 0.

ROY LOW 1964/65-1966/67

Utility player. BORN: Watford, Hertfordshire, 8.7.44.
GAMES: 6 (2). GOALS: 1.
OTHER CLUBS: Watford 66/7-68/9 (26, 4).

BILLY DODGE

FRED SHARPE

JIMMY COLLINS

ROY LOW

STEVE PITT

JOHN COLLINS

ROY WOOLCOTT

ROGER HOY

ROY BROWN

KEN HANCOCK

RAY CLARKE

TERRY LEE

STEVE PITT 1965/66

Winger. BORN: Willesden, London, 1.8.48.
GAMES: 1. GOALS: 0.
OTHER CLUBS: Colchester United 69/70 (6, 0).

ROGER HOY 1965/66-1967/68

Centre-half. BORN: Bow, London, 6.12.46.
GAMES: 12. GOALS: 0.
OTHER CLUBS: Crystal Palace 68/9-69/70 (53, 6);
Luton Town 70/1 (32, 0); Cardiff City 71/2-72/3 (16, 0).

JOHN COLLINS 1965/6-1967/68

Full-back. BORN: Rhymney, Monmouthsire, 21.1.49.
GAMES: 2. GOALS: 0.
OTHER CLUBS: Portsmouth 71/2-73/4 (74, 0);
Halifax Town 74/5-75/6 (82, 1); Sheffield Wednesday 76/7 (7, 0);
Barnsley 76/7-79/80 (129, 1).

ROY BROWN 1966/67

Goalkeeper. BORN: Hove, Sussex, 15.10.45.
GAMES: 1. GOALS: 0.
OTHER CLUBS: Reading 68/9-69/70 (63, 0);
Notts County 70/1-74/5 (113, 0); Mansfield Town 75/6 (1, 0).

ROY WOOLCOTT 1969/70

Forward. BORN: Leyton, London, 29.7.46.
GAMES: 1. GOALS: 0.
OTHER CLUBS: Gillingham *on loan* 71/2 (13, 5).

KEN HANCOCK 1969/70-1970/71

Goalkeeper. BORN: Hanley, Staffordshire, 25.11.37.
GAMES: 4. GOALS: 0.
OTHER CLUBS: Port Vale 58/9-64/5 (240, 0);
Ipswich Town 64/5-68/9 (163, 0); Bury 71/2-72/3 (35, 0).

RAY CLARKE 1972/73

Forward. BORN: Hackney, London, 25.9.52.
GAMES: 0 (1). GOALS: 0.
OTHER CLUBS: Swindon Town 73/4 (14, 2);
Mansfield Town 74/5-75/6 (91, 52); FC Bruges, Belgium;
Brighton 79/80 (30, 8); Newcastle United 80/1 (14, 2).

TERRY LEE 1973/74

Goalkeeper. BORN: Stepney, London, 20.9.52.
GAMES: 1. GOALS: 0.
OTHER CLUBS: Torquay United 75/6-77/8 (106, 0);
Newport County 78/9 (1, 0).

JOE KINNEAR

A pal's misfortune presented Joe Kinnear with the chance to prove his worth at White Hart Lane, though the talent, toughness and self-belief with which he capitalised on his windfall confirmed that, sooner or later, he would have reached the top regardless. The charming, dark-haired Dubliner had played a handful of senior games at the end of 1965/66 but, having been troubled by a blood clot on his thigh, appeared to face a lengthy wait in the reserves, when Phil Beal broke his arm in February 1967. Thus Joe inherited the right-back berth and retained it till the end of that season, which he climaxed as the popularly acclaimed man of the match in the FA Cup Final victory over Chelsea.

The former apprentice printer who had been discovered playing amateur football in St Albans - the Kinnear family had crossed the Irish Sea when he was seven - brought a comprehensive range of qualities to his game. Quick and bursting with untold energy, Joe was an exhilarating overlapper and polished passer, but didn't lose sight of his prime responsibility, that of defence. To that end he bit incisively in the tackle and covered his colleagues shrewdly, as he showed in the occasional accomplished display as sweeper.

Having made the first team, however, Joe was not to experience a smooth ride. In January 1969 his leg was broken in two places during a home clash with Leeds, and he was out for a year. On recovery, he was linked with Manchester United but that came to nothing, and he reclaimed his place for the League Cup triumphs of 1971 and 1973, and the UEFA Cup success of 1972. Both between and after these highs, though, the Eire international was kept out on merit by Ray Evans and in August 1975, with Terry Naylor ready to don the number-two shirt, he joined Brighton. After retirement he assisted his mentor, Dave Mackay, as coach at Doncaster, his uplifting personality fitting him well for the management career he began subsequently with Wimbledon.

BORN: Dublin, 27.12.46.
GAMES: 251 (7). GOALS 2.
HONOURS: UEFA Cup 71/2; FA Cup 66/7; League Cup 70/1, 72/3.
26 Republic of Ireland caps (67-76).
OTHER CLUBS: Brighton 75/6 (16, 1).
MANAGER: Wimbledon (91-).

1965/66 - 1975/76

TERRY VENABLES

Terry Venables was a debonair schemer, extravagantly skilful and brimming with self-belief, whose prospects for glory seemed boundless when he crossed the capital from Chelsea to Tottenham in May 1966. At Stamford Bridge, as the League's youngest skipper, he had been a vital influence in the Tommy Docherty-led revival and, at 23, had won two England caps. The £80,000 switch to White Hart Lane, a bastion of soccer sophistication, was surely tailor-made to suit his talents. Yet after three seasons of moderate accomplishment, Terry departed to Queen's Park Rangers, leaving behind an inescapable impression of anti-climax.

What went wrong? In retrospect, the answer appears simple enough - it was merely a matter of style. As the Blues' creative fulcrum, he was accustomed to deliberating on the ball before dispensing the immaculate passes that were his trademark; he was the conductor of an orchestra in which the musicians were well attuned to his promptings. But Spurs did things a different way, espousing a more fluid, one-touch game which thrived on constant movement; thus when the ball reached Terry, who had stamina in plenty but lacked pace, he interrupted the momentum. Naturally this frustrated the fans, who never really warmed to the solidly-built newcomer with the distinctive rolling gait, comparing him unfairly but not unexpectedly to the revered John White.

Even so, Terry had his moments - notably at the climax of his first full season when he helped lift the FA Cup at the expense of his former club - and not even his sternest critic could question his devotion to the job. Scrupulous about his physical fitness, Terry also thought deeply about the game, ever analysing systems of play and devising free-kick routines, and his considered approach served him well after his £70,000 move to Loftus Road in June 1969. Way ahead was a high-profile career as a manager, and a loudly heralded return to White Hart Lane.

BORN: Bethnal Green, London, 6.1.43.
GAMES: 139 (2). GOALS: 9.
HONOURS: FA Cup 66/7. 2 England caps (64).
OTHER CLUBS: Chelsea 59/60-65/6 (202, 26); Queen's Park Rangers 69/70-74/5 (179, 19); Crystal Palace 74/5 (14, 0).
MANAGER: Crystal Palace (76-80); Queen's Park Rangers (80-84); Barcelona, Spain (84-87); Tottenham Hotspur (87-91).

1965/66 - 1968/69

ALAN MULLERY

Despite a career of high achievement, Alan Mullery has remained somehow underrated in comparison to many of his peers. In considering his merits, often there has been an element of 'Steady old Alan, he always did a reliable job.' Well so he did, but there was much more to it than that. In fact, throughout most of his eight-year White Hart Lane tenure, there was no more consistently excellent outfield player at the club, and after the departure of Dave Mackay in 1968, he became not only the side's captain, but also its heart. From the moment in March 1964 when Spurs paid Fulham £72,500 for his services - Bill Nicholson made an unsuccessful attempt to sign full-back George Cohen in the same deal - Alan knew he faced a struggle for acceptance. Having inherited the number-four shirt vacated by the much-loved Danny Blanchflower, he was expected to replace the virtually irreplaceable. Soon some so-called fans were letting him know they felt he wasn't up to it; as well as the inevitable catcalls from the terraces, he encountered insults on the street and hate mail at home.

But if the morons thought they could frighten off the brash Londoner, they reckoned without the tempered steel at the core of both his character and his game. Rejecting the soft option of asking for a move, Alan buckled down to reveal the all-round qualities that made him one of the most effective wing-halves in the land. Sturdily built and with stamina to burn, he was never the most graceful of movers as he ferried his talents to every corner of the pitch, but such was his strength and skill that he was devilishly difficult to dispossess. In addition, he tackled abrasively, passed fluidly and packed a walloping shot, but equally important was his value as a motivator. Consumed by an insatiable desire to win, he drove on his colleagues and could be bitingly critical, which didn't exactly make him the most popular man at White Hart Lane but had a marked effect on team performance.

A landmark in the Mullery career was the 1967 FA Cup Final defeat of Chelsea, in which he was outstanding, and after which he appeared to gain in stature. Indeed, that year he secured a regular place in the England side that might have been his in 1964 had he not contrived to rule himself out of a tournament in Brazil by ricking his back while shaving, thereafter fading temporarily from the scene as Nobby Stiles staked his claim. In 1968 he became club skipper and entered his finest playing phase, which took in a stirring contribution to England's 1970 World Cup campaign. However, after holding aloft the League Cup in 1971, Alan began to suffer from a deep-seated pelvic strain, often finishing games in agony, and needed a four-month lay-off in the middle of the subsequent term.

On recovery he went on loan to Fulham and there were fears that he was finished, but they seemed laughable as he was recalled to lead Spurs into their UEFA Cup semi-final with AC Milan. Not for the first time, Bill Nicholson had pulled a masterly stroke, his revitalised captain clinching the tie with a brilliant 20-yard volley at San Siro, then going on to secure the trophy with a brave header - he knocked himself out in the process - in the second leg of the final against Wolves. Afterwards, cut off from his team-mates by milling fans, he embarked on a solo lap of honour with the Cup he had done so much to win. That summer, still only 30, he returned to Craven Cottage for £65,000. Three terms on, as Footballer of the Year, he led Fulham to the FA Cup Final and still had a season's football left in him. It was difficult not to conclude that Alan Mullery - by then an MBE and on the brink of a managerial career - had been allowed to leave Tottenham far too soon.

BORN: Notting Hill, London, 23.11.41.
GAMES: 373. GOALS: 30.
HONOURS: UEFA Cup 71/2; FA Cup 66/7; League Cup 70/1.
35 England caps (64-71).
OTHER CLUBS: Fulham 58/9-63/4 (199, 13) and 71/2-75/6 (165, 24).
MANAGER: Brighton (76-81); Charlton Athletic (81-82);
Crystal Palace (82-84);
Queen's Park Rangers (84);
Brighton (86-87).

1963/64 - 1971/72

DENNIS BOND

Few, if any, players at White Hart Lane in the late sixties were blessed with sweeter skills than Dennis Bond - and in a squad that included the likes of Greaves, Gilzean and Venables, that was saying something. The problem was that the young midfielder was not a natural athlete, his outstanding ability being concentrated more in his feet than his body, and he never achieved the consistency necessary for a top-level career.

Twenty-year-old Dennis was seen as a gilt-edged investment when he was signed from Watford for £20,000 in March 1967. In training, he looked positively brilliant, his control, vision and passing accuracy enough to make the purists drool. He packed a tremendous shot, too, but it was seen all too rarely in games, in which he appeared to lack stamina in spite of a sturdy physique. Occasionally, as in the home Cup Winners' Cup clash with Olympique Lyonnais in December 1967, he looked the part, but competition for places proved too hot and in October 1970 he moved to Charlton Athletic.

A popular, breezy individual who enjoyed life to the full, he later returned to Watford and served them splendidly, but that could not disguise the fact that the tale of Dennis Bond was one of potential unrealised.

BORN: Walthamstow, London, 17.3.47.
GAMES: 23 (4). GOALS: 1.
OTHER CLUBS: Watford 64/5-66/7 (93, 17);
Charlton Athletic 70/1-72/3 (75, 3);
Watford 72/3-77/8 (179, 20).

1966/67 - 1970/71

DAVID JENKINS

The demands on any young man joining a club of Spurs' stature are bound to be massive, but for David Jenkins the challenge was always going to be that little bit stiffer than the norm. The reasons were two-fold: first, the talented but inconsistent forward was arriving from Arsenal, the old enemy; second, he had been swapped for Jimmy Robertson, a proven and popular player.

In the eyes of many Tottenham fans, Bill Nicholson had dropped a rare transfer-market clanger, and in truth the Bristolian did little to dissuade them from that view following the surprise deal in October 1968. Though his goals at Stoke and at home to QPR that winter were each worth a point, the former schoolboy star just did not convince.

David possessed a strong shot, good control and adequate pace, but sadly these ingredients in a potentially excellent mix never gelled. In addition there was a feeling that he lacked a bit of 'devil', and as the criticism mounted, so his confidence appeared to wither. New players were signed, he dropped in the pecking order, and in July 1972 he accepted a move to Brentford. However, neither with the Bees nor his subsequent clubs could David fulfil his youthful promise.

BORN: Bristol, 2.9.46. GAMES: 13 (4). GOALS: 2.
OTHER CLUBS: Arsenal 67/8-68/9 (17, 3);
Brentford 72/3 (18, 1); Hereford United 72/3-73/4 (22, 3);
Newport County *on loan* 73/4 (6, 1);
Shrewsbury Town 74/5 (2, 1); South African football;
Workington Town 75/6 (6, 0).

1968/69 - 1969/70

ROGER MORGAN

Bill Nicholson's decision to pay £110,000 to QPR for Roger Morgan in February 1969 had most White Hart Lane fans bubbling with enthusiasm. They didn't doubt that the identical twin of fellow winger Ian - also linked with Spurs but destined to remain a Ranger - could create for Tottenham's marksmen the same abundance of opportunities he had provided for former team-mate Rodney Marsh. After his first outing - at Loftus Road, curiously - in which he set up a goal for Jimmy Greaves, and his home debut against Wolves, on which he scored, they had little reason to revise their opinions.

However, after a brief settling-in period, the terrace mutterings began. Roger exhibited commendable skill and could be an accurate crosser, usually finding space to dispatch the ball by jockeying for an angle rather than speeding past defenders, but lacked consistency. Stepping up from Rangers - bound for a swift return to Division Two at the time of the deal - to a club with designs on the top prizes, the England under-23 international had something to prove; sadly, he never quite managed it.

To be fair, the second half of his Tottenham career was blighted by injury, which ruled him out of contention between October 1970 and January 1972. On his return there was some promise, including an enterprising display and a goal on his European debut against Arad in Rumania, but fitness eluded him and he bowed out of the professional game. For the happy-go-lucky Londoner - who admitted to modelling his image on George Best yet somehow never cut the most athletic of figures - this was a bitter pill after months of pain and hard work. A natural ball-player - both he and brother Ian had been talented young cricketers who had excited interest from three counties - Roger retained his sporting connection by becoming a Football In The Community officer at West Ham.

BORN: Walthamstow, London, 14.11.46.
GAMES: 77 (3). GOALS: 12.
OTHER CLUBS: Queen's Park Rangers 64/5-68/9 (180, 39).

1968/69 - 1971/72

CYRIL KNOWLES

Cyril Knowles was a born entertainer. To the thousands of doting fans with whom he enjoyed a gleeful rapport, he exuded charisma, even in the traditionally unspectacular position of full-back; to his team-mates he was a zestful companion, beloved for his perpetual good cheer and addiction to practical jokes, but also respected for the toughness, dedication and sheer ability that lurked behind that contagious humour.

Indeed, it would be shameful to underplay the distinctive footballing merits that can be overlooked all too easily amid the strains of 'Nice One, Cyril', the pop record which he inspired and which earned him national cult status in 1973. The Knowles game was a cocktail of swashbuckling adventure, lithe athleticism and jarring power, though it was principally the last-mentioned ingredient which transfixed the attention of his new colleagues after the one-time Yorkshire pitman arrived from Middlesbrough as a £45,000 virtual unknown in May 1964. In his first training session, the eager 19-year-old ran amok, tackling anything that moved with a wild abandon that had Dave Mackay calling for calm! Accordingly, Cyril applied restraint - you didn't argue with Dave - though throughout his career faint-hearted opponents were to quail at the vigour of his challenges, while acknowledging them to be fair.

But most vivid in the memory are images of his raiding overlaps, cultured distribution (after early rashness had been ironed out) and coolness in defensive crises. Cyril was in his element speeding down the flank, like some rampant premonition of Stuart Pearce, before releasing a made-to-measure cross, a service that proved particularly productive when the two Martins, Chivers and Peters, were in their prime. As his experience grew, so did the renown of his left foot as an instrument of culture, picking out his targets with impeccable accuracy, though it must be admitted that there were moments when his confidence - some might say arrogance - in possession caused Tottenham hearts to flutter. Cyril had an occasional, disconcerting tendency to trap the ball on his own goal-line, then swagger forward selling outrageous dummies as he waltzed towards safety. Inevitably, such an eccentric talent was doomed to periodic aberrations, but it would be hard to find a fan who didn't reckon them a small price to pay for so much that was captivating. Cyril's one obvious weakness was a lack of aerial prowess, surprising in a six-footer and on which canny opponents such as Don Revie's Leeds were wont to prey. Overall though, he proved to be one of Bill Nicholson's best bargains, and only the brilliance of Ray Wilson and Terry Cooper prevented him from playing more times for England.

At club level, he spent his initial North London season at right-back, moving to the left to replace his erstwhile partner, Ron Henry, at the start of 1965/66. Thereafter he rarely relinquished the number-three shirt until a knee injury in December 1973 sidelined him for five months and warned of future problems. Still ahead, however, was perhaps his most cherished display, at home to Leeds on the last day of 1974/75. Spurs had to win to be certain of staying up, and Cyril was the hero of the hour, cracking home a free-kick and a penalty as well as tormenting the visitors' defence incessantly in a 4-2 victory.

The Knowles knee broke down repeatedly during the first half of 1975/76, and he was forced to retire, having shared in four cup triumphs during a stirring career. Keen to remain in football - unlike his gifted brother Peter, the Wolves forward who had left the game at 24 to concentrate on his faith as a Jehovah's Witness - Cyril went on to become a successful coach and manager. But calamity was lying in wait; in August 1991 Cyril Knowles died of a brain tumour at the tragically early age of 47. The soccer world was distraught; it seemed impossible to believe that such a fervent lover of life was no more.

BORN: Fitzwilliam, Yorkshire, 13.7.44.
GAMES: 504 (2). GOALS: 17.
HONOURS: UEFA Cup 71/2; FA Cup 66/7; League Cup 70/1, 72/3.
4 England caps (67-68).
OTHER CLUBS: Middlesbrough 62/3-63/4 (37, 0).
MANAGER: Darlington (83-87);
Torquay United (87-89);
Hartlepool United (89-91).

1964/65 - 1975/76

ALAN GILZEAN

The difference between Alan Gilzean and the majority of his peers was the gulf between a Van Gogh and a competent, even excellent painting by a lesser artist. A cursory glance at the canvases by anyone but a true connoisseur might offer the impression that there was little to choose between them; closer examination, of course, would reveal the subtlety of colour, composition and texture that lifted the Dutch master into a class of his own. So it was with 'The King of White Hart Lane', who provided Tottenham fans with everything they demand of their idols - sheer quality invested with character and style.

Pale, balding and frequently besuited, the intelligent Scot fitted the popular image of stockbroker or accountant rather than that of star centre-forward. Indeed, one irreverent team-mate reckoned that, even in his twenties, Alan looked the League's oldest player, while others spoke of an ungainly figure with one shoulder higher than the other. But dress him in football kit, give him a ball and suddenly the butterfly emerged from the chrysalis. What made Alan special was a supreme delicacy of touch, especially with his head, that often defied belief. No one equalled his accuracy in nodding the ball in any direction, invariably employing the most minimal of glancing deflections rather than power. One moment there would seem little danger as a hopeful punt sailed towards the penalty area with 'Gilly' surrounded by a forest of huge opponents; the next he had timed his leap to perfection, letting the ball slide from his pate at whatever angle was required to wreak havoc.

On the ground, too, he was a professor of stealth and technique, creating an illusion of strolling as he slipped into space, controlled the ball deftly and laid it off with infinite cunning. So gently did Alan caress a football that he might have been wearing carpet slippers; in fact, he soaked his boots in hot water before every match to make them soft and ensure added feeling. Sometimes in the heat of action, the players around him failed to read his intentions, but rarely would he appear ruffled, instead merely resuming his beat across the Spurs front line. Inevitably such a performer received copious punishment from desperate opponents, but he was not lacking in heart and accepted the blows as part of his job, preferring to retaliate with skill rather than violence. He was helped in this by enviable fitness which belied that superficially non-athletic appearance; in reality, he regularly outdid younger men in ten-lap races around the training ground.

Alan joined Tottenham in December 1964, a £72,500 capture from Dundee, with whom he had scored prolifically as a conventional spearhead, helping them win the Scottish title and reach the European Cup semi-finals. Dens Park boss Bob Shankly, brother of Bill, was not keen to part with his prize asset, but the persuasive Bill Nicholson - seeking to rebuild as his 'double' side broke up - beat off opposition from Sunderland and Torino of Italy to strike a deal. Soon it became evident that he could make goals as well as take them, and he featured in two celebrated partnerships without ever scoring heavily himself. First came 'The G Men' with Jimmy Greaves, his close friend; then, arguably to even more marked effect, he linked with Martin Chivers, whose colossal throw-ins he met so cleverly at the near post. Alan served Tottenham until he was nearly 36, his deathless craft compensating royally for declining pace, and signed off with a goal at Newcastle on the final day of 1973/74. Thereafter Gilzean senior - his son Ian was a Spurs junior before switching to Dundee - played in South Africa and managed Southern League Stevenage before taking a job outside the game. Never, though, will Alan be forgotten at White Hart Lane, where he gave so much pleasure. The fans loved him then, and they love him still.

BORN: Coupar Angus, Perthshire, 22.10.38.
GAMES: 429 (10). GOALS: 133.
HONOURS: UEFA Cup 71/2; FA Cup 66/7;
League Cup 70/1, 72/3.
22 Scotland caps (63-71).
OTHER CLUBS: Dundee 59/60-64/5 (134, 113);
Highland Park, South Africa.

1964/65 - 1973/74

PETER COLLINS

It was like some verdant, young, giant oak crashing to the forest floor, while alongside him the gnarled survivors of many a storm continued, for the moment, to wave their branches in the breeze. When injury and consequent arthritis forced Peter Collins to retire from top-level football at the age of 26, it spelled calamity not only for a talented performer who looked capable of becoming the backbone of Spurs' defence for five more years at least, but also for a team in urgent need of long-term replacements for the experienced Mike England and Phil Beal.

It was little consolation that Peter had been something of a windfall in the first place, costing just £5,000 from non-League Chelmsford City in January 1968, with a further £4,000 to pay if he made ten senior appearances. In the event, the second instalment fell due during the following season when the strapping 6ft 1in stopper enjoyed 33 outings as injuries disrupted Bill Nicholson's plans.

Enormously strong, fearsomely hard and very quick for a big man, Peter couldn't equal Mike's ball skills, but he matched him in the air and his all-round game was improving steadily. The youngster's most rewarding term was 1970/71 when he shone in an early stint as deputy for Phil, then stood in for the sidelined Welshman from midwinter onwards and pocketed a richly deserved League Cup winners' medal for his pains.

Having returned to the reserve ranks in 1971/72, Peter continued to distinguish himself whenever called to the first-team colours, as against Rapid in Bucharest that December. But then ankle and knee problems developed and by the mid-seventies it was clear that the popular centre-half - dubbed 'Spud' and 'Farmer' by irreverent team-mates in reference to his rural roots - had no future at White Hart Lane. He went on to become player-boss of Southern League Folkestone, while Tottenham strove unavailingly for the rest of the decade to find a fitting successor to Mike England.

BORN: Chelmsford, Essex, 29.11.48.
GAMES: 91 (10). GOALS: 5.
HONOURS: League Cup 70/1.

1968/69 - 1972/73

MIKE DILLON

The experience of central defender Mike Dillon highlights the uncertainty of football as a career, even for the most promising of youngsters who sample life in the senior ranks. An England schools and youth international, he helped Spurs win the FA Youth Cup in 1970, displaying all-round ability and abundant confidence, and praise was heaped upon him. At that stage, Mike looked a banker to make the grade.

All was well on his senior debut, too, standing in for Phil Beal in a 4-1 victory at Old Trafford in the autumn of 1972, and over the next season and a half he proved a competent deputy both for Phil and for Mike England, including appearances in two European encounters. But despite the opportunity afforded by the impending departure of several senior rivals, Mike failed to progress at the rate demanded by the Spurs management, illustrating the truisms that individuals develop at different speeds and that nothing can be taken for granted. Perhaps a trifle short for his role at 5ft 10in, he was unable to dominate larger and more seasoned opponents, and after brief loan stints with Millwall and Swindon, Mike left for New York to ply his trade alongside Pele.

BORN: Highgate, London, 29.9.52.
GAMES: 25 (4). GOALS: 1.
OTHER CLUBS: Millwall *on loan* 74/5 (4, 0);
Swindon Town *on loan* 74/5 (9, 0);
New York Cosmos, USA.

1972/73 - 1973/74

TONY WANT

The shadows of Cyril Knowles and Joe Kinnear loomed large and dark for Tony Want. The gutsy little Londoner was a quick, aggressive left-back who played as if his life depended on it, but throughout his five-year sojourn on the fringe of Tottenham's senior squad he never quite made the breakthrough from reliable deputy to regular first-teamer. England youth international Tony, a stalwart of Spurs' successful Football Combination side of the late sixties, made his debut when Joe was omitted for the home encounter with West Bromwich Albion in March 1968, playing in the number-three shirt with Cyril switching flanks.

But it was not until 1969/70, when the Irishman had broken his leg, that the loyal reserve was given a settled run. Tackling tigerishly and passing assuredly with his left foot, Tony let no one down but failed to cement his place. It would have been understandable if he had become disheartened, but he battled on until he ousted Cyril on merit in 1971/72, only to perform disappointingly and be dropped again. That summer he joined newly-promoted Birmingham City for £60,000, serving the Blues for six years before trying his luck in the United States.

BORN: Shoreditch, London, 13.12.48.
GAMES: 52 (4). GOALS: 0.
OTHER CLUBS: Birmingham City 72/3-77/8 (101, 1);
Minnesota Kicks, USA;
Philadelphia Fury, USA.

1967/68 - 1971/72

MARTIN CHIVERS

The words seem extravagant in stark black-and-white, yet the case is so strong that it deserves to be made: for a couple of seasons in the early seventies, Martin Chivers was the best all-round centre-forward in the world. There, it's said, and there is no shortage of vivid memories or expert opinion to support a contention certain to attract wider support with the addition of one simple qualification: when he was in the mood. In terms of attributes for the job, Martin lacked either none or only one, depending on your viewpoint. About his power and technique, flair and balance there could be no argument, and it was rare to find such a rich combination of qualities in a big man. Add intelligence and speed - he could seem ponderous, but it was a dangerous illusion as countless defenders left stranded by that ground-gobbling lope could testify - and the picture of an exceptional performer is almost complete.

And so to the one factor which some believe prevented Martin from attaining true greatness - the absence of devil, a killer streak, call it what you will. Certainly Bill Nicholson despaired at times, reckoning his gifted, muscular number-nine needed an injection of Bobby Smith-style aggression to fulfil his vast potential. The frustrated manager even urged defenders to clatter Martin on the training field in a bid to provoke the flashes of fire he so longed to see, and as a result, his relationship with the sensitive striker became strained. It all served to heap extra pressure on a man already carrying a massive burden of expectation due to the inescapable fact that if he didn't score, then Spurs' chances of victory were drastically reduced.

Martin joined Spurs from Southampton in January 1968, valued at £125,000 in the deal that took Frank Saul to The Dell. After early goals, the newcomer hit a barren patch as the team struggled, but was picking up form when, that September at Nottingham Forest, he twisted his knee and was sidelined for a year. Now his very career was in doubt, and on his return he had to rebuild confidence as well as fitness. Perhaps the turning point came in spring 1970 with the departure of Jimmy Greaves; Martin appeared to relish fresh responsibility as chief goal-getter and over the next two terms his game ascended to new heights.

Meshing delightfully with Martin Peters and Alan Gilzean - how often that subtle duo capitalised on the long throw that became a Chivers hallmark - or going it alone, he was frequently unstoppable. His two goals won the 1971 League Cup Final against Aston Villa, there were two more - a stunning 25-yarder after beating two men, and a soaring header - in the first leg of the 1972 UEFA Cup Final against Wolves at Molineux and, still more spectacular, a 35-yard free-kick of phenomenal velocity that provided a crucial away goal against Vitoria Setubal in March 1973. But no single strike epitomised his blend of strength and delicacy more than one in a home clash with Stoke in October 1970, when he surged infield from the left flank like some rampant tank before shrugging off the combative Denis Smith and outwitting Gordon Banks with the sweetest of 20-yard curlers.

It must be admitted that between such peaks were troughs of inconsistency, and it was then that the lack-of-bite brigade delivered their most poisonous barbs, notably when he failed to score as Poland dumped England out of the World Cup in 1973. Thereafter Martin was never quite the same irresistible force, and in 1976 he joined Servette Geneva for £80,000. Come the early nineties, he was a successful businessman involved in promoting Spurs' image; meanwhile, though arguments about his precise position in the club's order of merit might continue, few could deny that, on his day at least, Martin Chivers was unequalled among his contemporaries.

BORN: Southampton, 27.4.45.
GAMES: 355 (12). GOALS: 174.
HONOURS: UEFA Cup 71/2; League Cup 70/1, 72/3.
24 England caps (71-73).
OTHER CLUBS: Southampton 62/3-67/8 (175, 97);
Servette Geneva, Switzerland;
Norwich City 78/9 (11, 4);
Brighton 78/9-79/80 (5, 1).

1967/68 - 1975/76

GRAEME SOUNESS

Every club has suffered the mortification of letting a young player slip from their grasp only to see him re-emerge as a star on some rival stage. But that offered scant consolation to Spurs fans as they cast envious eyes towards Anfield, Italy and Ibrox, and noted the awesome progress of Graeme Souness. Even given the heroic deeds of Hoddle and Ardiles, the Tottenham cause could hardly afford to lose such a talent.

Having helped Spurs win the FA Youth Cup in 1970, the precocious Scot progressed quickly to the first-team fringe, making his one senior appearance as a substitute for Alan Mullery in Keflavik in September 1971. Already Graeme's game was stamped with that familiar swagger: there was little pace but his passing was immaculate and his tackling brisk; undeniable, too, was a hint of petulance, though in fairness, at that age he was more sinned against than sinner.

With so much ability for all to see, the young man grew impatient on the sidelines, apparently believing he could do better than the established stars. Thus after returning homesick to Scotland, he signed for Middlesbrough before developing into one of the most influential British play-makers since the War. Of that magnificent career, all Tottenham followers had to savour was 26 minutes in Iceland . . .

BORN: Edinburgh, 6.5.53. GAMES: 0 (1). GOALS: 0.
HONOURS: 54 Scotland caps (74-86).
OTHER CLUBS: Middlesbrough 72/3-77/8 (176, 22);
Liverpool 77/8-83/4 (247, 38);
Sampdoria, Italy, 84/5-85/6 (56, 8);
Glasgow Rangers 86/7-89/90 (50, 3).
MANAGER: Glasgow Rangers (86-91); Liverpool (91-).

1971/72

PHIL HOLDER

Phil Holder was consumed by enthusiasm, slaving constantly throughout every match, and was brave to a degree that made hardened professionals wince; he lacked nothing in terms of skill or strength, either, and there was a time in the early seventies when the squarely-built England youth international had a chance of overcoming the disadvantage of standing only 5ft 3in to fashion a top-flight career with Spurs. That was during the regime of Bill Nicholson and his assistant, Eddie Baily - as demanding a duo as ever ran a football team - who honoured Phil for his phenomenal spirit. Indeed Bill, not noted for dispensing light-hearted nicknames, unbent sufficiently to accord the effervescent Londoner, who was one of 13 children, the title of 'Chief'.

But come autumn 1974, new boss Terry Neill found him surplus to requirements and, in the next February, Phil moved to Crystal Palace. In truth, he had never risen above the rank of reserve at White Hart Lane - impressing on occasions as a midfield deputy for his best friend, Steve Perryman - and was troubled both by injuries and a tendency to gain weight when unable to train. A natural motivator, Phil became a coach when his playing days ended, and worked under Steve at Brentford until taking over as manager in 1990.

BORN: Kilburn, London, 19.1.52.
GAMES: 9 (10). GOALS: 1.
OTHER CLUBS: Crystal Palace 74/5-77/8 (95, 5);
Bournemouth 78/9-79/80 (58, 4).
MANAGER: Brentford (90-93).

1971/72 - 1973/74

RAY EVANS

If achievement were measured purely by speed, fitness and enthusiasm, then Ray Evans would have been England's right-back. As it was, he will be remembered as a strong and eager dasher, practically a winger in disguise, whose defensive qualities never quite equalled his invaluable attacking attributes.

Ray was at his most effective sprinting down the touchline before releasing any manner of centre - now long and raking to a distant Martin Chivers, then curving wickedly to Alan Gilzean on the near post - a ploy which created plenty of goals. He struck the ball with resounding crispness and his booming, accurate passes into the traditional inside-forward channels could transform defence into instant attack, while the fierce Evans shot was a potential threat to any goalkeeper within 30 yards of his right boot.

At the back, however, he was more adequate than outstanding, a tackler of variable precision and rather disappointing in the air for a tallish, solidly-built individual who deputised occasionally in central defence. At need, though, the former youth international could be a limpet-like marker, as he showed against Red Star Belgrade's Dragan Djajic at the Lane in November 1972.

After making his senior debut in March 1969, Ray was to spend three years as faithful understudy to Joe Kinnear before playing so well during a lengthy stint in 1971/72 that the more polished Irishman couldn't reclaim his place on regaining fitness. During the following season, the two men were given equal opportunities in the number-two shirt, before Ray established the ascendancy, missing only two games in 1973/74. Frustratingly for the ebullient North Londoner, Joe was the incumbent for all three cup triumphs during the early seventies, with his own 1974 UEFA Cup loser's medal offering little consolation. Come January 1975, with new boss Terry Neill bringing change, Ray joined Millwall for £40,000, later performing solidly for Fulham and Stoke City.

BORN: Edmonton, London, 20.9.49.
GAMES: 174 (7). GOALS: 4.
OTHER CLUBS: Millwall 74/5-76/7 (74, 3);
Fulham 76/7-78/9 (86, 6);
Stoke City 79/80-81/2 (94, 1).

1968/69 - 1974/75

MIKE ENGLAND

Bill Nicholson acquired the services of Britain's best centre-half when he bought Mike England from newly relegated Blackburn Rovers in the summer of 1966. That, at least, was the judgement of most contemporary pundits - the merits of Jack Charlton of Leeds and Sunderland's Charlie Hurley notwithstanding - and it was reflected in the £95,000 fee, then a Football League record for a defender. A further indication of the big Welshman's worth was the identity of Spurs' chief rival in the race for his signature - a certain Matt Busby, who for months had been favourite to recruit Mike and had withdrawn surprisingly from negotiations at a late stage. Perhaps Spurs' immediate need was greater than Manchester United's - a recent injury had ended Maurice Norman's career, while veteran Old Trafford stopper Bill Foulkes was still in harness - but there was no doubt whose decision proved soundest in the long term.

For their money, Tottenham brought strength, stability and style to the heart of their defence, as well as adding a fearsome new option to their attacking armoury. Most instantly eye-catching of the England assets was his aerial might, which owed as much to intelligent timing as it did to a bonily angular 6ft 2in frame and a wide forehead which propelled the ball vast distances. But unlike many traditional centre-halves, Mike could offer a respectable turn of pace and a degree of ball control and passing expertise of which many a midfielder would have been proud. If not under direct challenge, he could 'kill' a 70-yard drop-kick from the opposing goalkeeper with a single touch and his penetrating through-balls fashioned many an opening for the front-men.

In fact, apart from a slight vulnerability on the turn when faced by a nippy adversary, the only criticism to be levelled against the long-striding pivot's all-round expertise was a certain awkwardness in the tackle. He appeared to close clumsily on his target, often falling in a tangle which occasionally resulted in conceding free-kicks in perilous situations, as well as placing undue strain on his joints. This last-mentioned consequence might have been a factor in the knee problems that plagued him for years, to the extent that at times he played with heavy strapping and was known to take hot baths *before* games to aid mobility.

After his move from Ewood Park, Mike took several outings to settle before striking a vein of majestic form that was typified by his utter dominance of the dangerous Tony Hateley in that season's FA Cup Final victory over Chelsea. In 1968/69, as Spurs struggled to find the net, he demonstrated his versatility with a six-game stint at centre-forward, partnering Jimmy Greaves and scoring twice; indeed thereafter, having returned to the back, he seemed keener than ever to lend his power to the attack in timely exhilarating sorties. The new decade started with frustration for Mike as injury deprived him of a League Cup medal in 1971, but - despite frequently playing through considerable pain, which was etched on his features during matches - he made up for it in 1973 and excelled in the UEFA Cup triumph of the intervening term.

A forthright character who insisted on doing things right - back in 1966 he had threatened to quit football when Blackburn initially blocked his move - he rocked fans by departing suddenly in spring 1975, reportedly disillusioned with the regime of new manager Terry Neill. Two spells in Seattle and one with Cardiff rounded off his exploits on the pitch, before he spent most of the eighties in charge of the national side he had served so nobly as a player. Where does he stand in the pantheon of Spurs stars? Suffice it to say that when Bill Nicholson selected his dream XI, he pondered the hefty claims of Maurice Norman before opting for Mike England. In Tottenham terms, there could be no more meaningful tribute.

BORN: Holywell, Flintshire, 2.12.41.
GAMES: 397. GOALS: 19.
HONOURS: UEFA Cup 71/2; FA Cup 66/7; League Cup 72/3.
44 Wales caps (62-74).
OTHER CLUBS: Blackburn Rovers 59/60-65/6 (165, 21);
Seattle Sounders, USA;
Cardiff City 75/6 (40, 1);
Seattle Sounders, USA.
MANAGER: Wales (80-88).

1966/67 - 1974/75

JIMMY PEARCE

The Tottenham team-mates of Jimmy Pearce had always believed he was a star in the making, and by 1972/73 he was beginning to prove them right. After four seasons of bright, promising contributions had fallen marginally short of establishing an automatic first-team slot, the skilful utility attacker was finally adding consistency to his comprehensive range of assets. Then, at 26 and on the threshold of his prime, Jimmy suffered persistent knee pain that was linked to a rare bone condition, and he never played top-level soccer again.

Perhaps part of the reason for the fitful early progress was that the mild, self-deprecating local lad didn't realise just how good he was. Those who watched him as an England schoolboy had no such doubts, predicting a full international future, and he did enough in 1968/69, his first senior season, to confirm that here was a talent worth monitoring. In full flight, Jimmy was a thrilling performer, able to control the ball at high speed and blessed with a characteristic shimmy which took him gliding past defenders almost as if they weren't there. A crisp finisher with his right foot and physically strong, he gave his most satisfying displays as a winger with a predilection for cutting inside, though he doubled effectively as a central striker.

However, he continued to flit in and out of the side, a frustrating situation underlined when he came on as substitute to score in the 1971 League Cup semi-final against Bristol City, yet was denied a place at Wembley. It was two years before Jimmy made up for the disappointment, winning a medal for his part in the victory over Norwich in the same competition. At last, it seemed, his confidence was matching his ability and he was poised to become a major influence - then came that shattering diagnosis. Jimmy rested for a year before making a comeback with non-League Walthamstow; meanwhile, a declining Tottenham were left to rue the departure of a talent they could ill afford to lose.

BORN: Tottenham, 27.11.47.
GAMES: 141 (52). GOALS: 35.
HONOURS: League Cup 72/3.

1968/69 - 1972/73

Jimmy Neighbour was a winger of considerable natural gifts, a twister and turner who could mesmerise an opponent and bring a crowd to its feet, yet he remains something of a 'nearly man' in the Tottenham story.

Having risen through the club's junior ranks and turned professional in 1968, he found himself competing for a flank berth with Roger Morgan and Jimmy Pearce. This was no easy option and when Morgan suffered a long-term injury in 1970/71, then Pearce was tried and temporarily discarded, it was an opportunity on which the inexperienced Neighbour needed to capitalise convincingly. That he did so to such effect - earning a place in the League Cup Final triumph over Aston Villa - reflected great credit on the slightly-built 20-year-old, whose cause was strengthened by his ability to play on either flank.

Sadly for Jimmy, his momentum was halted abruptly by the purchase of Ralph Coates and a switch of formation from 4-3-3 to 4-4-2. Thereafter his opportunities were limited, and it was not until the appointment of Terry Neill as manager that he was given the extended senior sequence he craved. Even then his elevation to first-team regular was delayed until 1975/76, but once in place he responded with the most captivating form of his career. Though he held on to the ball too long at times, his nimble footwork paved the way for a stream of accurate crosses, and he was ever willing to chase back when possession was lost.

Yet for such a clean striker of the ball, Jimmy did not score enough goals - three in 44 starts that term was a woeful return - which was a factor, presumably, in the decision of new boss Keith Burkinshaw to sell him to Norwich for £75,000 in September 1976. The move was greeted with dismay by some fans who preferred Jimmy to his replacement, Peter Taylor, their discontent being fuelled by that season's relegation and their former favourite's fine service at Carrow Road.

BORN: Chingford, Essex, 15.11.50.
GAMES: 134 (22). GOALS: 11.
HONOURS: League Cup 70/1.
OTHER CLUBS: Norwich City 76/7-79/80 (106, 5);
West Ham United 79/80-82/3 (73, 5);
Bournemouth *on loan* 82/3 (6, 0).

1970/71 - 1976/77

MARTIN PETERS

Martin Peters was a sleek, ultra-professional performer who won the minds of Tottenham supporters without, perhaps, managing always to warm their hearts. That is no sleight on a man blessed liberally with every skill in the textbook, but whose mode of operation tended towards the subtle and unobtrusive. Cool and seemingly detached from the hurly-burly, Martin played the game with his brain, frequently seeing things that escaped his fellow players, let alone those watching from the stands and terraces. Accordingly, despite the cornucopia of honours that came his way during a fabulous career, it was not universally appreciated just *how* good he was.

Indeed, his willingness to leave West Ham, aged 26 and approaching his prime, might have had plenty to do with a desire to escape from the all-encompassing shadows cast by Bobby Moore and Geoff Hurst, his co-heroes of England's 1966 World Cup triumph. Whatever the motivation, it was in March 1970, close to the transfer deadline, that Martin became Britain's first £200,000 footballer in the transaction which took Jimmy Greaves to Upton Park.

Though he scored with a header on his debut, a home defeat by Coventry, Martin took time to gain widespread acceptance, but gradually the sheer quality of almost every Peters touch convinced the doubters of his pedigree. A clean striker of the ball, he underpinned his accurate distribution and lethal finishing by supreme positional awareness which enabled him to drift into space, creating danger from unexpected angles. A lean, wiry six-footer, he was magnificent in the air, whether timing spring-heeled leaps to perfection or leaning forward imperceptibly to make wicked near-post deflections. Ever thoughtful, he could turn a game with a flash of intuition, a swift pass here, a little run there, without stirring a crowd with the more overt vigour of, say, a Mackay or a Mullery.

Thus doing his job quietly, elegantly, and sometimes courageously - his refusal to be intimidated by Rapid Bucharest's strong-arm tactics in Rumania in December 1971 offered comprehensive proof of his steel - Martin became an increasingly influential part of the Tottenham set-up as trophy followed trophy in the early seventies. He was the natural successor as captain when Alan Mullery left in 1972, earning the respect of his team-mates through personal example, tactical shrewdness and unquestionable integrity. Though it is inevitable that victories linger longest in the memory, one of Martin's most inspirational displays came on a night of aggregate defeat, against Liverpool at White Hart Lane in the 1973 UEFA Cup semi-final second leg. The skipper was everywhere, prompting ceaselessly and scoring twice in a stirring fightback which was not quite enough to prevent the Merseysiders going through on the away-goals rule.

Martin maintained his standards admirably into mid-decade, but the side's fortunes slumped, leading to the resignation of Bill Nicholson and the surprise appointment of Terry Neill. The young Irishman found himself at odds with certain senior players and in March 1975, while a relegation battle was raging, a disagreement resulted in the ex-Hammer's £40,000 departure to Norwich City. It might be argued that the price was fair for a 31-year-old, but Martin demonstrated that he had been released prematurely in the most effective way possible - by giving the Canaries five years of impeccable service, most of them in the top flight. At the end of the decade he switched to Sheffield United, with whom he tried management before opting for a future in insurance. One thing was certain, however; the player whom Alf Ramsey had once described as ten years ahead of his time had done enough to suggest that, no matter in what era he played, he would have excelled.

BORN: Plaistow, London, 8.11.43.
GAMES: 260. GOALS: 76.
HONOURS: UEFA Cup 71/2; League Cup 70/1, 72/3.
67 England caps (66-74).
OTHER CLUBS: West Ham United 61/2-69/70 (302, 81);
Norwich City 74/5-79/80 (207, 44);
Sheffield United 80/1 (24, 4).
MANAGER: Sheffield United (81).

1969/70 - 1974/75

PHIL BEAL

If Bill Nicholson had ever felt moved to take out insurance against conceding goals through recklessness among his back four, it is easy to imagine the policy being delivered by Phil Beal; after all, the blond, moon-faced defender was guaranteed never to make a drama out of a crisis. A shrewd anticipator who was at his best sweeping up alongside centre-half Mike England, Phil tended to go unnoticed yet so often it was he who defused dangerous situations. Frequently it would be well after a game was over that Spurs' more reflective fans would begin to recall his timely interceptions, the cool efficiency in everything he did; indeed, that he had barely put a foot wrong.

The Beal footballing philosophy appeared to be based on a safety-first method in which over-elaboration had no place and the ball was returned carefully to 'keeper Pat Jennings if there was the slightest risk of squandering possession through a more ambitious option. Some observers felt him to be over-cautious and reckoned he did not make the most of commendable ball control, albeit with a heavy right-foot bias, and a sharp soccer brain; presumably he believed he *was* using his ability in the best way possible, and could cite his longevity at the top level as compelling evidence.

Phil's path to recognition as a leading player was not an easy one. After being spotted by Spurs' assistant boss Harry Evans in county football, the England youth international, who had been considering a career in the Merchant Navy, signed as an amateur in 1960. He turned professional two years later but it was not until 1963 that he made his senior debut, deputising at right-half for Danny Blanchflower at Aston Villa. The arrival of Alan Mullery in 1964 seemed to leave him in the cold, but fate took a hand when he came on at right-back for the seriously injured Maurice Norman in a home friendly against a Hungarian XI in November 1965. Phil impressed, was given a lengthy run in the number-two shirt, and by early 1967 appeared to be well established.

However, it was not to last. A broken arm put him out for the rest of the season, costing him an FA Cup Final appearance against Chelsea, and the following term found him changing roles regularly, filling every defensive position except goal and also excelling as an adhesively attentive one-on-one midfield marker. Yet despite missing few matches, Phil remained something of a 'bits-and-pieces' player and in January 1968 he was linked with Southampton as part of the deal that took Martin Chivers to North London. Nothing came of that, though, and the departure of Dave Mackay in the summer brought about the turning point of his career. Now he settled into a sound and complementary central defensive partnership with Mike England; Phil was merely adequate in the air but with Mike around that didn't matter, while his own speed, durability and decisiveness offered crucial support to the big Welshman.

Of course, it took the fans who had idolised Mackay some time to accept his replacement and Phil endured unwarranted helpings of terrace stick, but eventually he wore down the critics to win both acceptance and affection. That landmark campaign of 1968/69 also saw his only senior goal, at home to QPR in January, and a memorable one it was; picking up the ball deep in his own half, he ran some 75 yards and completed a slick one-two interchange with Jimmy Greaves before clubbing an unstoppable drive from just outside the box.

Phil went on to play a major part in one UEFA Cup and two League Cup triumphs, while his extrovert, mickey-taking personality became ever more central to maintaining team morale. When he left for Brighton in July 1975, it became apparent that the merits of Phil Beal had long been taken for granted. He was sorely missed, both by a struggling side and by supporters who were becoming increasingly desperate.

BORN: Godstone, Surrey, 8.1.45.
GAMES: 417 (3). GOALS: 1.
HONOURS: UEFA Cup 71/2; League Cup 70/1, 72/3.
OTHER CLUBS: Brighton 75/6-76/7 (10, 0);
Memphis Rogues, USA;
Crewe Alexandra 79/80 (4, 0).

1963/64 - 1974/75

PAT JENNINGS

It was like George Best being shunted off to Liverpool or Geoff Boycott dispatched across the Pennines to take guard for Lancashire; the world went crazy for Tottenham fans on that terrible day in August 1977 when Pat Jennings, the man they revered as the world's greatest goalkeeper, was sold to Arsenal - yes, Arsenal - for a piffling £45,000. Coming just three months after relegation to the Second Division, it seemed too much to take; and to rub salt into the most gaping of wounds, the man to whom Spurs boss Keith Burkinshaw had practically gift-wrapped Pat was Terry Neill, his less than universally popular predecessor at White Hart Lane.

It was a bizarre incident, and a decision which Burkinshaw - while maintaining that the sale of the 32-year-old Ulsterman had appeared a reasonable option at the time - was later big enough to admit that, in retrospect, he would have reversed. Yet it served to highlight not only the glorious unpredictability of sport, but also the notoriously short memories of many supporters. It seems unthinkable now, but the fact was that after Bill Nicholson paid Watford £27,000 for 19-year-old Pat in June 1964, the one-time tree-feller and Gaelic footballer made such a nervous start that he became a target for mindless barrackers who demanded - and got temporarily- the recall of the popular Bill Brown. So potentially damaging was the abuse that the manager was forced to appeal to the boo-boys to lay off, and it is a tribute to the Nicholson acumen that even in that dark hour, he retained faith in his man.

For Pat there followed two seasons of sharing senior duty with Brown, gradually gaining confidence as his talent blossomed. Rangy, muscular and supremely fit, he was, it seemed, born to keep goal, albeit with an unorthodox style that was all his own. One moment he was a benign but immovable giant who might have been plucking fruit in his orchard, that huge reach and safe pair of hands dominating the air around his net; the next he was a snake-charmer, hypnotising some unfortunate forward into shooting precisely when and where the master wished. Pat was a master of angles, an improviser supreme, adept at saving with feet, elbows or any other part of his anatomy. All this, combined with a composed, dignified bearing, made the job look easy, which was an absurd illusion, as all those privy to his thorough physical preparation and his tension as he built concentration before a match could testify.

The Jennings career was studded with spellbinding displays too numerous to mention, but there are examples which will lodge forever in this writer's memory: a series of fabulous saves over the two legs of the 1972 UEFA Cup Final against Wolves, including one astonishingly elastic stretch to tip over a chip after racing back 15 yards to reach the ball; the two penalty saves at Anfield in March 1973, diving right to frustrate Kevin Keegan, left to defeat Tommy Smith; and the drop-kicked goal against Manchester United in the 1967 Charity Shield.

Pat helped Spurs lift four trophies and broke the club's appearance record (since eclipsed by Steve Perryman). On a wider front, he won player of the year accolades from writers (1973) and his fellow professionals (1976), and was awarded the MBE (1976) before heading for Highbury with nine years of top football - during which he stretched his international cap total to 119, then a world record - ahead of him. Sadly, he left the Lane with the feeling that he was no longer wanted. He never asked to go, but was not offered a new deal, a silence which upset and disappointed him. Soon it emerged that Keith Burkinshaw was in a telling minority in believing that Pat's day was done. Manchester United and Aston Villa both moved to sign him, but he opted to join the Irish enclave at Arsenal where, significantly, Neill handed him a four-year contract. One of sport's most modest, yet enduring heroes had been allowed to depart prematurely from the scene of his greatest triumphs. In 1985/86 Pat returned to serve Spurs briefly as first-team cover (he gave Everton similar assistance) and to hone his fitness for the 1986 World Cup.

BORN: Newry, Northern Ireland, 12.6.45.
GAMES: 590. GOALS: 0.
HONOURS: UEFA Cup 71/2; FA Cup 66/7; League Cup 70/1, 72/3.
119 Northern Ireland caps (64-86).
OTHER CLUBS: Watford 62/3-63/4 (48, 0);
Arsenal 77/8-84/5 (237, 0).

1964/65 - 1976/77

TERRY NAYLOR

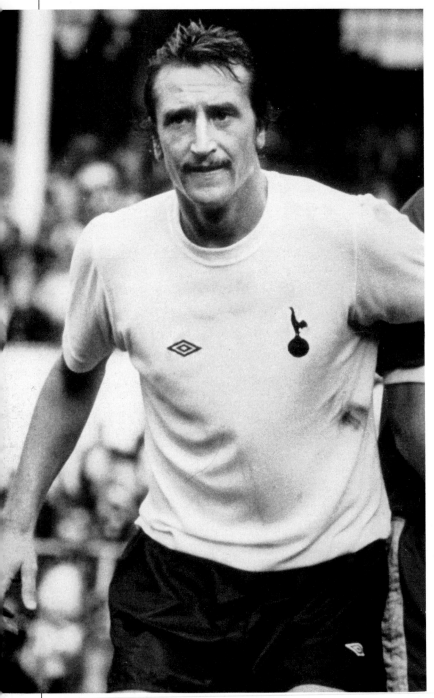

Terry Naylor was hard and he was funny, a pugnacious, wise-cracking gladiator who gave sterling service in the Spurs back line during one of the leaner periods of White Hart Lane history. The blond, brash North Londoner, a one-time porter at Smithfield Market, lacked plenty in finesse but nothing in confidence, as he showed at his first training session after turning professional with Tottenham. Walking calmly into the dressing room, he announced in matter-of-fact tones to the assembled stars: 'Anyone fancy dying today? 'Cause if they do, they should tackle me.' Terry revelled in taking opponents on, both physically and verbally, and even on the practice field he was not a man with whom to trifle.

His senior breakthrough came in spring 1970, when he stood in for Phil Beal, and there followed several years spent primarily as a central defensive deputy - with occasional outings as a combative midfield trouble-shooter - before injury to left-back Cyril Knowles in December 1973 afforded him his longest sequence to date. Terry took his chance avidly and thereafter filled every outfield defensive role, becoming a regular until the late seventies.

As well as such splendid versatility, his chief assets were fitness, strength and an earthy refusal to accept defeat - all particularly priceless in the 1977/78 dogfight to rise from Division Two - but also he read the game with a shrewdness for which he received scant public credit. Admittedly, Terry's skills were not dainty, though he loved to get forward and his cross for Martin Peters to score the winner in the 1974 UEFA Cup quarter-final in Cologne was typical of many successful sorties.

That competition yielded his only medal - sadly of the loser's variety - but neither his spirit nor his humour flagged and when he left for Charlton in November 1980, the White Hart Lane scene was duller for his absence. Terry Naylor would never have won a place in a great Spurs side, but in times of struggle he was an absolute nugget.

BORN: Islington, London, 5.12.48.
GAMES: 290 (14). GOALS: 1.
OTHER CLUBS: Charlton Athletic 80/1-83/4 (73, 0).

1969/70 - 1979/80

KEITH OSGOOD

Keith Osgood was one of an alarmingly large White Hart Lane contingent during the mid-seventies - players who appeared on the verge of long and satisfying Tottenham careers, but who for a variety of reasons slipped anti-climactically from the scene.

The promising central defender, an England schoolboy and youth international, was three days past his 19th birthday when he received his senior call-up, leaving the bench to replace Phil Beal at Newcastle in May 1974. There followed a handful of stand-in appearances during the following autumn, but the key moment in Keith's continued rise came that February when Mike England left the club. The youngster stepped up, impressing immediately with his speed, agility and composure, and cementing his position with a courageous display at home to Leeds in April. Only a win would provide insurance against the drop to Division Two, and when Keith played on with painful head and ankle injuries, deserving enormous personal credit for his part in a 4-2 victory, he signalled that a character of substance had arrived at the heart of Spurs' defence.

However, though he was competent in the air, at 5ft 11in Keith did not dominate in the manner of his predecessor, and big Willie Young was drafted in alongside him. In other respects, his game developed satisfactorily, his smooth distribution and his knack of cracking home free-kicks from anything up to 35 yards drawing widespread approbation, leaving only the occasional lapse in concentration on which to work.

Thus, after two ever-present terms - with heavy speculation that he would follow Terry Neill to Arsenal having proved incorrect, and despite Spurs' relegation in 1976/77 - his White Hart Lane future seemed assured. But in midwinter 1978, a difference of opinion with boss Keith Burkinshaw preceded a £130,000 move to Coventry, after which the Osgood career failed to fulfil all that early potential.

BORN: Isleworth, London, 8.5.55.
GAMES: 126 (1). GOALS: 14.
OTHER CLUBS: Coventry City 77/8-78/9 (25, 1);
Derby County 79/80-81/2 (69, 10); Orient 81/2-83/4 (36, 0);
Cambridge United 84/5-85/6 (35, 1).

1973/74 - 1977/78

JOHN PRATT

Only the valiant, it's been said, should contemplate a life in football, a profession which demands steely resolution in all manner of ways. It needs obvious physical bravery to confront a ferocious tackle, or to play on with an injury; a different kind of courage is required to risk a piece of outrageous skill when the stakes are high, and yet another brand of fortitude to own up to a calamitous blunder; the list could go on. But could there be anyone more stout-hearted than the player who faces concerted, frequently prolonged and mindless criticism from the terraces, yet who never hides or shirks, just keeps coming back for more? Such a man was John Pratt, who believed unshakeably in his own ability and whose appearance record for Spurs - more than 400 outings over 12 seasons - speaks volumes for both his strength of character and the esteem in which he was held by a succession of managers.

John was an unselfish workhorse of the type every side needs, but who lacked the extravagant natural skills possessed by the majority of Tottenham midfielders down the years. Hence when the tide of battle was flowing the wrong way, he was a convenient scapegoat, for a time becoming a particular target of a vitriolic section on The Shelf. In fact, as well as being prodigiously industrious - which *did* win him admirers, witness the 24,000 attendance for his testimonial game with Arsenal in 1978 - John knew the game comprehensively and had a marvellous eye for an attacking opening. The problem was that he could not always make the most of it, his more ambitious passes tending to go astray, and that's when the condemnation would begin.

What the detractors chose to ignore was that although he gave the ball away a lot, he won it a lot, too, challenging combatively both in the air and on the ground. In addition, John was a magnificent motivator, coaxing some team-mates while driving others, refusing to yield while the slightest shred of hope remained. Then there were his goals, many of which were unleashed suddenly, spectacularly and at moments of vital importance, as Liverpool discovered when his unstoppable blast into the top corner of Ray Clemence's net set Spurs on the victory trail in a White Hart Lane League Cup quarter-final clash in December 1972. He went on to play a prominent part in lifting that trophy, though his sole Wembley appearance was marred by an injury which forced him out of the action after 20 minutes.

North Londoner John - a former centre-half who deputised occasionally at the heart of Tottenham's rearguard - had spent a year in Brentford's youth team when he joined Spurs as an amateur on the recommendation of Terry Medwin. He made his League debut at Highbury in March 1969, but had to wait until 1971/72 for a settled senior stint, coming in for the sidelined Alan Mullery and finishing the campaign with a UEFA Cup winner's medal. For the rest of the decade, John's name was rarely absent from the teamsheet - in 1977/78 he was an ever-present as Spurs climbed out of the Second Division at the first attempt - and his standard of performance remained commendably consistent.

In the summer of 1980, aged 32 and having been displaced by new arrival Terry Yorath, John opted for a fresh challenge across the Atlantic, starting a three-year association with Portland Timbers. Next came a return to the Lane, at first running the youth side, then the reserves, before a spell as assistant manager, which ended when Peter Shreeves was sacked in 1986. Thus Spurs bade farewell for a second time to one of their most dedicated loyalists.

BORN: Hackney, London, 26.6.48.
GAMES: 381 (34). GOALS: 49.
HONOURS: UEFA Cup 71/2; League Cup 72/3.
OTHER CLUBS: Portland Timbers, USA.

1968/69 - 1979/80

RALPH COATES

The devastation of Burnley fans when Ralph Coates was sold to Tottenham for £190,000 in May 1971 was overwhelming; at 25, the thickset midfielder-cum-flankman appeared to be on the verge of fully-fledged soccer stardom. Despite the Clarets' relegation, he had just completed a season of majestic personal performances, and Alf Ramsey had rewarded him with an England call-up. There were even some observers ready to extend a comparison with fellow north-easterner Bobby Charlton beyond the obvious similarity in hair-do, though such a parallel always reeked of wishful thinking. Sadly, in the event, Ralph was not to find a platform for greatness at White Hart Lane; rather his seven-year tenure was characterised by ceaseless, honest graft, illuminated by only the periodic shaft of brilliance. In the final analysis, without being a flop, he never quite matched his billing.

Certainly, expectations had been elevated to the skies, not only by the gnashing of teeth emanating from Turf Moor, but also because invariably Ralph had looked a potential world-beater when Burnley had met Spurs. Anticipation was fuelled further by melodramatic rumours of how Bill Nicholson, alarmed at competition from other clubs, had dashed north to meet his quarry at a secret rendezvous; the fans felt that if their manager, whose judgement they trusted implicitly, was so keen then this fellow Coates must be quite a player.

Accordingly, Ralph's early contributions were seen as a marked anti-climax. Playing as an orthodox winger, he appeared over-anxious and even clumsy at times, his pace and strength not matched by his ball control and sense of direction. However, after a brief rest from the limelight he returned as a midfielder and, apparently revelling in the added responsibility for chasing back, proved far more effective. On his day, there was no doubt that Ralph could turn a match, most often through a sudden burst of acceleration or a flowing body-swerve that left defenders leaden-footed. He could cross well under pressure, too, but was prone to give a disappointing final ball when time and space were his. Equally frustrating was the Coates shot, a fearful weapon when delivered accurately but frequently lacking in precision, fizzing wide and wild like a bullet from the gun of a blindfolded cowboy.

The best of Ralph was seen at Highbury in the final League match of his first campaign in North London, when he picked up the ball inside his own half, ran past several defenders and gave Arsenal 'keeper Geoff Barnett no chance with a high-quality finish. Less spectacular but even more welcome than a strike against the old enemy was his Wembley winner some ten months later in the League Cup Final against Norwich, a stinging cross-shot after coming on as substitute for John Pratt. The fact that Ralph had been omitted from the starting line-up was an apt illustration of his fluctuating fortunes at that time, and it came as a timely boost for a modest, honest and personable character. Now some of the tension seemed to lift from his game and 1973/74 saw a succession of freer, more confident displays - notably an inspired effort, both going forward and defending, against Dinamo in Tbilisi - along with four goals during Spurs' progress to the UEFA Cup Final, which was lost to Feyenoord.

For three seasons thereafter, Ralph remained more often in the senior side than out of it, sometimes struggling on bravely while carrying injuries, without wielding the overall influence once expected. The relegation term of 1976/77 saw his last major involvement and he started only one Second Division match before a brief spell in Australia preceded a free transfer to Orient in October 1978. Two admirable seasons at Brisbane Road completed a career that had flourished most productively away from the merciless microscope under which all those seeking success at White Hart Lane must perform.

BORN: Hetton-le-Hole, County Durham, 26.4.46.
GAMES: 229 (19). GOALS: 24.
HONOURS: UEFA Cup 71/2; League Cup 72/3.
4 England caps (70-71).
OTHER CLUBS: Burnley 64/5-70/1 (216, 26);
St George's, Sydney, Australia *on loan*;
Orient 78/9-80/1 (76, 12).

1971/72 - 1977/78

IAN MOORES

Big, blond and bewhiskered, Ian Moores strode out at Old Trafford for his Tottenham League debut in September 1976 like some time-warp Viking bent on an afternoon of plunder. He snatched some booty, too, scoring as Spurs transformed a two-goal deficit into victory, but all too soon the pickings were to grow desperately thin, the rather cumbersome front-man struggling to hold his place, even as his new club dropped a division.

Ian had cost £75,000 from Stoke City following an enthusiastic recommendation from England trainer Les Cocker, who had been hugely taken with his showings as an under-23 international. As well as being an aerial threat in the penalty box, the ex-Potter could drop deep to play his part in building attacks, sometimes supplying a classy touch. Unfortunately he tended to ruin the effect by botching something basic, perhaps a straightforward one-two passing movement, and before long the fans lost patience with him.

The most bountiful day of Ian's disappointing White Hart Lane sojourn was in October 1977, when he contributed a hat-trick towards the 9-0 demolition of Bristol Rovers. However, a year later he was gone, a £55,000 fee taking him to Orient, whom he served competently for four seasons before his career petered out.

BORN: Chesterton, Staffordshire, 5.10.54.
GAMES: 28 (4). GOALS: 8.
OTHER CLUBS: Stoke City 73/4-75/6 (50, 14);
Orient 78/9-81/2 (117, 26);
Bolton Wanderers 82/3 (26, 3); Burnley *on loan* 82/3 (3, 0).

1976/77 - 1978/79

CHRIS McGRATH

The term 'enigma' is over-used when discussing gifted footballers who fail to do justice to their talent, but in the case of Chris McGrath it is singularly apt. The dark, softly-spoken Ulsterman had exquisite skill that might have graced either Tottenham flank for a decade, and he made a stirring start to his White Hart Lane career; but then, inexorably, he faded into obscurity.

Chris was introduced to the senior ranks as an 18-year-old challenger for Jimmy Neighbour's wing role in autumn 1973 and soon was impressing with his ability to flow past defenders on either the outside or inside. Though he disappeared up his share of blind alleys and didn't always choose the right moment to pass, it was felt that such flaws were due merely to inexperience. Chris proved particularly potent in that term's progress to the UEFA Cup Final, scoring five goals, including one that climaxed a thrilling dribble at home to Aberdeen.

But in the next two seasons, the Irish international's confidence appeared to evaporate and his form fizzled. In October 1976, still only 21, he joined Manchester United for £30,000, but fared no better at Old Trafford. A subsequent American sojourn offered scant consolation for what might have been.

BORN: Belfast, 29.11.54.
GAMES: 38 (9). GOALS: 10.
HONOURS: 21 Northern Ireland caps (74-79).
OTHER CLUBS: Millwall *on loan* 75/6 (15, 3);
Manchester United 76/7-80/1 (28, 1);
Tulsa Roughnecks, USA.

1973/74 - 1975/76

JOHN DUNCAN

It might surprise many who recall John Duncan as an unorthodox, rather awkward centre-forward whose method of finishing sometimes owed as much to knee or shin as it did to instep or forehead; yet the fact remains that over the past three decades, only a select few Spurs strikers boasted a better goals-to-games ratio than the angular Scot.

When new Tottenham manager Terry Neill signed Dundee's top marksman for £125,000 in October 1974, he was following a fruitful precedent - ten years earlier one Alan Gilzean had taken the same path from Dens Park to White Hart Lane, with fabulous results. However, the two players could hardly have offered a more vivid contrast. Where Alan had been the subtlest of artists, a master of the game's finer points, John daubed his canvas with the broadest of brushes.

There was no doubt, though, that the newcomer delivered the goods. So what if, on occasion, he would shape to shoot one way and the ball would slew in an unexpected direction; the chances were that it would end in the net. Certainly, his control was not of the silky variety, but he *could* bring the ball down and shoot in one explosive movement, his predatory positional instinct was second to very few, and that distinctive stiff-backed run generated deceptive pace as he peeled away suddenly from defenders who never knew quite what to expect.

In his first term as a Spur, John's goals played a crucial part in staving off relegation, then his quarter-century of League and Cup strikes in 1975/76 provoked unheeded calls for an international call-up. Significantly, he was sidelined by a back injury for most of 1976/77, when Tottenham went down, but was regularly on target as they bounced back at the first attempt. With Keith Burkinshaw planning a radical team overhaul, John joined Derby for £150,000 in September 1978, later doing well as one of British soccer's more articulate managers.

BORN: Lochee, Angus, 22.4.49.
GAMES: 118 (2). GOALS: 62.
OTHER CLUBS: Dundee 68/9-74/5 (124, 62);
Derby County 78/9-80/1 (36, 12); Scunthorpe United 81/2-82/3 (9, 0).
MANAGER: Scunthorpe United (81-83); Hartlepool United (83);
Chesterfield (83-87); Ipswich Town (87-90); Chesterfield (93-).

1974/75 - 1978/79

CHRIS JONES

One stark statistic offers the most telling comment on the Spurs career of striker Chris Jones: over more than half a decade of being in first-team contention, he never stretched his end-of-season goal tally into double figures. Drawing attention to that sorry fact is not intended to belittle the popular Channel Islander, but is rather an attempt to explain why a player of undoubted talent was discarded when still in his mid-twenties.

In fact, there was no shortage of mitigating circumstances. For most of his senior tenure Chris was playing in a side that fell below the club's traditional quality, and only twice did he exceed 30 League outings in one term. Then there was the little matter of competition, at various times, from Messrs Chivers, Duncan, Armstrong, Moores, Lee, Falco, Archibald, Crooks and Gibson!

Yet Chris was by no means the poor relation when it came to qualifications for the job. Though slightly built, he made up for any short-fall in power with speed, effort and a splendid touch, which he employed intelligently to retain possession until a passing option materialised. Good in the air and a specialist in shrewd off-the-ball runs, he roamed productively to the flanks, from which he would whip in wickedly dipping shots and crosses.

One vivid instance of Chris at his best came against Aston Villa at the Lane in April 1977: back to goal and closely policed near the byline, he controlled a Hoddle pass on his thigh before swivelling to hit a fierce half-volley into the far top corner of the net. Of course, such a strike needs a dash of luck, and often that was one commodity Chris lacked, his shots seeming to rebound from the woodwork with depressing frequency. Come September 1982, with Crooks and Archibald rampant, his time ran out and he was freed to join Manchester City. But only later, with Orient, did his performances come close to matching his ability.

BORN: Jersey, 18.4.56.
GAMES: 166 (19). GOALS: 42.
OTHER CLUBS: Manchester City 82/3 (3, 0);
Crystal Palace 82/3 (18, 3);
Charlton Athletic 83/4 (23, 2);
Orient 84/5-86/7 (107, 19).

1974/75 - 1981/82

WILLIE YOUNG

Raw talent, with the accent firmly on the 'raw': that was Willie Young in September 1975 when Terry Neill crossed the Scottish border in his quest for a long-term successor to Mike England. Clearly, despite the reservations of some observers, the Spurs boss was deeply impressed by the potential of the towering red-headed stopper. He parted readily with the £100,000 needed to prise him away from Aberdeen and was undeterred by a lurid reputation which owed something to a fiery playing style, but more to a recent lifetime ban imposed on the under-23 international by his country following an alleged incident in a Copenhagen nightclub.

Soon Willie, though cumbersome and with ball skills which might charitably be described as basic, was winning the Spurs fans' approval with his aerial dominance, crunching strength and infectious enthusiasm. However, by mid-1976/77, after some shaky displays, the Scot was dropped by new boss Keith Burkinshaw and, still disinclined to bow his head to authority, he was ready to leave White Hart Lane. Accordingly that March he joined Arsenal in an £80,000 deal that saw him reunited with Terry Neill. At Highbury, 'Big Wullie' became something of a cult hero, prospering in a more settled side before assisting Nottingham Forest and sampling lower-division life, then leaving the game.

BORN: Edinburgh, 25.11.51.
GAMES: 64. GOALS: 4.
OTHER CLUBS: Aberdeen 70/1-75/6 (132, 10);
Arsenal 76/7-81/2 (170, 11); Nottingham Forest 81/2-82/3 (59, 5); Norwich City 83/4 (6, 0);
Brighton *on loan* 83/4 (4, 0); Darlington 84/5 (4, 0).

1975/76 - 1976/77

ALFIE CONN

Alfie Conn had so much to offer, yet in the end delivered so little. When Bill Nicholson bought him from Rangers for £150,000 in 1974, he was hailed as a magical talent, a beguiling goal-maker and ruthless finisher who, at 22, had limitless potential. In truth, he made a better first impression with the fans, who were rapturous over his skills, than Bill, who made no secret of his loathing for Alfie's hippy-length locks.

Fitness worries delayed his full debut until January at Newcastle, where he responded with an impudent hat-trick, his blend of pace and control making the imagination reel. But his inconsistency and attitude could be infuriating: he demurred when new boss Terry Neill asked him to switch from roving entertainer to the left of midfield, and when he was asked for more effort, it was not always forthcoming. Alfie's two sides were illustrated against Leeds in April 1975. With victory imperative to stave off relegation, he dribbled past three men to score brilliantly, then re-motivated the flagging visitors by sitting on the ball!

His form that term won him two Scotland caps, but then injuries restricted his appearances during the next two seasons, before he joined Celtic for £60,000 in 1977. What a shame that, in recollecting the deeds of Alfie Conn, the negative so firmly outweighs the positive.

BORN: Edinburgh 5.4.52.
GAMES: 38 (5). GOALS: 7.
HONOURS: 2 Scotland caps (75).
OTHER CLUBS: Glasgow Rangers 69/70-73/4 (92, 23);
Celtic 76/7-78/9 (39, 8); Pittsburgh, USA; Hearts 80/1 (17, 3);
Blackpool 80/1 (3, 0); Motherwell 81/2-82/3 (27, 3).

1974/75 - 1976/77

JOHN GORMAN

Even as the storm clouds of impending relegation gathered over White Hart Lane in the early winter of 1976, manager Keith Burkinshaw demonstrated by the purchase of John Gorman that Tottenham were seeking to play, rather than clog, their way out of trouble. That the battle was destined to be lost reflected no discredit on the swarthily dark left-back who, but for persistent knee problems, must surely have become a classy medium-term replacement for the recently retired Cyril Knowles.

John had cost £60,000 from Carlisle, with whom he had enjoyed one term in the top flight before returning to Division Two. He was neither quick, nor graceful - his jerky, almost stuttering running action was unmistakable - but he was the possessor of an astute soccer brain. No hell-for-leather tackler, he preferred to jockey opponents away from the danger area, though it was his assured control and long, accurate passes down the left flank that spoke most eloquently of his quality.

Unfortunately, injury limited the Scot to 16 games in his first season at the Lane, wiped out the whole of his second and truncated his third, before he sought better luck in the Florida sunshine. By the nineties, John had recrossed the Atlantic to become assistant manager to his friend, Glenn Hoddle, at Swindon.

BORN: Winchburgh, West Lothian, 16.8.49.
GAMES: 32. GOALS: 0.
OTHER CLUBS: Carlisle United 70/1-76/7 (229, 5);
Tampa Bay Rowdies, USA.

1976/77 - 1978/79

JIMMY HOLMES

Jimmy Holmes had everything it took to become a long-term fixture on the left flank of Tottenham's defence; everything, that is, except luck. The amiable Dubliner was an emergency £120,000 acquisition from Coventry City on transfer deadline day in 1977, following a serious injury to John Gorman. Despite winning their two most recent matches, Keith Burkinshaw's men were in dire peril near the foot of the table and time was running out. The Republic of Ireland international was quick to display his footballing pedigree. In attack he was an intelligent overlapper whose left-foot delivery to his forwards was outstanding, while his work at the back was brisk and decisive, based on sound positioning and a firm tackle.

However, despite Jimmy's goal in a home victory over Leicester in the season's last game, Spurs went down. An exemplary professional who applied himself unstintingly as they bounced straight back, he enjoyed an enterprising return to the top flight, his all-round skill proving effective during two spells in midfield. But then fate dealt a cruel blow: Jimmy broke his leg on international duty in Bulgaria, and never played for Spurs again. Brief service with other clubs preceded a coaching post at Northampton Town.

BORN: Dublin, 11.11.53.
GAMES: 92. GOALS: 2.
HONOURS: 30 Republic of Ireland caps (71-81).
OTHER CLUBS: Coventry City 71/2-76/7 (128, 7);
Vancouver Whitecaps, Canada; Leicester City 82/3 (2, 0);
Brentford 82/3 (4, 0); Torquay United 82/3-83/4 (25, 3);
Peterborough United 83/4-85/6 (49, 7).

1976/77 - 1978/79

DON McALLISTER

Pace, strength and versatility were the hallmarks of Don McAllister, whose football would never have won commendations for culture, but who deserves an honourable mention in dispatches for doughty work during a period of Tottenham travail. Terry Neill signed the blond Lancastrian from Bolton in February 1975, and for his £80,000 he got an honours graduate from the Burnden Park academy of tough tackling, made famous in the fifties by Messrs Roy Hartle, Tommy Banks and assorted hard nuts.

Initially Don slotted in as a midfield ball-winner, then went on to give half a decade of solid service in the back four, performing at various times in every outfield defensive position. Some of his finest displays came in a central role alongside Steve Perryman during a 1977/78 campaign spent in the Second Division, though he could hold his own in the top flight, too, as he proved with two consistent seasons as the seventies drew to a close. He was used also as an occasional, extremely single-minded one-on-one marker, oozing implacable aggression and constituting an obstacle not to be taken lightly by any opposing play-maker.

If Don could have used the ball more creatively himself, he might have retained his place into the eighties and taken his part in the exciting era then dawning at White Hart Lane. As it was, he was overtaken by more accomplished all-round footballers and his status slipped to that of reliable reserve, causing him to miss the two epic 1981 FA Cup Final encounters with Manchester City. Thus it became clear that if Don wanted first-team football - and at 28 he was far from washed-up - his future lay elsewhere. Accordingly that August he crossed London to join Charlton Athletic for £40,000, half his purchase price, leaving Tottenham to feel they had got their money's worth from a man who had clocked up a double-century of senior outings.

BORN: Radcliffe, Lancashire, 26.5.53.
GAMES: 197 (5). GOALS: 10.
OTHER CLUBS: Bolton Wanderers 69/70-74/5 (156, 2);
Charlton Athletic 81/2-82/3 (55, 6);
Tampa Bay Rowdies, USA; Rochdale 84/5 (3, 0).

1974/75 - 1980/81

93

PETER TAYLOR

One crucial flaw in Peter Taylor's footballing make-up prevented him from maturing into a Tottenham star whose lustre would have lit up White Hart Lane well into the eighties. What the multi-talented, goal-scoring winger lacked during lengthy periods of his North London sojourn was confidence, a commodity of huge importance to all players but which to Peter was the very lifeblood of his game.

When he arrived as a £200,000 recruit from Crystal Palace in September 1976, he was flying high. At Selhurst Park that flamboyant psychologist Malcolm Allison had kept Peter bubbling by informing him constantly what a marvellous player he was, thus extracting the last ounce of performance. Indeed, so scintillating had the Taylor form been that recently he had made light of his Third Division base to win four England caps.

But at Tottenham, he was under Keith Burkinshaw, a good manager but one whose comparatively dour style could hardly have been in greater contrast to Malcolm's. Now Peter faced the daunting task of replacing the popular Jimmy Neighbour without his regular fixes of confidence, and in a team doomed to relegation in his initial term, he struggled at times. Not that he could be dubbed a flop, totalling 30 League goals in his first three campaigns - a prolific return for a flankman and testimony to a venomous shot in either foot - and displaying, intermittently, a thrilling ability to beat a defender and deliver an accurate cross.

But *so* much was expected, and by the turn of the decade his consistency had dipped alarmingly. Thus in November 1980 - out of the Spurs side and his international prospects in ruins at the tender age of 27 - Peter joined Orient for £150,000. After playing on in the lower divisions, then sampling the non-League scene, he left the game before returning as Steve Perryman's number-two at Watford, bursting with enthusiasm. Then, in May 1993, Peter moved into management with Hendon.

BORN: Rochford, Essex, 3.1.53.
GAMES: 128 (12). GOALS: 33.
HONOURS: 4 England caps (76).
OTHER CLUBS: Southend United 70/1-73/4 (75, 12); Crystal Palace 73/4-76/7 (122, 33);
Orient 80/1-82/3 (56, 11); Oldham Athletic *on loan* 82/3 (4, 0);
Maidstone United (non-League); Exeter City 83/4 (8, 0).

1976/77 - 1980/81

NEIL McNAB

Once upon a time - it seems worlds away now, but actually happened in the mid-seventies - Neil McNab was the recipient of what many considered to be the ultimate seal of soccer approval.
He was pronounced, by a certain Bill Shankly, to be as fine a midfield prospect as there was in the land. Yet despite joining Spurs when he was only 16 and too young to turn professional, Neil was destined to spend the bulk of his career outside the top flight. Certainly such an outcome would have been unthinkable to Morton boss Hal Stewart, who waxed so lyrical about his prodigy that in February 1974 Bill Nicholson took a look for himself, then gambled £75,000 to take the boy south.

Though short and thin, Neil was deceptively powerful, a fiery character who dug hard in the tackle and had immense stamina; but the real appeal of the McNab game was his lovely skill. In training he could stroll the length of the pitch and back, casually bouncing the ball from foot to foot without letting it touch the ground; more practically, in matches he could worm his way past opponents and pass superbly. He was not rushed, however, being nursed in the reserves with the occasional taste of the big time, until Terry Neill gave him a six-week senior run at the start of 1975/76. Judged to be not ready still, he continued to play most of his football in the Combination until 1977/78 when, with Spurs in Division Two, Keith Burkinshaw used him in every match.

Then came the turning point of Neil's career. Back in the top flight, Tottenham made their bold Argentinian investment and he was dropped. That November he joined Bolton for £250,000, going on to serve four more clubs, his performances improving as he matured. Some say he was a brilliant youngster who failed to progress at the expected rate; others maintain that letting him go at 21 was a criminal waste. That he never scaled the game's loftiest peaks tends to bear out the Burkinshaw judgement, but had he remained at White Hart Lane, who knows?

BORN: Greenock, Scotland, 4.6.57.
GAMES: 70 (10). GOALS: 3.
OTHER CLUBS: Morton 72/3-73/4 (14, 0); Bolton Wanderers 78/9-79/80 (35, 4);
Brighton 79/80-82/3 (103, 4); Leeds United *on loan* 82/3 (5, 0);
Manchester City 83/4-89/90 (221, 16); Huddersfield Town *on loan* 91/2 (11, 0);
Tranmere Rovers 89/90- (105, 6).

1973/74 - 1978/79

MARK KENDALL

Mark Kendall was the dark horse in the three-man race to replace Pat Jennings and become Tottenham's goalkeeper of the eighties. But though he had youth on his side - the Welshman was junior by some seven years to both Barry Daines and Milija Aleksic - he couldn't make it count, and it can have been of precious little consolation that his rivals, too, were unable to step into the void filled eventually by Ray Clemence.

By far Mark's most successful season was 1978/79, in which he missed only one League game between November and April and won an under-21 cap into the bargain. At that time there were hopes that the personable six-footer, who was not helped by a constant struggle to control his weight, might add much-needed consistency to all-round competence.

But errors, particularly of the positional variety, continued to mar otherwise excellent displays, and in September 1980 Mark joined Newport for £45,000. After six years at Somerton Park, he played some of his finest football for Wolves before bowing out of the League at Swansea City.

BORN: Blackwood, South Wales, 20.9.58.
GAMES: 36. GOALS: 0.
OTHER CLUBS:
Chesterfield *on loan* 79/80 (9, 0);
Newport County 80/1-86/7 (272, 0);
Wolverhampton Wanderers 86/7-89/90 (147, 0); Swansea City 90/91-91/2 (12, 0);
Burnley *on loan* 91/2 (2, 0).

1978/79-1980/81

MICKY STEAD

Though all-round footballers inferior to Micky Stead have enjoyed lengthy First Division stints, it must be conceded that the sturdy full-back was not quite of top-flight calibre. Highly competitive in the tackle and a reliable passer, the blond Londoner was not the quickest of movers and in the three seasons in which he lurked on the fringe of the senior side, a regular berth seemed likely to remain beyond his compass.

When 19-year-old Micky made his first-team bow at Stoke in February 1976, he played well enough to retain his place for three matches, until injured first-choices Terry Naylor and Don McAllister regained fitness. Then he enjoyed a six-match run at the end of the following season as Jimmy Holmes' deputy.

But his future at White Hart Lane was clearly limited and, after a loan spell at Swansea, he joined Southend for £45,000 in September 1978. At Roots Hall Micky found his true level, serving United doughtily before ending his playing days at Doncaster Rovers, where he became a coach.

BORN: West Ham, London, 28.2.57.
GAMES: 14 (1). GOALS: 0.
OTHER CLUBS:
Swansea City *on loan* 76/7 (5, 1);
Southend United 78/9-85/6 (297, 5);
Doncaster Rovers 85/6-87/8 (85. 0).

1975/76-1977/78

COLIN LEE

As dream starts go, Colin Lee's at Tottenham was decidedly on the extravagant side. Two days after joining Spurs in a £60,000 move from Torquay in October 1977, the tall Devonian scored four times in the 9-0 annihilation of Bristol Rovers in front of the *Match Of The Day* cameras at White Hart Lane. It is almost superfluous to note that he never attained such heights again.

With an injury crisis at its height, the young marksman had arrived at a time of rare opportunity: instead of taking his place in a queue, as a raw newcomer from the bottom flight might expect, Colin won a regular place in the Second Division promotion fray. However, though wholehearted, he proved limited, an effective leaper for high balls beyond the far post but lacking the required sharpness on the ground. Still, he helped achieve the immediate objective, and made 26 starts - including a few as a makeshift defender - in Spurs' first term back among the elite. Then, in January 1980, a £200,000 fee took Colin to Chelsea, with whom he was converted eventually into a capable full-back.

BORN: Torquay, Devon, 12.6.56.
GAMES: 65 (6). GOALS: 21.
OTHER CLUBS: Bristol City *no games;*
Hereford United *on loan* 74/5 (9, 0);
Torquay United 76/7-77/8 (35, 14);
Chelsea 79/80-86/7 (185, 36);
Brentford 87/8-88/9 (24, 1).
MANAGER: Watford (90).

1977/78-1979/80

BARRY DAINES

It is Barry Daines' misfortune to be remembered principally as the man in whom Keith Burkinshaw had so much confidence that he sold Pat Jennings to Arsenal in August 1977. It was a decision which enraged many Spurs fans, who were mystified on two counts: if Barry was *that* good, why had he not been hunted by other clubs since his debut in 1971, and why had he been content to remain an understudy for more than half a decade?

In fact, Barry was a competent all-rounder - better, perhaps, at stopping shots than claiming crosses - and the pick of the 'keepers tested by Tottenham during the interregnum between the Irishman and Ray Clemence. But despite the bold backing of his manager - based on some impressive displays when Pat was injured during the relegation season of 1976/77 - and an admirable, ever-present contribution to the subsequent promotion campaign, Barry appeared to lack self-belief. This became evident on Spurs' return to the top flight, and culminated in Burkinshaw's preference of Milija Aleksic for the 1981 FA Cup Final.

Concluding understandably that the future could hold little for him at White Hart Lane, Barry opted to try his luck in Hong Kong, later serving Mansfield. However, despite the anti-climax, it would be wrong to under-value his loyal, ten-term contribution to the Tottenham cause; true, he was never in the Jennings class, but then who was?

BORN: Witham, Essex, 30.9.51.
GAMES: 173. GOALS: 0.
OTHER CLUBS: Hong Kong; Mansfield Town 83/4 (21, 0).

1971/72 - 1980/81

GERRY ARMSTRONG

When Gerry Armstrong crossed the Irish Sea to join Tottenham in 1975, he was raw, hungry and ready for action - and without being disrespectful to one of the game's best-loved and most genuine characters, it might be said that the big striker had barely altered when he left for Watford five years later. Of course, there had been certain refinements to his method, but essentially Gerry would always remain a prodigiously strong, unendingly selfless workaholic, not overburdened with ball skills but a colossus in the air and with heart enough for ten men.

Not that he was devoid of technique: his colleagues knew that they could knock the ball towards him and, having fought for it and won it, he could retain possession until reinforcements arrived. But as the Argentinian influence placed extra emphasis on touch play, Gerry was not in his element at the Lane, and he didn't help his standing with the fans by battling on uncomplainingly when he was injured, thus unable to do himself full justice. As stars were bought, his departure became inevitable, but a place in folklore was awaiting him. The Ulsterman's spirited exploits in the 1982 World Cup, including the winning goal against Spain, earned him an award as British Player of the Tournament - and a more popular accolade is difficult to imagine.

BORN: Belfast, 23.5.54.
GAMES: 74 (24). GOALS: 16.
HONOURS: 63 Northern Ireland caps (77-86).
OTHER CLUBS: Bangor, Northern Ireland;
Watford 80/1-82/3 (76, 12); Real Mallorca, Spain;
West Bromwich Albion 85/6 (8, 0); Chesterfield *on loan* 85/6 (12, 1);
Brighton 86/7-87/8 (42, 5); Millwall *on loan* 87/8 (7, 0).

1976/77 - 1980/81

MILIJA ALEKSIC

The ups and downs of football life were illustrated poignantly by the three-and-a-half-year White Hart Lane sojourn of goalkeeper Milija Aleksic. His ride on the Tottenham roller-coaster began with a £100,000 transfer from Luton Town in December 1978, joining Barry Daines and Mark Kendall as contenders for the job between Spurs' posts. His fortunes dipped as he was injured after two matches, declining even more drastically in January 1980 when he broke his jaw in a collision with Manchester United's Joe Jordan in an FA Cup replay at Old Trafford.

Now poor Milija was due an upturn, but it did not come until the spring of 1981 when a knock to Barry Daines gave the Midlands-born son of a Yugoslavian father the opportunity to shine. He seized it avidly, playing so well that he retained his place for both FA Cup Final clashes with Manchester City. Now, his stock never higher, he had concrete hopes of becoming Tottenham's number-one, but suddenly Ray Clemence arrived and his prospects at the club took a final plunge. In truth, Milija was no more than a competent all-round 'keeper, brave and with the sharp reflexes of a natural shot-stopper, but seemingly nervous when dealing with crosses. After returning to Luton on loan, he took up coaching in South Africa.

BORN: Newcastle-under-Lyme, Staffordshire, 14.4.51.
GAMES: 32. GOALS: 0.
HONOURS: FA Cup 80/1.
OTHER CLUBS: Plymouth Argyle 73/4-75/6 (32, 0);
Luton Town 76/7-78/9 (77, 0);
Luton Town *on loan* 81/2 (4, 0).

1978/79 - 1981/82

TERRY YORATH

Mention Terry Yorath and most football fans will think of Leeds, where he spent nine seasons as an often under-appreciated member of one of post-war soccer's finest squads, or of Wales, whom he has managed for five years. Yet somewhere between those peaks was an interlude at Tottenham which, though relatively uneventful, was completed with characteristic, full-blooded application. Keith Burkinshaw signed Terry from Coventry for £275,000 in August 1979, seeing in him the battle-hardened warrior he desired to play alongside his centre-half. In this role, and in the more familiar midfield holding berth to which he was to revert, the rugged, blond Welsh international brought the abrasive tackle and nagging persistence which had served him so well at Elland Road.

Though his pace was sluggish, Terry's distribution was more accomplished than many pundits would allow, and he possessed a shrewd grasp of tactics that he was not slow to share with colleagues on the pitch. However, after suffering injuries early in 1980/81, he was unable to reclaim a regular place in the face of stiff competition, and that summer he moved to Vancouver Whitecaps, later returning to these shores before launching a successful career in coaching and management.

BORN: Cardiff, 27.3.50. GAMES: 58 (4). GOALS: 1.
HONOURS: 59 Wales caps (69-81).
OTHER CLUBS: Leeds United 67/8-76/7 (143, 10);
Coventry City 76/7-78/9 (99, 3); Vancouver Whitecaps, Canada;
Bradford City 82/3-84/5 (27, 0); Swansea City 86/7 (1, 0).
MANAGER: Swansea City (86-89); Bradford City (89-90);
Swansea City (90-91); Wales (88-).

1979/80 - 1980/81

RICARDO VILLA

The two sides of Ricardo Villa were laid bare in the 1981 FA Cup Final. In the first, drawn encounter with Manchester City he was sluggish, brooding, almost sulkily ineffective; in the replay he came alive, was suddenly bright and inventive, contributing two goals including a winner that will stand forever as one of the finest Wembley has witnessed.

Though he had made two substitute appearances as his country had lifted the World Cup that summer, Ricky was little known to British fans when, valued at £375,000, he accompanied Osvaldo Ardiles to White Hart Lane in July 1978. After outdoing his star stable-mate in pre-season training, the so-called 'Dark Horse of the Pampas' was quickly out of the starting stalls with a goal on his Spurs debut at Nottingham Forest, but soon found the going tougher than expected. Taking longer than Ossie to settle in a strange land and hampered by injuries in his first English autumn, his form was patchy.

However, when Ricky *was* on song, he was a stylish swashbuckler. Tall and bulky, his bullish strength made him hard to dispossess and his apparent ponderousness belied skills fit to grace any stage. His scorn for the orthodox took him swerving away from two defenders to plant a booming 30-yarder into the Wolves net in the 1981 semi-final, and it surfaced even more gloriously in the final replay. On receiving the ball in the inside-left slot, he was confronted by a wall of opponents and most men would have passed. But Ricky surged on, went past Caton, Ranson and Caton again before gulling keeper Corrigan to give Spurs the Cup.

Yet this headiest of moments proved no cure for inconsistency and Ricky's confidence, never noticeably resilient, took a further fearful buffeting when he was abused by opposing crowds over the Falklands conflict. Understandably, he left England in June 1983, taking his unpredictable talents to the USA. At the Lane, meanwhile, memories of Ricky Villa grow ever warmer in the rosy glow of retrospect.

BORN: Argentina, 18.8.52
GAMES: 168 (11). GOALS: 25.
HONOURS: FA Cup 80/1. Argentina caps.
OTHER CLUBS: Quilmes, Tucuman and Racing Club, all Argentina;
Fort Lauderdale Strikers, USA.

1978/79 - 1982/83

PAUL MILLER

For those purists who demand culture from their Spurs, Paul Miller was close to anathema. But as even the most savage critic of the rough-and-ready central defender would have to admit, he was a born survivor. For a large proportion of the time between his senior debut in spring 1979 and his ultimate unseating by Richard Gough in August 1986, Paul seemed on the verge of being replaced. John Lacy, Paul Price, Gary Stevens, they all might have been expected to sabotage the loquacious Londoner's first-team ambitions, but each time he rose to meet the challenge, pocketing three major cup medals in the process.

Though Paul's game boasted barely a shred of refinement, in certain circumstances he was mightily effective, his ruthless tackling and aerial power equipping him as an opponent with whom no one relished a confrontation, particularly when he was operating in tandem with the formidable Graham Roberts. But - and it was a sizeable but - he could be exposed mercilessly by clever, elusive forwards who laid off him or who ran at him with the ball, and he could be drawn out of position too easily for comfort. As a result, Paul was subjected to periods as a crowd scapegoat that would have scuppered less buoyant characters, but he would emerge from them with his confidence and drive undiminished, cheerfully ready for whatever the football fates had in store for him.

To be fair, Paul's footwork improved with experience, and he became relatively adept at picking out his attackers with long, raking passes. He could play at full-back, too, and loved to get forward, contributing one of Tottenham's most valuable goals of the decade, a powerful header from a Mike Hazard corner in the drawn first leg of the 1984 UEFA Cup Final against Anderlecht in Belgium. Paul - dubbed 'Max' by team-mates after the music-hall comedian with whom he shared both a surname and an aptitude for patter - left White Hart Lane for Charlton in February 1987, later seeing out his career in the lower divisions.

BORN: Stepney, London, 11.10.59.
GAMES: 281 (4). GOALS: 10.
HONOURS: UEFA Cup 83/4; FA Cup 80/1, 81/2.
OTHER CLUBS: Charlton Athletic 86/7-88/9 (42, 2); Watford 88/9 (20, 0); Bournemouth 89/90-90/1 (47, 1); Brentford *on loan* 89/90 (3, 0); Swansea City 90/1 (12, 0).

1978/79 - 1986/87

CHRIS HUGHTON

Chris Hughton was a thoroughly modern full-back, as far removed from the outmoded tradition of hulking clogger as it is possible to imagine, his game based on smoothness and movement without the hint of a jagged edge. Small and neat, light and searingly quick - at his peak, wingers tended to struggle in *his* wake, rather than vice versa - he was a potent overlapper and careful crosser, a legacy of his teenage days as a flankman.

When Spurs had possession, Chris was ever ready to receive the ball, then keep the game flowing with thoughtful distribution, and when scoring opportunities presented themselves he could oblige skilfully. At the back he was equally calm and resourceful, more disposed to jockeying opponents out of position than robbing them with a thundering tackle. Versatility was another Hughton asset, at least to the extent of being able to play on either defensive flank, though the right-footer's preference for playing on the left - an increasingly common vogue - did not win universal approval. Certainly he could be seen frequently switching the ball to his stronger side, but such was his dexterity that momentum was sacrificed only rarely.

Chris, who qualified to play for Eire as his mother hailed from Limerick, was working as a lift engineer when Spurs spotted him in junior football. After he turned professional in the summer of 1979, his impact was instant, and he missed only three League games during the season that followed. Thereafter he shared in all Spurs' cup triumphs of the early eighties, though as the decade grew old his form became fitful and he grew less assured of his place. Accordingly Chris, whose brother Henry played for three League clubs, was given a free transfer in 1990, joining West Ham before lending his experience to Brentford in the new First Division.

At Griffin Park, as throughout an exemplary White Hart Lane career, he remained a credit to himself and to his sport.

BORN: West Ham, London, 11.12.58.
GAMES: 389 (9). GOALS: 19.
HONOURS: UEFA Cup 83/4; FA Cup 80/1, 81/2.
53 Republic of Ireland caps (79-91).
OTHER CLUBS: West Ham United 90/1-91/2 (33, 0);
Brentford 91/2- (32, 0).

1979/80 - 1989/90

MARK FALCO

It's an unpalatable fact but surely one for which his own teenage years as a denizen of The Shelf must have prepared Mark Falco: simply that being born in North London and graduating through Tottenham's junior ranks is anything but a passport to acceptance from the White Hart Lane faithful. Local boys, it seems, are expected to do that little bit more to satisfy fans who are sometimes willing to make generous allowances for star imports. Thus despite a commendable goals-to-games ratio - the product of unceasing honest endeavour and vast strength coupled with rather more natural ability than he was credited with - the former England youth international never received the terrace acclaim that was his due.

Part of the problem was that Mark's style was not easy on the eye. Tall and strappingly built, he could appear cumbersome, and in all fairness, compared to quicksilver contemporaries Archibald and Crooks, so he was. But when he ran on to a through-ball in his favoured inside-left slot, it took a good man to stop the Falco surge, which was apt to climax in a venomous low shot. Fearless and a constant menace in the air, he was effective at retaining possession, too, frequently taking the knocks and contributing the legwork that paved his colleagues' way to goal.

After scoring on his senior debut in May 1979, Mark lingered on the fringe of Spurs' squad until August 1981, when two Charity Shield goals against Aston Villa signalled the start of a five-week purple patch. But injury intervened and it was not until 1983/84 that Mark won a regular place. Then came three prolific terms in which his tally never dipped below 20, yet always there was the feeling that just around the corner was an expensive buy and that Mark would have to make way. So it proved when Nico Claesen arrived and David Pleat dispatched the faithful Falco to Watford for a bargain £300,000 in October 1986. Maybe he fell short of the highest class, but Mark was an underrated asset to Tottenham and to each of the string of clubs he went on to serve.

BORN: Hackney, London, 22.10.60.
GAMES: 217 (19). GOALS: 90.
HONOURS: UEFA Cup 83/4.
OTHER CLUBS: Chelsea *on loan* 82/3 (3, 0);
Watford 86/7 (33, 14); Glasgow Rangers 87/8 (14, 5);
Queen's Park Rangers 87/8-90/1 (87, 27);
Millwall 91/2 (21, 4).

1978/79 - 1986/87

Lean, lanky Liverpudlian John Lacy might be described as Tottenham's 'silent signing'. He joined in the summer of 1978, at the height of the commotion surrounding the arrival of Ardiles and Villa from Argentina, and thus tended to be overlooked. In fact, the 6ft 3in stopper was making his own piece of history as the first man whose fee - in the region of £200,000 - was fixed by a Football League tribunal after Spurs and his former club, Fulham, failed to agree terms.

John had profited much at Craven Cottage from the tutelage of Alan Mullery and Bobby Moore, alongside whom he had played in the 1975 FA Cup Final, yet there was no disguising the truth that his work with the ball at his feet was no match for his commendable aerial prowess. In those early days at White Hart Lane his control and passing were poor and an impatient crowd let him know it in time-honoured heartless fashion.

But where lesser men might have made their excuses and left, John - an economics graduate who had not taken up football seriously until his university days - worked hard on his skills and, imperceptibly at first, attitudes began to change. Hard-boiled terrace critics who had protested that 'this mug can't play' ended up swallowing their words, even professing affection towards a player who had been willing to learn.

Of course, the improvement was relative, and after a niggling thigh injury had ruled him out of contention for the 1981 FA Cup Final, in which the vigorous young central defensive partnership of Graham Roberts and Paul Miller had performed effectively, the long-term prospects of a man approaching 30 were not bright. However John remained at the Lane until August 1983, making 27 senior starts in his final season before moving to Crystal Palace for a year, then linking up with former Fulham team-mate John Mitchell at non-League St Albans and embarking on a career outside the game.

BORN: Liverpool, 14.8.51.
GAMES: 126 (6). GOALS: 3.
OTHER CLUBS: Fulham 72/3-77/8 (168, 7);
Crystal Palace 83/4 (27, 0).

1978/79 - 1982/83

STEVE PERRYMAN

Steve Perryman was that rarest of gems, a sure thing in an uncertain world. He remained the one constant factor as Spurs lifted a clutch of cups in the early seventies, then slumped to relegation before rising to win further trophies and, at last, make a sustained title challenge. Throughout that dramatic decade-and-a-half, Steve shone as a footballer of superior all-round ability and, no less important, a character whose strength and honesty, affability and intelligence, were of incalculable value to the Tottenham cause. That he won more medals and made more senior appearances - in excess of a thousand, including friendlies - than any other Spur, and counts an MBE (1986) and a Footballer of the Year award (1982) among his honours, is hardly surprising. That he won just one England cap, and that as a substitute, is a mystery to which only Don Revie and Ron Greenwood could ever have supplied a solution; Alf Ramsey, as the Perryman under-23 record shows, was grooming Steve for an international future when he lost his own job in 1974.

The marathon top-level tenure began in September 1969 when the baby-faced 17-year-old was pitchforked into League action after a handful of reserve games. Nothing too unusual about that, except that most such youngsters return to the 'stiffs' to continue the learning process. Not so the tough, enthusiastic midfielder, who kept his place among the stars, becoming indispensable through a biting tackle, persistence and a maturity beyond his years while rendering irrelevant a certain deficiency in pace. Steve fitted perfectly into the Spurs style, winning the ball, moving it on and making himself available for an instant return pass. Some felt his elevation had come too early, and that by slaving so assiduously he was not doing justice to his impressive ball skills. Yet having broken through on the back of work-rate, he was in no mind to slacken off and, certainly, Bill Nicholson wasn't complaining.

However, in 1971/72 Steve endured a hiatus in form which, combined with a lack of goals that was to dog him throughout his career, gave grounds for concern. The challenge was met with typical fortitude as he battled on, underlining his recovery that spring with two beautifully volleyed edge-of-the-box strikes at home to AC Milan in the UEFA Cup semi-final. Nevertheless, with Spurs struggling early in 1974/75, the unthinkable almost occurred when he came close to joining Coventry, but the move fell through after the shock resignation of the manager.

Changes *were* afoot for Steve, though. First, in March 1975, the departure of Martin Peters signalled his promotion to captain, a role in which he was to revel for ten years; then, towards the climax of the relegation dogfight in March 1977, he switched to a central defensive berth that might have been made for him. Now the game opened up for Steve, the more considered approach demanded at the back enabling his talents to blossom, and though he was not as aerially dominant as bigger men, his impeccable reading of situations could be trusted to neutralise the quickest and wiliest of opponents.

Though he revitalised the rearguard, it was too late to avoid the drop, and at season's end Liverpool tried to lure him north. Making a decision that encapsulated his personality, Steve opted to stay at the Lane, reasoning that as he had led his men down, it was his duty to lead them back, and so he did, going on to reap rich reward in the eighties. By then, he had become an overlapping right-back, tackling as implacably as ever but relishing also the long-delayed taste of adventure as he galloped forward to keep his strikers supplied with crosses. Steve closed a Spurs career of unparalleled achievement in March 1986, serving Oxford briefly before entering management. It is work for which he is eminently well-equipped, with his vast knowledge, sane values and commendable ethics. No parents with a son on the verge of a life in football could place their lad's future in more trustworthy hands.

BORN: Ealing, London, 21.12.51.
GAMES: 851 (3). GOALS: 39.
HONOURS: UEFA Cup 71/2, 83/4; FA Cup 80/1, 81/2; League Cup 70/1, 72/3.
1 England cap (82).
OTHER CLUBS: Oxford United 85/6-86/7 (17, 0); Brentford 86/7-89/90 (53, 0).
MANAGER: Brentford (87-90); Watford (90-).

1969/70 - 1985/86

OSVALDO ARDILES

It might have been an old Argentinian proverb, more likely it was the product of his own shrewd soccer brain. Either way, Osvaldo Ardiles had a saying: 'Some people play with a round ball, others use a square one'. What he meant was that while certain players make life easy for themselves and their team-mates, creating time and space by delivering intelligent passes, unfortunately there are those who make a simple game deucedly difficult by not using their heads. Ossie, of course, was the living, breathing embodiment of the former category, a footballing philosopher whose intellect and instinct evoked memories of Danny Blanchflower, no less, bringing a new dimension to Spurs while making a vast impression on the English game as a whole.

When Keith Burkinshaw bought Ossie from Huracan of Buenos Aires in July 1978, it was hailed as both a coup and a gamble. Tottenham fans were delighted at the acquisition of a performer who only weeks earlier had sprung to international celebrity as a leading light in his country's World Cup triumph. At £325,000, a comparatively modest fee facilitated by Argentina's financial recession, many felt that Tottenham had a rare bargain, though there was no shortage of cautionary voices questioning how Ossie and his compatriot Ricky Villa would settle in North London.

Certainly as far as the diminutive schemer was concerned, doubt on that score was short-lived. Charming and articulate - he was trained as a lawyer - Ossie swiftly secured a social niche, while showing all the dedication and mental strength his new life demanded. On the pitch, he worked hard to become accustomed to the extra pace of the First Division and was quick to learn certain unfamiliar defensive responsibilities. But more significantly, even as those minor adjustments were being made, Ossie's creative game blossomed gloriously at White Hart Lane. The 'Little Master' brought to his work perfect ball control, distribution that was at once both artistic and workmanlike, and what seemed like his own radar system - 'I hear feet coming' was his deadpan explanation to colleagues mystified by his knack of detecting and avoiding unexpected challenges.

Ossie's trademark was the instantly dispatched 15-yard pass, sometimes piercing a defence at a single stroke but more frequently the centrepiece of a quickfire midfield interchange. He was that rare phenomenon in England, a 'head-up' player, one who could make the ball do his bidding without glueing his eyes to it, thus having more chance to spot an opening; and all the time he *wanted* that ball, scooting everywhere in tireless search of it. Inevitably there were opponents who, gulled by his bird-like frame, believed that force could stem his flow, but they were wrong, reckoning without a wiry strength allied to beautiful balance and feisty determination.

By the time of his first English club honour, a 1981 FA Cup winner's medal, Ossie was beloved of the Spurs supporters, and his integration into the local scene heightened his distress as nationalist fervour ran amok during the Falklands War. As a result of the conflict, he moved temporarily to Paris St Germain, missing the 1982 FA Cup triumph and not 'coming home' until January 1983. Then began an epidemic of injuries that was to plague him for more than three years and the return to something near his best form in 1986, following two broken legs and a cartilage operation, was a comeback as remarkable as Dave Mackay's in the sixties. In 1987/88, aged 35, Ossie was loaned to Blackburn before joining QPR on a free transfer the following summer. There followed a managerial career that began brightly, then faltered, before picking up new momentum. But whatever lies ahead for Ossie Ardiles - and some see him as a future Spurs boss - few would deny his status as the British game's most successful foreign import.

BORN: Cordoba, Argentina, 3.8.52.
GAMES 293 (18). GOALS: 25.
HONOURS: UEFA Cup 83/4; FA Cup 80/1. Argentina caps.
OTHER CLUBS: Instituto de Cordoba and Huracan, both Argentina;
Paris St Germain *on loan* 82/3; Blackburn Rovers *on loan* 87/8 (5, 0);
Queen's Park Rangers 88/9 (8, 0); Swindon Town 89/90 (2, 0).
MANAGER: Swindon Town (89-91); Newcastle United (91-92);
West Bromwich Albion (92-).

1978/79 - 1987/88

STEVE ARCHIBALD

He was the darling of the White Hart Lane faithful; some of his team-mates warmed to him while others remained distinctly cool; manager Keith Burkinshaw, having paid handsomely for his services, rowed bitterly with him. But one thing was certain about Steve Archibald - *everyone* recognised his outstanding talent. The slim, sandy-blond Glaswegian joined Spurs from Aberdeen in May 1980, fresh from playing a star role in taking the Scottish title to Pittodrie. The £800,000 fee was the biggest to pass between clubs on opposite sides of the border, but soon - as Steve netted 25 times and tasted FA Cup glory at Wembley in his first English season - it became obvious that the North Londoners had sunk their capital into gilt-edged stock.

Here was a striker with wings on his heels: eternally alert, he could flash past a defender as suddenly and unstoppably as an arrow from a bow, and could finish with apparently nerveless efficiency. Steve boasted skill, subtlety and style in abundance, and was well served by a wiry resilience which enabled him to withstand heavy physical challenges. He brimmed with stamina, too, often roaming deep to join in the build-up to attacks, and could do a capable job in midfield at need. Crucially, the Scot employed his many assets cleverly, constantly adapting to the ever-changing options around him, and making the most of the sumptuous service emanating from Messrs Hoddle and Ardiles. Particularly bountiful for the Tottenham cause was the scoring partnership he enjoyed with Garth Crooks, and those who would chide Steve for a certain selfishness when confronted with the net - a required tendency for any successful marksman - should note that his deft touches supplied a more-than-acceptable number of 'assists'.

However, after that prolific introductory campaign, the Archibald bandwagon encountered a somewhat rockier road in 1981/82, when the winning of a second FA Cup medal was offset by injury absences and a leaner time in front of goal. There was one moment of archetypal Archibald to savour, though, when he held off two defenders before netting expertly in the League Cup Final defeat by Liverpool. The next term brought more consistent personal returns, but it was in 1983/84, his final season at White Hart Lane, that he reached his zenith - and that despite a well-publicised rift with Keith Burkinshaw. The apparent cause was the player's insistence on leaving the field after being injured at home to Coventry that August, while the manager, having used his substitute already, wanted him to stay on. Though quiet, Steve was strong-willed and there were heated exchanges which failed to clear the air. Even after the striker returned to action with a thunderous 25-yard goal at Watford, the relationship remained intensely strained, a situation hardly conducive to team needs, and Steve's attitude annoyed certain of his colleagues. Such unwelcome distractions did not put him off his own game, though; indeed, he struck his richest vein of form to date, scoring 29 goals and helping to secure the UEFA Cup, as well as showing his courage by playing through at least one game in severe pain.

Oddly, both men were due to leave White Hart Lane that summer, Keith resigning at season's end and Steve - dismaying the doting thousands who serenaded their hero with 'We'll Take More Care Of You, Archibald', to the strains of a topical TV advertising ditty - was sold to Barcelona in July for £1,150,000. Predictably for such an accomplished and self-confident performer, he flourished in Spain, before ending his career with further short spells in England and Scotland. Meanwhile, back on the Tottenham terraces, his memory is cherished still.

BORN: Glasgow, 27.9.56.
GAMES: 185 (4). GOALS: 78.
HONOURS: UEFA Cup 83/4; FA Cup 80/1, 81/2.
27 Scotland caps (80-86).
OTHER CLUBS: Clyde 74/5-77/8 (65, 7); Aberdeen 77/8-79/80 (76, 29);
Barcelona, Spain, 84/5-87/8; Blackburn Rovers 87/8 (20, 6);
Hibernian 88/9-89/90 (44, 15);
Espanol, Spain, 89/90-90/1; St Mirren 90/1 (16, 2);
Reading 91/2 (1, 0);
Clyde 92/3;
Fulham 92/3 (2, 0) .

1980/81 - 1983/84

GARTH CROOKS

'Black Magic in the box' - a typically glib tabloid newspaper tag, but when Garth Crooks was at his effervescent best it was an apt one. Somehow it summed up more than his quicksilver, explosive contributions to the Tottenham attack, carrying with it a hint of glamour and tapping into the zestful personality of a performer who thrived on life at a big-city club. While some players from the provinces seem overcome by the razzmatazz which is an inescapable part of the White Hart Lane scene, Garth appeared to be lifted by the limelight; indeed, when he was on a roll he exuded an infectious confidence that expressed a rare quality in the modern game, the sheer joy of playing football.

Born in the Potteries of Jamaican parents, Garth had made an exciting impression with Stoke, his hometown club, and as an established under-21 international was viewed as one of England's most promising young forwards when Keith Burkinshaw signed him for £600,000 in July 1980. He arrived in North London two months after the Scot, Steve Archibald, and before long the two had established a rapport which was to reap rich rewards. Friends off the field, they became a lethal strike combination on it, spearheading Tottenham's triumphant back-to-back FA Cup campaigns of the early eighties and, importantly, catching the fans' imagination.

Though not the equal of Steve in terms of ball control and all-round ability, the left-sided Garth was to be no junior partner, as he indicated by netting on each of his first three League outings. Bouncy, fleet-footed and brave, he provided an ideal, constantly moving target for the passing masters in Spurs' ultra-creative midfield, and when given a chance at goal he could take it with waspish vigour. One archetypal Crooks strike came in the 1981 FA Cup semi-final replay against Wolves, when he sprinted on to a supremely weighted through-ball from Glenn Hoddle before beating 'keeper Paul Bradshaw with ruthless accuracy. In fact, numerous memories of Garth at his most effective relate to the FA Cup, in which he played 17 games for the club before tasting defeat: there was the smartly dispatched equaliser in the 1981 final rematch against Manchester City, the slight miscue that knocked out Arsenal in January 1982 and the adroit volley that ended Leeds United's interest in the following round.

However, Garth's tenure at Tottenham was not spent solely on the crest of a wave. Injuries and the type of lean spell that plagues every marksman from time to time appeared to dent the Crooks confidence and 1983/84 saw him out of the side for long periods. That season, with the presence of Alan Brazil increasing the already keen competition for places, he was released on loan to Manchester United, but was given little chance to impress at Old Trafford and returned to the Lane understandably frustrated. Yet he still had much to offer, as he demonstrated during the next season as another new acquisition, Clive Allen, faced fitness problems. That autumn Garth grabbed two hat-tricks in eight days - one at Halifax in the League Cup, the other in a home UEFA Cup encounter with Sporting Braga - before going on to score in seven successive games at the turn of the year. Then, he netted the goal against Liverpool that secured Spurs' first win at Anfield for 73 years, and had he not sustained a springtime injury, Tottenham's title challenge might not have faded away in quite the anti-climactic manner it did.

Despite his 'second wind', though, it became clear that Garth's future lay elsewhere and that August he switched to West Bromwich Albion, later serving Charlton Athletic before retiring. An intelligent, articulate individual who had proved an able chairman of the Professional Footballers Association, he moved on eventually to a promising media career. On the air, as on the pitch, Garth Crooks was a bundle of unbounded vitality.

BORN: Stoke, 10.3.58.
GAMES: 176 (6). GOALS: 75.
HONOURS: FA Cup 80/1, 81/2.
OTHER CLUBS: Stoke City 75/6-79/80 (147, 48);
Manchester United *on loan* 83/4 (7, 2); West Bromwich Albion 85/6-86/7 (40, 16);
Charlton Athletic 86/7-90/1 (56, 15).

1980/81 - 1984/85

MIKE HAZARD

Mike Hazard was a richly gifted play-maker who decorated many games but dominated few, thus condemning himself to an in-and-out White Hart Lane existence languishing perplexedly in the shadow of Glenn Hoddle. In retrospect, and after drooling over film clips of the bubbly-haired Wearsider's bewitching skills, it would be easy to berate successive Tottenham managers for not using him more regularly - only once did Mike exceed 20 League starts in a season - but cooler consideration invites the unavoidable conclusion that neither Keith Burkinshaw nor Peter Shreeves can reasonably be blamed. Finding a regular place for one midfield artist whose contribution did not tally consistently with his talents may be expected of a club with Spurs' traditions, but accommodating two, surely, would have been unaffordably rash.

Certainly, though, it can be conceded that Mike was monstrously unlucky to encounter such a formidable rival in his own camp, and it is telling that the majority of his most influential displays were made in Glenn's absence, notably during early 1984/85. Then, he revelled in the role of chief creator, entertaining royally with an intoxicating combination of incisive passing and adventurous dribbles. In full flow, Mike was an enthralling sight, all swerves and feints and shimmies, capable of carving his way through apparently inpenetrable rucks of opponents, and he struck the ball well, too, crossing perceptively and shooting powerfully, many of his goals coming from outside the box.

Tantalisingly, there were occasions when the Hazard-Hoddle chemistry was perfect - they gelled most successfully during one heart-lifting spell in mid-1981/82 - which served only to whet the appetite for what might have been. Eventually, Mike lost patience with waiting for a regular slot and in September 1985 he joined Chelsea for £310,000. Yet, ironically, some of the finest form of the Hazard career was reserved for Swindon in the nineties . . . playing alongside a certain Glenn Hoddle.

BORN: Sunderland, 5.2.60.
GAMES: 113 (25). GOALS: 23.
HONOURS: UEFA Cup 83/4; FA Cup 81/2.
OTHER CLUBS: Chelsea 85/6-89/90 (81, 9);
Portsmouth 89/90-90/1 (8, 1);
Swindon Town 90/1- (110, 17).

1979/80 - 1985/86

TONY GALVIN

Tony Galvin was a rough diamond of a footballer whose presence among a collection of more sophisticated gems brought much-needed attacking balance to Spurs sides of the early and mid-eighties. In contrast to the subtlety and guile of Hoddle, Ardiles and company, the indefatigable Yorkshireman employed a full-frontal, hard-running approach that was apt to catch defenders cold by its sheer directness and simplicity. Indeed, especially on days when the artists were a little off-colour, there was something solidly reassuring in the sight of Tony - head down, elbows out and socks around his ankles - bustling purposefully along his flank.

Though the Galvin style has been called naive, that is hardly surprising in view of his lack of a conventional soccer apprenticeship. While the majority of his contemporaries were learning their craft, Tony was acquiring a university degree in Russian studies, only then joining Spurs as a £30,000 recruit from non-League Goole Town in January 1978. His early progress was interrupted by a pelvic injury which sidelined him for almost a year, and it was not until January 1981 that he sprang to prominence. Then, though still in considerable pain, he scored in the FA Cup third round replay victory over QPR and played a vigorous part during the rest of the campaign that ended triumphantly at Wembley.

Tony built on this, becoming invaluable not only for forward sallies but also for tenacity in tackling back, and shared in all Spurs' successes of that era while forging an international career thanks to a grandparent from the Irish Republic. Though naturally right-sided, he lined up most frequently on the left wing, from which he could cross ably with either foot or cut in and dash across the box before shooting. Some reckoned he was one-dimensional, but in context of the team's need, the only valid criticism would be his relatively meagre goal tally. When Tony Galvin left for Sheffield Wednesday in August 1987, Spurs lost both an underrated player and a welcome down-to-earth influence.

BORN: Huddersfield, Yorkshire,
12.7.56. GAMES: 262 (11). GOALS: 31.
HONOURS: UEFA Cup 83/4; FA Cup 80/1, 81/2.
29 Republic of Ireland caps (82-89).
OTHER CLUBS: Sheffield Wednesday 87/8-88/9 (36, 1);
Swindon Town 89/90 (11, 0).

1978/79 - 1986/87

GORDON SMITH

Injury marred the White Hart Lane career of Gordon Smith, an attacking full-back who never produced for Spurs the splendid form he had displayed for his former club, Aston Villa. Keith Burkinshaw paid the Midlanders £150,000 for the Scottish under-23 international in February 1979, content in the knowledge that he was acquiring a young defender with three seasons of experience in the top half of the First Division.

But after a handful of competent performances in 1979/80, both in the flank role and as a deputy for Paul Miller in the centre, Gordon succumbed to knee problems and needed an operation in the spring. Despite working hard on the road to recovery, he impressed only rarely in a settled sequence at the outset of the following season, and he was dropped, thus missing out on the FA Cup Final clashes with Manchester City.

Thereafter his all-round accomplishment appeared no better than average and he never again held a regular place during a period in which competition for full-back places came from Miller, Chris Hughton and Don McAllister. Gordon, who played in contact lenses, was allowed to join Wolves in August 1982, but suffered further injuries and bowed out of Molineux two years later.

BORN: Glasgow 3.7.54.
GAMES: 40 (5). GOALS: 1.
OTHER CLUBS: St Johnstone 72/3-75/6 (118, 11);
Aston Villa 76/7-78/9 (79, 0);
Wolverhampton Wanderers 82/3-83/4 (38, 3).

1978/79 - 1981/82

PAUL PRICE

When Paul Price left Luton Town for Tottenham in June 1981, the 27-year-old central defender was at the crossroads of his career. For a recently-established Welsh international with nearly a decade of League experience behind him, the £250,000 move looked like the ideal turning; sadly, it was to prove a frustrating dead end. Paul suffered an early blow when an injury in his second match, at home to West Ham, sidelined him for several months, and when he returned the expectant crowd gave him little time to settle. However, he played well in the second half of the season, helping Spurs reach Wembley twice, suffering League Cup defeat at the hands of Liverpool, then pocketing an FA Cup winner's medal at the expense of Queen's Park Rangers.

It might have been the platform for consolidation, but even allowing for fitness setbacks, Paul's form thereafter was patchy. At his best he was a competent all-rounder, without ever suggesting he might become the dominant figure Tottenham needed. His final performance, in the morale-sapping League Cup reverse against Arsenal at White Hart Lane in November 1983, was particularly disappointing and it was hardly a surprise when he left for Minnesota the following summer. Later Paul returned to the British scene at Swansea, then Peterborough.

BORN: St Albans, Hertfordshire, 23.3.54.
GAMES: 58 (4). GOALS: 0.
HONOURS: FA Cup 81/2. 25 Wales caps (80-84).
OTHER CLUBS: Luton Town 72/3-80/1 (207, 8);
Minnesota Strikers, USA; Swansea City 84/5-85/6 (61, 1);
Peterborough United 86/7-87/8 (86, 0).

1981/82 - 1983/84

ALAN BRAZIL

There was no shortage of envious rivals when Keith Burkinshaw secured the signature of Alan Brazil in March 1983. Indeed, the Scottish international striker, a £450,000 buy from Ipswich Town, was one of the most wanted men on the First Division scene, a billing he justified with six goals in 12 outings for his new club that spring. Skilful and quick, Alan boasted a wicked sidestep that could leave the tightest marker floundering as he bore down on goal, usually from his favoured left side, and was adept at confusing defenders by intelligent, curving runs.

However, his confidence was fragile, and when it dried up after a barren spell early in 1983/84, he was unable to rise above a combination of injuries and stiff competition for places. When he was dropped, Alan - essentially an easy-going fellow - clashed with his manager, and despite some valuable contributions, notably a goal in either leg of the UEFA Cup quarter-final against Austria Vienna, he departed to Old Trafford for £700,000 in June 1984. Thus, while failing to get the best out of him, Spurs had profited financially from a player who was perhaps more suited to life at a relatively small-town club where the spotlight was less intense, a theory supported by his subsequent struggles with Manchester United.

BORN: Glasgow, 15.6.59.
GAMES: 33 (5). GOALS: 13.
HONOURS: 13 Scotland caps (80-83).
OTHER CLUBS: Ipswich Town 77/8-82/3 (144, 70); Manchester United 84/5-85/6 (31, 8); Coventry City 85/6 (15, 2); Queen's Park Rangers 86/7 (4, 0); FC Baden, Switzerland.

1982/83 - 1983/84

TERRY GIBSON

Striker Terry Gibson goes down as one of the unluckiest players who failed to make the grade at White Hart Lane. On most of his senior outings, the 5ft 4in dasher showed all the qualities that once made him the hottest property in local youth football. Sharp and fiery, he made light of his lack of inches, buzzing everywhere across the front line, ferreting for defensive mistakes and often inducing them. But if he didn't happen to get a goal - and his ratio wasn't bad considering the fragmentary nature of his Spurs career - the fans, bred on expensive stars, called for the manager to brandish his chequebook.

Consequently Terry, an archetypal chirpy Londoner who showed admirable spirit throughout his travails, was almost always near the end of the queue for a first-team berth. Many wondered why, especially those who saw him during his one settled run, some 19 games in early 1983 when he netted six times and demonstrated enormous potential. That August, his Tottenham future clearly limited, Terry accepted a £100,000 move to Coventry, where he shone so brightly that Manchester United procured his signature.
At Old Trafford, sadly, he was confronted once more by the star syndrome, being given few chances before leaving for Wimbledon, where injury blighted his progress.

BORN: Walthamstow, London, 23.12.62.
GAMES: 22 (4). GOALS: 7.
OTHER CLUBS: Coventry City 83/4-85/6 (98, 43); Manchester United 85/6-86/7 (23, 1); Wimbledon 87/8-92/3 (86, 22); Swindon Town *on loan* 91/2 (8, 1).

1979/80 - 1982/83

IAN SMITH

NOEL BROTHERSTON

ANDY KEELEY

GIORGIO MAZZON

IAN SMITH 1975/76

Full-back. BORN: Rotherham, Yorkshire, 15.2.57.
GAMES: 2. GOALS: 0.
OTHER CLUBS: Rotherham United 77/8 (4, 0).

STEVE WALFORD 1975/76

Defender. BORN: Highgate, London, 5.1.58.
GAMES: 1 (1). GOALS: 0.
OTHER CLUBS: Arsenal 77/8-80/1 (77, 3);
Norwich City 80/1-82/3 (93, 2); West Ham United 83/4-86/7 (115, 2);
Huddersfield Town *on loan* 87/8 (12, 0); Gillingham *on loan* 88/9 (4, 0);
West Bromwich Albion *on loan* 88/9 (4, 0).

NOEL BROTHERSTON 1975/76

Winger. BORN: Belfast, 18.11.56. GAMES: 1. GOALS: 0.
HONOURS: 27 Northern Ireland caps (80-85).
OTHER CLUBS: Blackburn Rovers 77/8-86/7 (317, 40);
Bury 87/8-88/9 (38, 4); Scarborough *on loan* 88/9 (5, 0).

MARTIN ROBINSON 1975/76-1977/78

Midfielder. BORN: Ilford, Essex, 17.7.57.
GAMES: 5 (1). GOALS: 2.
OTHER CLUBS: Charlton Athletic 77/8-84/5 (228, 58);
Reading *on loan* 82/3 (6, 2); Gillingham 84/5-86/7 (96, 24); Southend
United 87/8-88/9 (56, 14); Cambridge United 89/90 (16, 1).

ANDY KEELEY 1976/77

Defender. BORN: Basildon, Essex, 16.9.56.
GAMES: 5 (1). GOALS: 0.
OTHER CLUBS: Sheffield United 77/8-80/1 (28, 0);
Scunthorpe United 81/2-82/3 (77, 1).

STUART BEAVON 1978/79-1979/80

Midfielder. BORN: Wolverhampton, 30.11.58.
GAMES: 3 (2). GOALS: 0.
OTHER CLUBS: Notts County *on loan* 79/80 (6, 0);
Reading 80/1-89/90 (396, 44); Northampton Town 90/1- (98, 14).

PETER SOUTHEY 1979/80

Full-back. BORN: Putney, London, 4.1.62.
GAMES: 1. GOALS: 0.
Died 1983.

GIORGIO MAZZON 1980/81-1982/83

Defender. BORN: Cheshunt, Hertfordshire, 4.9.60.
GAMES: 4 (3). GOALS: 0.
OTHER CLUBS: Aldershot 83/4-88/9 (195, 6).

STEVE WALFORD

MARTIN ROBINSON

STUART BEAVON

PETER SOUTHEY

PAT CORBETT

ROBERT BRACE

PAT CORBETT 1981/82 - 1982/83

Defender. BORN: Hackney, London, 12.2.63.
GAMES: 3 (2). GOALS: 1.
OTHER CLUBS: Orient 83/4-85/6 (77, 2).

SIMON WEBSTER 1982/83-1983/84

Defender. BORN: Hinckley, Leicestershire, 20.1.64.
GAMES: 2 (1). GOALS: 0.
OTHER CLUBS: Exeter City *on loan* 83/4 (26, 0);
Huddersfield Town 84/5-87/8 (118, 4);
Sheffield United 87/8-89/90 (37, 3);
Charlton Athletic 90/1- (171, 11).

ROBERT BRACE 1983/84

Forward. BORN: Edmonton, London, 19.12.64.
GAMES: 0 (1). GOALS: 0.

IAN CULVERHOUSE 1983/84

Full-back. BORN: Bishop's Stortford, Hertfordshire, 22.9.64.
GAMES: 1 (1). GOALS: 0.
OTHER CLUBS: Norwich City 85/6- (254, 0).

ALLAN COCKRAM 1983/84

Midfielder. BORN: Kensington, London, 8.10.63.
GAMES: 2. GOALS: 0.
OTHER CLUBS: Bristol Rovers 85/6 (1, 0);
Brentford 87/8-90/1 (90, 14); Reading 91/2 (6, 1).

DAVID LEWORTHY 1984/85-1985/86

Forward. BORN: Portsmouth, 22.10.62.
GAMES: 8 (4). GOALS: 4.
OTHER CLUBS: Portsmouth 81/2 (1, 0);
Oxford United 85/6-88/9 (37, 8); Shrewsbury Town *on loan* 87/8 (6, 3);
Reading 89/90-91/2 (44, 7).

TIM O'SHEA 1986/87-1987/88

Defender. BORN: Pimlico, London, 12.11.66.
GAMES: 1 (2). GOALS: 0.
OTHER CLUBS: Newport County *on loan* 86/7 (10, 0);
Leyton Orient 88/9 (9, 1); Gillingham 88/9-91/2 (112, 2);
Eastern, Hong Kong

SHAUN CLOSE 1986/87-1987/88

Forward. BORN: Islington, London, 8.9.66.
GAMES: 6 (6). GOALS: 2.
OTHER CLUBS: Bournemouth 87/8-89/90 (39, 8);
Swindon Town 89/90- (38, 1).

SIMON WEBSTER

IAN CULVERHOUSE

ALLAN COCKRAM

DAVID LEWORTHY

SHAUN CLOSE

TIM O'SHEA

RICHARD COOKE

Small, slim and with legs that might have been borrowed from a sparrow, Richard Cooke looked in danger of being snapped in half by the first crunching tackle that came his way. However, the speedy North Londoner was deceptively resilient, managing to ride most challenges and, on his day, his non-stop running posed a threat to most defenders. One of two young wingers pushing for senior recognition in the mid-eighties - his direct style on the right offering an effective contrast to the trickier approach of left-flank partner Alistair Dick - he enjoyed a promising debut at Luton in November 1983, netting crisply from the edge of the box after being set up by Steve Perryman. But after a four-match run, the 18-year-old found it impossible to hold his place in the face of fierce competition, and during subsequent sporadic appearances Richard's rather frenetic efforts made little impact.

By 1986/87 his senior prospects had receded and, after a loan spell with Birmingham, he moved to Bournemouth. At Dean Court Richard forged a worthy career outside the top flight, but it was something of an anti-climax for a one-time England youth and under-21 international whose signature Tottenham had beaten Arsenal and Chelsea, among others, to secure. Worse was to come, however, when injury ended his playing days in 1993.

BORN: Islington, London, 4.9.65.
GAMES: 12 (5). GOALS: 2.
OTHER CLUBS: Birmingham City *on loan* 86/7 (5, 0);
Bournemouth 86/7-88/9 (72, 16);
Luton Town 88/9-90/1 (17, 1);
Bournemouth 90/1-92/3 (53, 2).

1982/83 - 1985/86

ALISTAIR DICK

When Ally Dick was dancing past defenders for Scotland schoolboys like some latter-day Jimmy Johnstone, there was never the slightest doubt of his ability to reach the top. Duly he continued to dazzle at youth level and when he made his League debut at home to Manchester City in February 1982, still three months short of his 17th birthday and professional status, the slim left-flanker's accession to fully-fledged stardom seemed only a matter of time.

But somehow it never happened. Despite the skill and pace, the talent for crossing and the powerful shot, there was something missing. Perhaps Ally lacked the necessary hunger for success, maybe he received too much attention too soon, possibly he was not strong enough to withstand the injuries that came his way. Whatever the reason, after some promising performances in 1983/84 - when he picked up a UEFA Cup winner's medal as a substitute for Gary Mabbutt in the second leg of the final against Anderlecht - he faded from contention and in the summer of 1986 joined Ajax on a free transfer. The identity of his purchasers bore eloquent testimony to the young Scot's potential, but he never made the grade in Amsterdam, either, and after unsuccessful attempts to break through at Wimbledon and Brighton, Ally Dick was lost to the game.

BORN: Stirling, Scotland, 25.4.65.
GAMES: 21 (4). GOALS: 2.
HONOURS: UEFA Cup 83/4.
OTHER CLUBS: Ajax, Holland.

1981/82 - 1985/86

GARRY BROOKE

If making the grade for Spurs could be likened to a 20-hurdle race, then only at the 19th obstacle did Garry Brooke take a tumble. As a teenager, the bright, chunky midfielder was a fabulous prospect, and the two FA Cup winner's medals he won as a substitute in 1981 and 1982 seemed unlikely to remain his only honours. But, hampered by both soccer injuries and those sustained in a car crash, he never stepped up from invigorating number 12 to first-team regular.

Garry's first senior impact came on Boxing Day 1980 when, fresh from a beneficial loan spell in Sweden, he netted twice on his full debut at home to Southampton. Indeed, his powerful long-range shooting, for which he employed negligible backlift and thus was apt to catch defences unawares, was a lethal asset, but he was no one-trick merchant. His control was impeccable, he crossed well from his habitual berth on the right flank and his quick-stepping, almost comical running style generated deceptive pace. But too often he would choose the wrong passing option or fail to find space at the right time, accordingly interrupting the flow of attacks, and in July 1985 he was allowed to join Norwich. After a brief stint at Carrow Road, the shrewd little Londoner drifted, somewhat surprisingly, towards footballing obscurity.

BORN: Bethnal Green, London, 24.11.60.
GAMES: 63 (38). GOALS: 18.
HONOURS: FA Cup 80/1, 81/2.
OTHER CLUBS: Gais, Sweden, *on loan* 80/1;
Norwich City 85/6-86/7 (14, 2); Groningen, Holland;
Wimbledon 88/9-89/90 (12, 0); Stoke City *on loan* 89/90 (8, 0);
Brentford 90/1 (11, 1); Reading 90/1 (4, 1).

1980/81 - 1984/85

GARY O'REILLY

Gary O'Reilly played international football for two countries, captaining England schoolboys and then, thanks to a parental qualification, representing the Republic of Ireland at youth level. But he found making the First Division grade an altogether more formidable proposition.

Intelligent and confident, Gary was a tall, long-striding full-back with the powerful physique to double as a centre-half. Though aerially effective, strong in the tackle and adept at thrusting forward to join in attacks, he hindered his cause by an occasional tendency to dwell on the ball in dangerous situations, a habit that can be self-destructive even for those with more skill than he had at his disposal.

Gary's senior career had begun promisingly with isolated stand-in duties and seemed poised for take-off when he excelled in the 1982 Charity Shield clash with Liverpool. That term was his best, with 30 first-team starts, but as his fallibility became apparent he lost ground in the ever-brisk struggle for a regular place, and in August 1984 he joined Brighton.

Gary's finest hour was to come at Wembley in 1990 when he gave Crystal Palace the lead against Manchester United in the FA Cup Final, though a loser's medal was his only reward.

BORN: Isleworth, London, 21.3.61.
GAMES: 47 (8). GOALS: 0.
OTHER CLUBS: Brighton 84/5-86/7 (79, 3);
Crystal Palace 86/7-90/1 (70, 2);
Birmingham City *on loan* 90/1 (1, 0);
Brighton 91/2 (28, 3).

1980/81 - 1983/84

GRAHAM ROBERTS

The question that echoed around Highbury on New Year's Day 1986, roared from the throats of several thousand exulting Spurs fans, could have only one answer. 'Who put Charlie in the stand?' they inquired of their Arsenal counterparts, in reference to a blitzkrieg of a tackle which had deposited a certain Mr Nicholas among the spectators. On receiving no satisfactory reply from the nonplussed North Bank, they filled the blank themselves with a thunderous homage to Graham Roberts. That incident illustrated luridly both the root and the nature of the ruthless central defender-cum-midfielder's popular appeal. And yet there was a paradox. Keith Burkinshaw once described Graham as being of 'the Duncan Edwards type', and while that ranks as one of the more hysterical managerial remarks of our time, the message that the Spurs boss was attempting to convey was valid: simply that his often-controversial ball-winner was a far better all-round player than most people allowed.

Graham cuts an unlikely figure as a fairy-tale hero, yet the sequence of events culminating in his elevation to the ranks of Tottenham Hotspur and England positively reeks of Boys' Own fantasy. In the spring of 1980, having been rejected by Southampton, Bournemouth and Portsmouth, he was plying his trade as a fitter's mate in a shipyard and playing part-time for Weymouth. He was recommended to Bill Nicholson, by then a scout, during a casual conversation with a stranger on a railway platform, and was signed subsequently for £35,000, then a record fee for a non-League player. Some 12 months later, having established himself at centre-half, he was helping his new club to victory over Manchester City in the 100th FA Cup Final.

On his graduation to the senior side, it became clear that Graham was the North Londoners' most formidable 'hard man' since Dave Mackay. Neither the tallest nor the quickest of defenders, nevertheless he would win challenges through sheer ferocious desire, and it must be said that there were occasions when his zeal got the better of him. He was prone to lose his temper, and while some opponents may have wilted, it's a fact that uncontrolled aggression can be counter-productive against wily operators with the nous to turn tantrums to their own advantage. Hence, when the 'red mist' descended, Graham was more likely to commit himself to tackles in dangerous situations or be drawn out of position. In general, of course, his physical might was of enormous value, yet it should not eclipse entirely his largely unsung creative ability, which was most evident during his mid-eighties spells as Glenn Hoddle's midfield 'minder'. In that role, Graham displayed habitually unplumbed depths of subtlety, controlling the ball with ease and passing both accurately and constructively. A further bonus from pushing the dreadnought on to the offensive accrued from his power of shot, as shown by long-range goals at home to Bruges in November 1984 and Everton five months later.

Often the option of using Graham as occasional midfielder proved profitable, notably when he plundered a hat-trick against his home town club, Southampton, in March 1982. But certainly the most valuable Roberts strike was reserved for a loftier occasion, the 1984 UEFA Cup Final against Anderlecht. Near the end of the home second leg, Graham - temping as captain in place of the suspended Steve Perryman - prodded the ball in from close range to set up the penalty shoot-out in which the spoils were claimed. His contribution that night, his stirring example in the van of a glorious fightback, typified all that was best about him. When a £450,000 fee took him to Glasgow Rangers in December 1986, it would have been a rare Spurs fan who did not experience a pang of regret for a departing hero. Whatever his critics may say, that is how Graham Roberts - who went on to manage non-League Enfield - will be remembered at White Hart Lane.

BORN: Southampton, 3.7.59.
GAMES: 276 (11). GOALS: 36.
HONOURS: UEFA Cup 83/4; FA Cup 80/1, 81/2.
6 England caps (83-84).
OTHER CLUBS: Glasgow Rangers 86/7-87/8 (55, 3); Chelsea 88/9-89/90 (70, 18);
West Bromwich Albion 90/1-91/2 (39, 6).

1980/81 - 1986/87

JOHN CHIEDOZIE

The merciless roasting John Chiedozie inflicted on Chelsea left-back Doug Rougvie at White Hart Lane in November 1984 stands as a telling microcosm of the fleet-footed Nigerian's career. That day John danced past the big Scot repeatedly and with an ease that embarrassed neutral observers. Yet just as Spurs didn't capitalise on the little winger's sparkling display - the match ended in a 1-1 draw - so he never made the most of a promising platform for long-term success.

John, whose family had left Africa for London when he was 12, had earned a glowing reputation with Orient before joining Spurs for £350,000 from Notts County in August 1984. That season he flourished on the right flank as Peter Shreeves' enterprising 4-2-4 system sustained Tottenham's title challenge into April. But next term his progress was hindered both by injury and the arrival of Paul Allen and Chris Waddle. All too soon, despite a moderately productive spell as a central striker, John lost momentum. Some felt his immense speed cost him quality of distribution, or maybe the physical knocks had taken their toll; arguably this nice, easy-going character - his grin of pleasure when he scored positively lit up the pitch - needed a little more drive. Whatever the root of his decline, John was freed in May 1988 and soon had left the professional game.

BORN: Nigeria, 18.4.60.
GAMES: 64 (11). GOALS: 14. HONOURS: Nigeria caps.
OTHER CLUBS: Orient 76/7-80/1 (145, 20);
Notts County 81/2-83/4 (111, 15); Derby County 88/9 (2, 0);
Notts County 89/90 (1, 0); Chesterfield 89/90 (7, 0).

1984/85 - 1986/87

TONY PARKS

One glorious night does not a career make, as few footballers know better than Tony Parks. The young goalkeeper's supreme moment came in May 1984, when he sealed UEFA Cup triumph for Spurs with his second save of the penalty shoot-out which climaxed the final at White Hart Lane. Springing to his feet, he celebrated ecstatically with his team-mates, but sadly for the North Londoner, there was to be no further joy from his Tottenham career.

His appearance against Anderlecht was the culmination of a splendid spell that spring as deputy for the injured Ray Clemence. But, perhaps unready to handle the limelight which followed his great achievement, Tony returned to Ray's shadow for the next three seasons, and when another chance came his way in 1987/88, there was little sign of his erstwhile confidence. An athletic, impressive shot-stopper who was not quite so reliable at claiming crosses, he soon found the supporters on his back and after a mid-season spell of 19 consecutive games he was dropped in favour of new signing Bobby Mimms. With his prospects at the Lane clearly bleak, Tony accepted a £60,000 move to Brentford that summer, but didn't settle and by 1992/93 was attempting to resurrect his fortunes with Falkirk.

BORN: Hackney, London, 28.1.63.
GAMES: 48 (1). GOALS: 0.
HONOURS: UEFA Cup 83/4.
OTHER CLUBS: Oxford United on loan 86/7 (5, 0);
Gillingham on loan 87/8 (2, 0); Brentford 88/9-90/1 (71, 0);
Fulham 90/1 (2, 0); West Ham United 91/2 (6, 0);
Stoke City on loan 92/3 (2, 0); Falkirk 92/3- (14, 0).

1981/82 - 1987/88

DANNY THOMAS

Those footballers who bemoan their luck at the slightest setback - and every profession is burdened with its share of whingers - would do well to remember the distressing case of Danny Thomas. In March 1987, while playing arguably the best football of his career, the 25-year-old full-back was cut down by a controversial tackle from Queen's Park Rangers' Gavin Maguire that provoked fury on the White Hart Lane terraces, and never played again. It was a savage blow for the sunny, universally-liked Midlander who had been tipped only recently to resume the England career he had begun while with his first club, Coventry City.

Keith Burkinshaw paid £250,000 to take Danny from Highfield Road in June 1983, and though he didn't settle immediately, by the middle of his first season he was showing the qualities that had elevated him to the international ranks. Capable of playing on either defensive flank, he was elastically athletic, an attacking overlapper of flashing pace and unending enthusiasm. He was no soft touch in the tackle, either, and was an effective one-on-one marker, a role in which he had been employed periodically during midfield days with the Sky Blues. However, though not unskilful, his control did not match his speed and he was not at his best when given time to deliberate on the ball, factors which contributed to the loss of his place for lengthy spells during the mid-eighties.

Undaunted, Danny worked hard and after new boss David Pleat restored him to the side in December 1986, he hit new peaks, linking smoothly with Chris Waddle and looking every inch a top-notch performer. Then came that fateful impact from Maguire's boot and ten months later, in January 1988, he was forced to retire. Ever positive, though, he refused to slink away in despair and qualified as a physiotherapist, going on to serve West Bromwich Albion in that capacity. The story of Danny Thomas offers an object lesson to everyone connected with the game.

BORN: Worksop, Nottinghamshire, 12.11.61. GAMES: 103 (13). GOALS: 1. HONOURS: UEFA Cup 83/4. 2 England caps (83). OTHER CLUBS: Coventry City 79/80-82/3 (108, 5).

1983/84 - 1986/87

RAY CLEMENCE

A few months earlier it would have seemed inconceivable, but suddenly in the autumn of 1981, one of the world's finest goalkeepers had something to prove. That August Ray Clemence, who with Liverpool had swept the honours board so clean and for so long, had joined Tottenham in a £300,000 deal - and he had made a distinctly shaky start. After a dose of uncertain handling in the Charity Shield clash with Aston Villa, seven goals flashed past him in his first two League games at White Hart Lane, and the whispers began. Was it possible that *anyone* might have looked good behind that superb Liverpool defence, and that all these years the England 'keeper had been overrated? Had he grown complacent in Anfield's pastures of plenty? Or, more bluntly, was he just plain past it? So much balderdash, of course, and before long he was back to his inspirational best, if anything stronger for the experience and having showed that his magnificent ability was matched by immense strength of character.

In fact, more fascinating than the temporary blip in Ray's form had been both his decision to head south in the first place and Keith Burkinshaw's choice of a 33-year-old custodian when, earlier in his managerial reign, he had dispensed with 32-year-old Pat Jennings, presumably on the basis of age. Ray explained his motivation for walking away from the near-certain prospect of continuing glory on Merseyside as the need for a fresh challenge, while clearly Keith had revised his views on the shelf-life of goalkeepers; taken together, these unexpected circumstances spelt marvellous news for Tottenham. However, even apart from that aforementioned indifferent start, Ray's first term in North London must go down as a bitter-sweet interlude. His quarter-final exploits against Eintracht Frankfurt had kept Spurs in the European Cup Winners' Cup, but one horrific bungle against Barcelona - allowing an innocuous 40-yarder to sneak through his hands - set them on the way towards semi-final elimination. Then there was a splendid League Cup Final performance against his old friends from Liverpool, which was to count for nothing as the Reds won in extra time. But at least the season was to end happily, with an FA Cup winner's medal - destined to remain Ray's only club honour in his playing days at the Lane - thanks to Wembley victory over Queen's Park Rangers.

As the eighties wore on, the Clemence standard showed no signs of slipping. As a 'sweeper-keeper' in the Anfield tradition pioneered by Tommy Lawrence, he needed a close understanding with his team-mates and achieved it, organising them vociferously and efficiently. With this system in place, Ray's agility, bravery and high-class handling, allied to a finely honed positional sense and fierce concentration, offered as formidable a last line of defence as could be found in the First Division. If there was a weakness to his game - and this is nit-picking, indeed - it was his poor kicking of a dead ball, but that was a tiny price to pay for so much that was outstanding.

In 1984/85 - after the disappointment of being sidelined for the previous term's UEFA Cup triumph - Ray was a prime factor in Tottenham's most credible Championship challenge for more than 20 years. Satisfyingly, he reserved one of his most memorable displays for the Kop, pulling off a string of acrobatic saves to preserve a 1-0 lead as the visitors recorded their first win at Anfield in almost three-quarters of a century. Even in his 40th year, Ray remained as consistent as ever and when he suffered a groin injury at Norwich in October 1987, the fans were not unduly alarmed, expecting to see him back between the posts within a couple of weeks. In the event, he was never to return, instead accepting a coaching post with the club, which led to his appointment as assistant to chief coach Doug Livermore in 1992. A breezy character who laughs a lot but who is deadly serious about the game, Ray Clemence has much to offer still to the cause of Tottenham Hotspur.

BORN: Skegness, Lincolnshire, 5.8.48.
GAMES: 330. GOALS: 0.
HONOURS: FA Cup 81/2. 61 England caps (72-83).
OTHER CLUBS: Scunthorpe United 65/6-66/7 (48, 0);
Liverpool 69/70-80/1 (470, 0)

1981/82 - 1987/88

IAN CROOK

Ian Crook was Glenn Hoddle's heir apparent as Spurs' schemer-in-chief, but he was denied the chance to prove that his slim shoulders could carry such an onerous mantle. The young wing-man-turned-midfielder was, quite simply, a superb technician with a football: he could drive it, clip it, bend it, chip it, or spin it any which way, and all with an astonishing accuracy that is profoundly rare in the modern game. The natural sweetness of the Crook passing repertoire was enhanced by contact with the likes of Hoddle and Ardiles, and when he was given his senior debut as a substitute in May 1982, his prospects glowed.

However, the three consecutive starts Ian made thereafter proved to be his longest first-team run and - amidst mutterings that he didn't chase and couldn't tackle - the gifted 23-year-old joined Norwich for £80,000 in June 1986. Of course, Glenn was to leave in 1987, and had he made his decision a year earlier it is possible that the younger man would have been retained. As it is he has matured gradually, habitually haunting his former employers with classy displays - his 30-yard winner at Carrow Road in spring 1991 was especially rewarding - and come 1992/93 Ian was making the play, subtly and delightfully, as the Canaries soared along blithely at the top of the Premier Division for much of that campaign.

BORN: Romford, Essex, 18.1.63.
GAMES: 11 (13). GOALS: 1.
OTHER CLUBS: Norwich City 86/7- (202, 14).

1981/82 - 1985/86

MARK BOWEN

Mark Bowen was an ordinary midfielder who became an excellent full-back - but not in time to carve out a career at White Hart Lane. Despite beavering enthusiastically and scoring a creditable number of goals for the reserves, it was not until the young Welshman dropped back that a senior breakthrough seemed feasible. After making his debut at home to Coventry in August 1983, Mark remained on the fringe of a crowded squad, enjoying short first-team stints in mid-1983/84 and spring 1985. By then playing on the left despite being right-footed, he rose above the trauma of gifting Trevor Steven a goal in the crucial title clash with Everton that April to impress with generally crisp defensive work and a voracious appetite for getting forward.

But his hopes were dashed by the purchase of Mitchell Thomas in the summer of 1986 and a year later, despite having underlined his promise by winning full caps, Mark was allowed to join Norwich. Subsequently, as he and other ex-Spurs flourished at Carrow Road, some Tottenham fans criticised their management over the exodus of talent. In fact, in most cases - and certainly in Mark's - the moans were not audible at the time of the move, being made only with the convenience of hindsight.

BORN: Neath, Glamorgan, 7.12.63.
GAMES: 17 (3). GOALS: 2.
HONOURS: 23 Wales caps (86-).
OTHER CLUBS: Norwich City 87/8- (212, 15).

1983/84 - 1986/87

RICHARD GOUGH

To most Tottenham fans, Richard Gough was a gift from the gods. They had been longing for a truly outstanding centre-half since the departure of Mike England some 11 years earlier, and in August 1986 the tall, red-haired Scot strolled down from Mount Olympus and got on with the job.

In the interests of strict accuracy, Richard arrived from Dundee United - after David Pleat had missed out on signing Terry Butcher - and from his coolly authoritative debut at Villa Park it was apparent immediately that the £750,000 international represented excellent value for money. The basic requisites of any standard stopper, aerial power and a stern tackle, were present and correct but, glory of glories, there was more. Here was a number-five with the skill to retain possession of the ball and pass it accurately, a player who seemed always to have time, a sure mark of class in any sport.

As matches went by, the evidence of Richard's prowess grew ever more conclusive. His astute positional sense, the certainty with which he marshalled the defence and the development of an intuitive partnership with Gary Mabbutt - both men got forward effectively, but such was their understanding that rarely did gaps appear at the back - all augured magnificently for the future. Indeed, Richard's appointment as skipper at Charlton on New Year's Day 1987 appeared to fall into the 'job-for-life' category, and his leadership was a telling factor in Tottenham's progress to the FA Cup Final in his first season.

Then disquieting rumours began to circulate in the Scottish press that Richard was set to re-cross the border and sure enough, that October, news broke that Spurs were to lose their new bulwark to Rangers for £1.5 million. Some pointed to the handsome profit, but there was black despair on the terraces. It seemed the Gough family could not settle in England, which was of little consolation to fans who would have moved heaven and earth to keep their hero - and five years without a fitting replacement was to render their reaction entirely understandable.

BORN: Stockholm, Sweden, 5.4.62.
GAMES: 65. GOALS: 2.
HONOURS: 61 Scotland caps (83-).
OTHER CLUBS: Dundee United 80/1-85/6 (165, 23);
Glasgow Rangers 87/8- (176, 13).

1986/87 - 1987/88

GLENN HODDLE

His touch was exquisite, his vision sublime; he was by a massive margin the most bounteously gifted English footballer of his age. Yet Glenn Hoddle will be remembered not only as a ball-playing master, but also as an unwitting vehicle for the Great Debate on the direction of modern soccer. Were his supreme, if sometimes sedate skills out of place in a game dominated increasingly by work-rate, pace and strength? Should he really have missed almost as many England games as he played? Because of those barren spells when the magic lay frustratingly dormant, was he a dispensable luxury? From White Hart Lane, where even to ask such questions might be seen as sacrilege, comes a thunderous negative on all three counts, a verdict echoed in the hearts and minds of all those who believe there is a place for beauty in sport.

The imagination and accuracy of the long-distance pass, the delicacy and precision of the unexpected chip, the sudden ferocity of the scoring volley, and the casual, yet inevitable curve of the free-kick around a defensive wall on its way into the net; truly such wonders were a joy to behold. Countless instances of artistry clamour for recollection, so where do we begin? Let's try his fourth full season, by which time he had already overcome a serious knee injury, tasted the despair of relegation, been tested in the hurly-burly of the Second Division, and made enough concessions to honest toil as might be deemed reasonable by any manager seeking a blend of complementary talents rather than a team of identical robots.

That term - it was 1979/80 - saw Glenn score 22 times for Tottenham, and one sensational edge-of-the-box volley at home to Manchester United might have been expected to win a 'Goal Of Any Season' competition; that is if the judges ignored an effort against Nottingham Forest which he clubbed home from 18 yards after the ball had travelled the length of White Hart Lane, from keeper Aleksic, to Armstrong, to Jones, to Hoddle and into the net without touching the ground. Of course, he created more than he scored, and this craft was illustrated breathtakingly in the 1981 FA Cup semi-final replay against Wolves, when he freed Garth Crooks with a raking through-ball with the outside of his left foot. But if future historians scour old video-tapes seeking one piece of footage to define the magic of Hoddle, then they will settle, surely, on his goal at Watford in 1983. Receiving the ball on the right side of the box, some 15 yards out and at an acute angle to goal, he feinted one way, made space with a deft back-flip, then half-swivelled to chip gently into the far corner of the net. It all seemed to happen in slow motion, and was so perfect in execution that it might have been choreographed.

But what of the other side of the coin? Undeniably, there were dog days when the action would pass Glenn by, and some felt that by the mid-eighties he was inclined to eschew the simple in favour of the needlessly spectacular. Admittedly, too, he had little pace, though after all, his passes allowed others to do his running for him; indeed, how lethal he was behind the jet-propelled Archibald and Crooks, and how tantalising to reflect on what he might have achieved in harness with the greyhound Lineker. Certainly there was no doubting his athleticism, as he proved as Spurs' emergency 'keeper, and those who questioned his desire for combat might ponder on a rare brand of courage which team-mates declare he possessed in abundance, that of taking responsibility for the ball, no matter how tight the situation.

When David Pleat sold Glenn to Monaco for around £1 million in July 1987, the loss to the Football League was colossal. Perhaps he felt stale, more likely unappreciated; whatever, Glenn flourished in France before injury threatened his future. His subsequent attainments at Swindon, both as father-figure on the pitch and as one of the country's most enlightened managers, gladdened the souls of purists everywhere.

BORN: Hayes, Middlesex, 27.10.57.
GAMES: 478 (12). GOALS: 110.
HONOURS: FA Cup 80/1, 81/2.
53 England caps (79-88).
OTHER CLUBS: Monaco, France, 87/8-90/1;
Swindon Town 91/2- (65, 1).
MANAGER: Swindon Town (91-).

1975/76 - 1986/87

CLIVE ALLEN

It was like a record with only one groove: 'And the first goal for Spurs was scored by number seven, Clive Allen!' In 1986/87, the striker's season of supreme grace, those words became a gloriously monotonous refrain from White Hart Lane announcer Willie Morgan, its inevitability reflecting the fans' confidence in their prolific hero. Quite simply, whenever Clive had a chance they *expected* him to hit the target and if he missed they were genuinely shocked. That term he netted 49 times in 54 appearances, including two as substitute, shattering Jimmy Greaves' club record for a single campaign that had stood for nigh-on quarter of a century and which, in the modern era of blanket defence, had appeared certain to remain inviolate.

In fact, without emulating the great Jimmy's all-round brilliance - no out-and-out goal merchant since the War has done that - Clive did possess certain Greaves-like characteristics. There was the instinct for taking up dangerous positions, the knack of twisting his body to shoot for goal no matter how awkwardly the ball fell, the ability to wrong-foot defenders with a single touch before turning in the tightest of spaces, and the accuracy of his finish, frequently with a firm sidefoot. There was also utter single-mindedness and a voracious edge that kept him sharp to the end of every match, no matter how many chances he might have squandered earlier - witness two hat-tricks, both plundered in the last ten minutes, against West Ham and Norwich in early 1987.

Clive, it seemed, had been put on this earth to score goals. The son of Les Allen, a leading marksman for Tottenham's revered League and FA Cup double-winning side, and nephew of Reading forward Dennis, he had absorbed soccer lore throughout his upbringing and made it tell from the moment he turned professional. He arrived at the Lane in August 1984, a £700,000 purchase from Queen's Park Rangers, a few weeks after winning his first full cap. In contrast to his decidedly lack-lustre international form, Clive's two-goal Spurs debut at Goodison installed him as an instant fans' favourite and he linked pleasingly with Mark Falco as Peter Shreeves' team topped the table that autumn. It was a heady period but it was not to last: that December Clive picked up a debilitating groin injury which was to keep him on the side-lines for a year. On his return, not surprisingly, he was slow to regain his momentum, and it was not until the spring of 1986 that the goals began to flow once more.

That, of course, was the prelude to Allen's Golden Season, which started fruitfully enough, then grew ever more bountiful after new manager David Pleat's November decision to play Clive as a lone raider in front of a five-man midfield. Revelling in the consequent space and helped by confusion among opponents uncertain about whom to mark, he capitalised ruthlessly on exceptional service from Messrs Hoddle, Waddle and Co, and the one regret come May - despite the personal consolation of the two major player of the year awards - was that Tottenham had no trophy to show for so much exciting football. Third in the League and losing semi-finalists in the League Cup, they had appeared on course to lift the FA Cup after Clive's near-post header had given them a second-minute Wembley lead, only for Coventry to fight back and deny them.

Nevertheless, 1987/88 dawned full of promise, only to prove traumatically anti-climactic. Clive, no doubt hindered by over-inflated expectations, struggled to find the net and at season's end, with the club sliding ever deeper into off-the-field travail, accepted a £1 million transfer to Bordeaux. A year later he was back in England, serving three clubs in as many seasons, playing well but with the game's peaks drifting ever more surely beyond his reach. It can be argued that, somehow, Clive Allen has not achieved all that might be expected of a man with his fabulous gift. But this much is sure: it will take one very fine striker to erase his name from the Spurs record books.

BORN: Stepney, London, 20.5.61.
GAMES: 124 (11). GOALS: 84.
HONOURS: 5 England caps (84-88).
OTHER CLUBS: Queen's Park Rangers 78/9-79/80 (49, 32);
Arsenal, no games; Crystal Palace 80/1 (25, 9);
Queen's Park Rangers 81/2-83/4 (87, 40);
Bordeaux, France, 87/8-88/9;
Manchester City 89/90-91/2 (53, 16);
Chelsea 91/2 (16, 7);
West Ham United 91/2- (31, 15).

1984/85 - 1987/88

JOHNNY METGOD

When Glenn Hoddle left White Hart Lane in the summer of 1987, Spurs needed a thoroughbred to fill the creative void in central midfield, and who could have seemed better qualified than a man who had operated in that role for those high priests of flair football, Real Madrid? Thus David Pleat paid Nottingham Forest £250,000 for Johnny Metgod and Spurs fans were anticipating eagerly the cultured passing for which the elegant Dutchman was renowned, while positively slavering over the prospect of his spectacular speciality, the dead-ball blast that created the optical illusion of gathering pace in flight.

The first surprise came when Johnny spent much of the season's opening game on the bench, and puzzlement increased when he made only three senior starts that autumn. But worse was to follow for the tall, balding play-maker, as Pleat departed and new boss Terry Venables' team selection made it clear that he was surplus to requirements. With his chances further hampered by injury, a move seemed inevitable and after returning to senior duty for the last four games of the season, Johnny joined Feyenoord for £175,000. Back in Holland, he specialised as a sweeper and it was in that position that he helped his countrymen remove Spurs from the European Cup Winners' Cup in 1991/92.

BORN: Amsterdam, Holland, 27.2.58.
GAMES: 7 (7). GOALS: 0.
HONOURS: Holland caps.
OTHER CLUBS: DWS Amsterdam, Haarlem, AZ 67 Alkmaar, all Holland; Real Madrid, Spain; Nottingham Forest 84/5-86/7 (118, 15); Feyenoord, Holland.

1987/88

NICO CLAESEN

Terrace opinion was sharply divided on the merits of Nico Claesen. There were those who reckoned the Belgian striker never fitted comfortably into English football, while others maintained that his industry, speed and a strike-rate that was highly respectable for a man still settling in a foreign country might have qualified him for an extended stay. He arrived in October 1986, a £600,000 acquisition from Standard Liege, having enhanced his reputation hugely in that summer's World Cup finals. Elusive to mark and with a strength that belied his lack of inches, he was used, at first, as a conventional front-runner alongside Clive Allen, impressing on his debut in a 1-0 win at Anfield. But soon David Pleat experimented with tactics and Nico suffered as a somewhat fitful member of the five-man midfield which served the Londoner so well.

When he was dropped periodically, he was unhappy and it showed - omission from the 1987 FA Cup Final starting line-up caused the deepest hurt - yet he shouldered his burden manfully and in 1987/88, back in his favoured forward role, he all but matched Allen's tally for that season despite playing far fewer games. However, new boss Terry Venables, struggling to stabilise a Spurs boat that was rocking alarmingly, preferred other options, and in August 1988 Nico returned to his homeland, joining Antwerp for £550,000.

BORN: Leut, Belgium, 1.10.62.
GAMES: 45 (18). GOALS: 23. HONOURS: Belgium caps.
OTHER CLUBS: Patro Eisden and Seresien, Belgium; Stuttgart, Germany; Standard Liege, Belgium; Antwerp, Belgium.

1986/87 - 1987/88

STEVE HODGE

The Spurs career of Steve Hodge caught fire in his first game but flickered only fleetingly thereafter, the flame soon to subside in dismal anti-climax. After the left-sided midfielder's admirable efforts for England in the 1986 World Cup finals, it seemed that David Pleat could congratulate himself for persuading Aston Villa to part with the skilful 24-year-old for £650,000 the following December. That impression was strengthened by his Boxing Day debut at home to West Ham in which he scored one fine goal and set up another. But after a two-goal flourish against his former club in January, and despite another brace against Watford in that term's FA Cup semi-final, he lost his way.

Blessed with boundless vitality and an insatiable desire to get forward, while not ignoring defensive chores, Steve seemed always to be about some urgent mission, and his incisive incursions into opposing penalty areas should have added a new dimension to Spurs' attack. But too often he scurried to little effect, rarely making optimum use of his lovely left-foot touch or supplying the lethal whipped crosses for which he was known. His disappointing form was linked, almost certainly, to his disenchantment with London life, and it was no surprise in August 1988 when he rejoined his first club, Nottingham Forest, for £550,000.

BORN: Nottingham, 25.10.62.
GAMES: 53 (1). GOALS: 9.
HONOURS: 24 England caps (86-91).
OTHER CLUBS: Nottingham Forest 81/2-85/6 (123, 30);
Aston Villa 85/6-86/7 (53, 12);
Nottingham Forest 88/9-90/1 (82, 20);
Leeds United 91/2- (46, 9).

1986/87 - 1987/88

BOBBY MIMMS

Poor Bobby Mimms! No professional footballer, indeed no human being, should be forced to endure public ridicule of the nature and degree heaped upon his head after Terry Venables drafted in the England under-21 goalkeeper to help stabilise Spurs' jittery defence in February 1988. For three games after his £375,000 move from Everton, all went well. But then he conceded a soft goal to Arsenal's Alan Smith at Highbury, several more errors followed and for the rest of the season he was pilloried mercilessly by press and fans alike.

The early months of 1988/89 brought no respite for Bobby, whose confidence had reached a low ebb. Though technically a sound all-rounder, he was now failing to dominate his six-yard box, let alone his penalty area, and suffered some horrible afternoons, notably during the home defeat by Derby in November. Despite the mounting pressure, raised a notch or two by the arrival of Erik Thorstvedt, Bobby kept a succession of clean sheets in December and might have been turning the corner, but then came a shock FA Cup exit at Bradford and the axe descended. Thereafter the Yorkshireman remained a reserve until December 1990 when a £250,000 transfer took him to Blackburn, where there awaited a renaissance and, perhaps, the last laugh.

BORN: York, 12.10.63. GAMES: 44. GOALS: 0.
OTHER CLUBS: Rotherham United 81/2-84/5 (83, 0);
Everton 85/6-87/8 (29, 0); Notts County *on loan* 85/6 (2, 0);
Sunderland *on loan* 86/7 (4, 0);
Blackburn Rovers *on loan* 86/7 (6, 0);
Manchester City *on loan* 87/8 (3, 0);
Aberdeen *on loan* 89/90 (6, 0); Blackburn Rovers 90/1- (109, 0)

1987/88 - 1989/90

CHRIS WADDLE

To Tottenham Hotspur fans in the late eighties fell the joy and the privilege of watching Chris Waddle mature from an exciting but wayward talent into one of the world's most accomplished forwards. Yet back in the autumn of 1985, that progress seemed anything but inevitable. Slouching diffidently, almost forlornly, on the fringe of the action, like some gauche farmhand longing for the end of an exhausting day in the fields, Chris cut an unlikely figure for a soccer hero. Even when he received a pass, the image of ungainliness persisted for a moment as he crouched wanly over the ball. But then a sloping shoulder would drop still further, the long, lean body would sway beguilingly before gathering pace, and he would be gone. On a good day defenders would fall away from him like chaff before the wind as he cut a swathe through their ranks; on a bad one he would disappear into some blind alley, there to be mugged, robbed and left wearing an expression of confusion. Contrast that with the confident, pulsating performer of 1988/89; now the ball came to him as a friend, a plaything, the instrument of his art, and in his use of it Chris Waddle became a genuine star.

The shy north-easterner, who had worked in a sausage-seasoning factory before winning England caps with Newcastle, had made a telling impact during the Magpies' first season back in the top flight when he joined Spurs in July 1985. Immediately he set about repaying his fee - £590,000, set by a transfer tribunal - with two headed goals on his debut at home to Watford, but then came that exasperating patch as he struggled to build self-belief. Come 1986/87 there were encouraging signs of consistency, and new manager David Pleat deserved credit for switching Chris from his original beat - on his natural left side and in the centre - to the right flank, from which he would cut inside to devastating effect, or roam free, creating havoc with his adhesive skills and intelligent distribution. It was, perhaps, in November 1986 at Oxford - where he scored twice, including a delicate curler after a delicious dribble - that the supporters accepted their gifted gangler as something special, and his verve was demonstrated to a wider audience in that term's FA Cup Final. Just two minutes into the game, his extravagant body-swerve wrong-footed a line of Coventry defenders before he crossed for Clive Allen to open the scoring in a match that was to end in such bitter disappointment.

Alas, there was further frustration lying in wait, for the player himself and for a side sorely in need of inspiration following the departure of Glenn Hoddle. Chris spent much of 1987/88 sidelined with heel and hernia problems but, happily, it was a prelude to pure gold. In 1988/89, he contributed what was arguably the most scintillating season of football by a Spurs player that decade, finally realising his full potential, becoming the team's fulcrum and accordingly being crowned by fans as the new 'King' of White Hart Lane. Some of his goals are etched indelibly on thousands of memories - the tight-angled drive after a surging run at home to Norwich in February, the 35-yard chip in the cloying mud at Southampton four days later, and the brilliant brace against Aston Villa that brought the Lane to its feet in March. Often it seemed that no one could take the ball from him, and as well as topping the goal chart with 14 he created countless chances for others.

Picture then the utter consternation among the fans when, that July, he moved to Marseille for £4.25 million. It is said that, desperately though they needed the cash, Spurs left the decision to Chris; he accepted the opportunity, overcame similar (but less protracted) problems of adjustment to those encountered at first in London, and went on to heady achievement in France before returning to England with Sheffield Wednesday. And what if he had stayed at the Lane with Messrs Gascoigne and Lineker? Well, it's conceivable that Spurs might have been the most beautiful-to-watch bankrupts British football has ever seen . . .

BORN: Felling, County Durham, 14.12.60.
GAMES: 172 (1). GOALS: 42.
HONOURS: 62 England caps (85-91).
OTHER CLUBS: Newcastle United 80/1-84/5 (170, 46);
Marseille, France, 88/9-91/2;
Sheffield Wednesday 92/3- (32, 1).

1985/86 - 1988/89

VINNY SAMWAYS

The pinched, sallow features still wore that characteristic expression of startled anxiety, the shoulders remained slightly hunched as if bearing some enormous burden, but the furrowed brows of bewildered opponents revealed an infinitely more telling story. Yes, in the spring of 1993, after years of flattering to deceive, the lovely play-making talents of Vinny Samways were approaching full bloom at last.

As a teenager, the skilful Londoner had excited rare anticipation among the White Hart Lane cognoscenti. Then skipper of Spurs reserves, he had shone in the Football Combination and exhibited such total command over the ball that he was slated for a starry future. Duly Vinny enjoyed his first settled sequence the following term, which confirmed the exquisite class of his passing, the sureness of his touch and the subtlety of his thinking, and he was accorded the status of an uncut jewel. In 1988/89, however, progress was expected at a more rapid rate than he managed, and it may be that he did not benefit from the all-enveloping midfield presence of new arrival Paul Gascoigne. Thereafter Vinny, already honoured by England at under-21 level, tended to float on the periphery, showing flashes of delightful insight but irritating fans by dallying while considering his next move. Often, too, he would take the safe option, acquiring for his pains the terrace tag of Vinny Sideways!

Come 1990/91 there was talk of a transfer, but then he dazzled in the FA Cup semi-final and final triumphs and was expected to flourish in Gascoigne's absence. Instead Vinny floundered, and after his delicate gifts were omitted from the side when pitches became heavy the following term, the spectre of eventual failure grew agonisingly real. Yet salvation was at hand. In 1992/93, roaming at will behind the front men, he ceased merely making pretty patterns and began consistently to lacerate defences with penetrating distribution. Appearing quicker and more competitive than ever before, Vinny had it within him to remain one of Spurs' prime creative influences until the decade grew old.

BORN: Bethnal Green, London, 27.10.68.
GAMES: 166 (33). GOALS: 15.
HONOURS: FA Cup 90/1.

1986/87 -

BRIAN STATHAM

When Tottenham's turbulent, sometimes desperate 1987/88 campaign was reviewed, there were precious few causes for satisfaction, but one, it seemed, was the emergence of young Brian Statham. After making his debut as a substitute at Southampton on Boxing Day, the African-born right-back won a regular place in February and retained it in some style until season's end, when he was rewarded with an England under-21 call-up. Neat, quick and skilful, Brian looked a fair bet to settle in as long-term successor to Danny Thomas, and he began 1988/89 in firm possession of Spurs' number-two shirt. But though he was not conspicuously poor, his form *had* declined and after six games, with the rearguard as a whole looking increasingly insecure, he was replaced by Gary Stevens.

Surprisingly in view of his earlier success, Brian never played another game for Spurs in major competition, a combination of injury and the club's plethora of defenders keeping him in the background for more than three years. His luck changed finally when Phil Holder took him on loan to Brentford in February 1992 and he helped the Bees win the Third Division title. A £70,000 transfer followed and Brian consolidated in the new First Division, forging an impressively consistent full-back partnership with former Tottenham team-mate Chris Hughton.

BORN: Zimbabwe, 21.5.69.
GAMES: 22 (5). GOALS: 0.
OTHER CLUBS: Reading *on loan* 90/1 (8, 0);
Bournemouth *on loan* 91/2 (2, 0);
Brentford 91/2- (63, 0).

1987/88 - 1988/89

CHRIS FAIRCLOUGH

Nottingham Forest fans saw it in the mid-eighties, supporters of Leeds came to swear by it, but in between at White Hart Lane, it was a vexingly elusive commodity. We're talking here about the best form of Chris Fairclough, an England under-21 centre-half who had long been coveted by Tottenham when he was signed by David Pleat in the summer of 1987. The transfer - a tribunal set the fee at £387,500 - mystified observers who saw no need to improve on the Gough-Mabbutt partnership, though the confusion was quick to lift as the Scot departed that October.

Chris was never an abject failure, rather something of a disappointment in view of his apparently vast potential. Brave and a superb athlete, he was extremely quick, competent on the ball and good in the air when well placed for headers. But there was the rub: his positioning within the Spurs defensive frame-work was at fault too often for comfort. Nevertheless, Chris was ever-present throughout Tottenham's troubled 1987/88 campaign, but after unconvincing performances the following term, he joined Leeds on loan in March, a £500,000 cheque later making the move permanent. At Elland Road he rediscovered his touch, and was outstanding as his new team lifted the title in 1992. Great for Chris, galling for Spurs.

BORN: Nottingham, 12.4.64.
GAMES: 70. GOALS: 5.
OTHER CLUBS: Nottingham Forest 82/3-86/7 (107, 1);
Leeds United 88/9- (148, 18).

1987/88 - 1988/89

GARY STEVENS

Tottenham fans who reckoned they knew a high-class footballer when they saw one were questioning their own judgement in the autumn of 1983. Just a few months earlier they had eulogised the FA Cup Final performance of Brighton's Gary Stevens, whose late equaliser had forced Manchester United to a Wembley replay, and had been overjoyed when Keith Burkinshaw had paid £300,000 for the 21-year-old central defender during the summer. But when understandable initial nervousness in the famous white shirt showed scant sign of abating, terrace indulgence was quick to evaporate and was replaced by something distressingly close to verbal bullying.

At this crucial juncture, with his expensive acquisition's confidence in tatters, the manager acted decisively by switching him to midfield, producing a marked improvement in form. That term Gary impressed in the latter stages of the successful UEFA Cup campaign, and by 1984/85 he was a revelation. Adopting the role of general factotum to the play-makers, he exerted such an influence, albeit unobtrusive, that by October he had won his first England cap.

Gary did the simple things well, tackling firmly and passing safely, and though he looked rather stiff and unimaginative on the ball, that hardly mattered alongside the likes of Glenn Hoddle or Mike Hazard. Indeed, there are shrewd observers who trace the first real cracks in Tottenham's title campaign to the moment that March when damaged knee ligaments ended his season.

Thereafter the Stevens career was plagued by injury, notably a broken shoulder sustained in an aerial challenge with Wimbledon's John Fashanu in November 1986 and further severe knee trouble, which dated from a notorious challenge by Vinny Jones some two years later. On his return Gary served at right-back but never became fully re-established and in March 1990 he was sold to Portsmouth for £250,000. Sadly, despite dedicated effort, fitness remained elusive and in 1991 he was forced to retire, staying close to the game as a media pundit.

BORN: Hillingdon, Middlesex, 30.3.62.
GAMES: 187 (13). GOALS: 9.
HONOURS: UEFA Cup 83/4. 7 England caps (84-86).
OTHER CLUBS: Brighton 79/80-82/3 (133, 2);
Portsmouth 89/90-90/1 (52, 3).

1983/84 - 1989/90

MITCHELL THOMAS

When David Pleat secured the services of Mitchell Thomas from Luton, his own former club, in the summer of 1986, it seemed that he had signed an outstanding prospect for a bargain fee. The Hatters had wanted £500,000 for their flamboyant England under-21 international left-back, but the new Spurs boss couldn't agree and a tribunal cut the asking price by half. The long term was to suggest this was a wise decision.

Yet Mitchell's form during his first season at White Hart Lane tended to support Luton's case. At that time reassuringly sound at the back, he was an ebullient attacker who belied his 6ft stature by fluid dribbles and high-speed dashes that could leave opponents in a heap. This enterprising start was marred slightly by his unsuccessful attempt to cope with Coventry's Dave Bennett in the FA Cup Final, but majority opinion saw this as an isolated off-day.

Thereafter Mitchell continued competently enough until, with Terry Venables now in charge, he was given opportunities in midfield. Strong and skilful, at times he appeared well equipped for the work but performed inconsistently, and occasionally with a certain eccentricity that earned him the terrace status of a minor cult figure.

In the end his contribution was not enough and, as he switched back and forth between roles, his standing as a first-team regular became eroded. The best and worst of Mitchell were illustrated in two home games during autumn 1988: against Manchester United he won a tackle outside his own area before splitting the Reds' rearguard with an incisive crossfield pass to Chris Waddle, who scored; then when Derby were the visitors, he was given a chasing by Ted McMinn, being fouled for two goals.

Inexplicably, as time went by the Thomas defensive technique appeared less reliable, his positional play provoking particular unease, and when West Ham came along with a £500,000 cheque in August 1991, it seemed in the best interests of both Mitchell and Spurs that he sought a fresh start at Upton Park.

BORN: Luton, Bedfordshire, 2.10.64.
GAMES: 176 (22). GOALS: 8.
OTHER CLUBS: Luton Town 82/3-85/6 (107, 1);
West Ham United 91/2- (38, 3).

1986/87 - 1990/91

PAUL ALLEN

Those who revel in graphs with zigzag lines depicting peaks and troughs would be less than fascinated by a diagram illustrating the level of Paul Allen's performances in the late eighties and early nineties. It would consist of little more than one straight line, a horizontal testimony to the diminutive midfielder's quite staggering consistency. Though public accolades have been sparse for an unspectacular contributor to the Tottenham cause, there is no doubt about his worth among those in the game; to them Paul has been, and remains, the perfect professional, an archetypal players' player. Traditionalists who would decry the fact that his habitual role, ferrying up and down the right flank, might have been filled in days of yore by a tricksy (but unpredictable) winger should not address their criticism to Paul, but to the modern game itself, of which he is a typical product.

Not that the third member of the footballing Allen family to play for Spurs - he was preceded at White Hart Lane by his uncle, Les, and cousin, Clive - has been denied his share of the media spotlight. His profile was high, indeed, as a rookie at West Ham in 1980 when, aged 17 years and 256 days, he became the youngest player in a Wembley FA Cup Final. Paul acquitted himself creditably as the Hammers beat Arsenal, receiving special attention as the victim of a cynical foul by Willie Young, and was hailed as a star of the future. Come the summer of 1985, by which time he had added England under-21 honours to his record 23 youth caps, both Liverpool and Arsenal were in the hunt for his signature, but a £400,000 fee - decided by a tribunal - took him to Tottenham.

Initially all went well, Paul performing effervescently and scoring on his debut at home to Watford, but soon his form dipped as he strove to fit into the Spurs set-up. Then, just as he showed signs of attaining the regular degree of excellence that was to become his hallmark, he was shaken by anxiety about his daughter's health. Eventually she recovered, Paul's relief was evident in his ever-growing confidence on the pitch and since then he has been, almost invariably, a welcome beacon of reliability in a mercurial, frequently-changing side. Even so, when big transfer targets are in the wind, such an unshowy individual can appear dispensable and in 1989 manager Terry Venables accepted a £700,000 bid from Millwall. But Paul, though temporarily out of favour, opted to stay and lost no time in regaining his place, going on to play arguably the most effective football of his career over the next three seasons. The Allen game is based on tireless running, gutsy determination in his challenges and shrewd positional play, but while he is not the man to lay waste to defences with Hoddlesque distribution, let no one belittle his all-round technique, which has improved steadily with experience. A modest character, ever willing to learn, Paul is versatile, too, capable of forsaking his usual right-sided role to become a driving force in central midfield, switching to the left to accommodate less adaptable colleagues or even filling in competently at full-back.

His touch and intelligence were never demonstrated more effectively than in the 1991 FA Cup semi-final victory over Arsenal, when he combined sweetly with Paul Gascoigne to set up the second goal for Gary Lineker, and in the final, when his incisive run paved the way for Paul Stewart's equaliser. Equally, when the tide is flowing against Spurs, Paul can be a heart-lifting figure, sprinting defiantly into enemy territory, searching for an opening when all seems lost. Then there is his pride, in himself and his club, so evident when the absence of Gary Mabbutt and Neil Ruddock elevated him to captain at home to Everton in September 1992. Typically, he responded with a spirited display and a goal to underline yet again that when, in the fullness of time, Paul Allen leaves the Lane, replacing him will be no mere formality.

BORN: Aveley, Essex, 28.8.62.
GAMES: 350 (19). GOALS: 28.
HONOURS: FA Cup 90/1.
OTHER CLUBS: West Ham United 79/80-84/5 (152, 6).

1985/86 -

TERRY FENWICK

Some footballers are cherished by fans in the manner of chosen sons, basking in favour even when playing like drains; others are eternal scapegoats, cast out as pariahs without hope of redemption. Not even the most casual visitor to the Lane could harbour doubts into which category Terry Fenwick fell. The game was given away not so much by the barrage of derision that greeted any mistake by the north-easterner, more the knowing groans from sizeable sections of the Tottenham 'faithful' even when he was performing well. Of course, it was unfair; 'Fen' was a competent enough defender much of the time. Certainly, Terry Venables thought so, having managed him at Crystal Palace and QPR, then paid £550,000 in December 1987 to make the versatile 28-year-old England defender his first major Spurs signing.

At the time, morale was low in a struggling side, and the Fenwick brief was to bring steel and method to a slack rearguard. But work-rate, professionalism and presentable technique could not disguise lack of pace, a tendency to stray out of position and tackling that could be crude. Starting at centre-half, he never looked the part and soon he was subjected to barracking (some critics using him, maybe, as a surrogate Aunt Sally for Venables). True, he embodied the backs-to-the-wall spirit needed in Spurs' current plight, but the point was that, even in the medium term, the fans didn't *want* a team with its back to the wall.

Later Terry, whose vocal imprecations to colleagues when he was playing badly himself sat ill with many observers (though not with his manager), performed more ably as sweeper and then right-back, but anonymously in occasional midfield outings. His strength of character was evident in the way he ignored the abuse, as it was in coming back after injuries (including a broken leg and a broken ankle) and a spell in prison for drink-driving. Come 1992/93 his day appeared to be done, but former team-mates should beware. With 'Fen' gone, there would be a lot of vitriol going spare . . .

BORN: Seaham, County Durham, 17.11.59.
GAMES: 90 (3). GOALS: 8.
HONOURS: 20 England caps (84-88).
OTHER CLUBS: Crystal Palace 77/8-80/1 (70, 0);
Queen's Park Rangers 80/1-87/8 (256, 33);
Leicester City *on loan* 90/1 (8, 1).

1987/88-

JOHN POLSTON

There was widespread disenchantment among Tottenham fans when 22-year-old central defender John Polston was sold to Norwich City in July 1990. The general feeling was that the blond Londoner was exactly the type of poised, stylish operator around whom the club's future should be built. The grievance was fuelled by the identity of John's new employers - the success at Carrow Road of Ian Crook, Ian Culverhouse and Mark Bowen had already caused considerable discontent, albeit retrospective - and also by the apparent folly of dispensing with a promising, home-grown youngster when transfer cash was in such short supply.

In fact, Spurs' financial plight was probably a major factor in the deal - any injection of funds was welcome at the time - though the board were considerably miffed when a tribunal fixed the fee at only £300,000. In further mitigation of the sale, it's true that John was at his best alongside a stopper, the role in which Gary Mabbutt excels. However, the skill and composure he revealed during a sequence of outings in early 1990 had convinced supporters of the Polston pedigree, and certainly his conception and execution of a goal at home to Charlton, which featured a flowing, end-to-end passing movement, supported their view. If John goes on to greater things, the recriminations will be bitter, indeed.

BORN: Walthamstow, London, 10.6.68.
GAMES: 20 (8). GOALS: 1.
OTHER CLUBS: Norwich City 90/1- (81, 6).

1986/87 - 1989/90

GUY BUTTERS

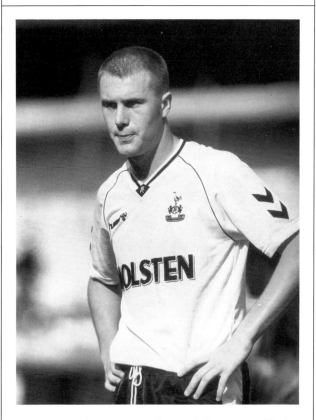

Guy Butters brought a gust of bracing fresh air to Spurs' back line when he was drafted in as a third centre-half in November 1988. No matter that he conceded an unlucky own-goal on his senior debut in a League Cup replay at Blackburn, the 19-year-old stopper's uncomplicated, uncompromising approach gave the rearguard a solidity which previously had been sadly lacking. Standing 6ft 3in, fearsomely strong and with limitless heart, Guy dominated in the air and tore into tackles with the minimum of ceremony. As a bonus, in his first League game he balanced his goal account with a powerful header at home to Wimbledon, but more important, he defended with a consistency that eluded some of his senior colleagues and retained his place deservedly until the end of the season.

Alas, the following term Guy looked a different player. After a succession of poor displays, culminating in a veritable stinker at Villa Park, he was left out to regain confidence, only to perform equally shakily on his return. In happier economic times, Tottenham might have been content to allow such a promising youngster to develop further in the reserves, but with cash at a premium and with Portsmouth offering £325,000, Guy headed south in September 1990.

BORN: Hillingdon, Middlesex, 30.10.69.
GAMES: 37 (2). GOALS: 1.
OTHER CLUBS: Southend United *on loan* 89/90 (16, 3); Portsmouth 90/1- (72, 3).

1988/89 - 1989/90

PAUL GASCOIGNE

Volatile and hyperactive, maniacally intense, even quite ludicrous at times - no, not Gazza, just a humble writer pondering how to do some sort of justice to the rarest, most enthralling talent of a footballing generation. Of course, all the above conditions have been ascribed to our hero at various junctures, and with every justification, but what matters most - all that *really* counts - is the spellbinding brilliance that flows from Paul Gascoigne when the ball is at his feet.

But what is it that makes this garrulous north-easterner of simple tastes, for whom Tottenham cheerfully wrote a £2 million cheque to Newcastle in July 1988, so different from the rest? His passing and vision can make the heart sing, his free-kicks can be savage or subtle but invariably sensational, he is strong, enthusiastic and is not afraid of hard work. But it is none of these things. No, Paul's uniqueness, the entire ethos of his game, is based on his mastery of the dying art of dribbling. During those three tempestuous but enchanting seasons with the Spurs cockerel carried proudly on his barrel chest, his surges from midfield that left a trail of bewildered defenders in his wake became as much a trademark as the Gazza nickname. When the Muse was with him, he could outwit opponents at will: now swerving past regally, keeping them at a distance as though refusing to admit mere commoners to his presence; next moving in tantalisingly close, before the toes twinkled, the ball was switched this way and that, and he was gone.

A telling microcosm of the Paul Gascoigne phenomenon was afforded by the 1991 FA Cup campaign, by which time his World Cup tears - whether they were shed in patriotism or in self-pity (or both) became irrelevant - had enshrined him as a media plaything more marketable than any personality British sport had yet known. Considering the inordinate pressure thus created, his contribution was astounding, and though it ignores the admirable tenet that football is a team game, for once it feels right to assert that one man took his side to the final.

After playing a merely mortal role in the third round victory over Blackpool, the once-portly play-maker - the roll of fat had receded since his Spurs debut, when Newcastle fans had pelted him with Mars bars - ascended to a more celestial plane. Against Oxford in the fourth and Portsmouth in the fifth, his extravagant skills and clinical finishing claimed the spoils; to Notts County in the quarter-final he offered the opening (by failing to clear his lines) from which they went ahead, before destroying them with a perfectly judged late strike - and all while carrying a groin injury that was to need an operation before the semi-final. Come *that* glorious day, Paul excelled even himself, giving Tottenham a fifth-minute lead over Arsenal with a 30-yard free-kick of awesome velocity that was to take its place in Wembley folklore, playing an inspired part in the second goal and generally holding centre stage.

And so to Gazza's blackest hour, the final against Nottingham Forest. Carrying an impossible burden of expectation, he made a fool of himself in front of the world, being lucky to escape dismissal for one early challenge, then crippling himself with a second wild tackle. He was stretchered away in discredit, a victim of self-destruction, and even as Spurs won the Cup their very future was in doubt, so desperately did they need the £8.5 million Lazio had agreed to pay for Paul. It's history now that after taking a year to recover, he moved for £5 million, showed the Italians what he could do and re-emerged as England's premier (only?) hope for international glory.

Off the pitch he is, by turns, funny, gross, endearing, petulant, almost always over the top - but no matter. It's as a footballer that he must be judged and ahead lies what should be his prime. May it be sullied as little as is realistically possible by controversy and the commercial machine. To hell with the hype and the money men; to the fan in the stand, Paul Gascoigne is a player beyond price.

BORN: Gateshead, County Durham, 27.5.67.
GAMES: 110 (2). GOALS: 33.
HONOURS: FA Cup 90/1. 25 England caps (88-).
OTHER CLUBS: Newcastle United 84/5-87/8 (92, 21);
Lazio, Italy, 92/3-.

1988/89 - 1990/91

NAYIM

Nayim is a connoisseur's delight, a true soccer thoroughbred whose presence brought spice and guile to the Tottenham midfield. Indeed, some seasoned observers maintain that, but for a certain lack of pace, the multi-talented, Moroccan-born Spaniard might have blossomed into an international star. Having been groomed at Barcelona by Terry Venables, Nayim - full name Mohammed Ali Amar - later became surplus to Catalan requirements and in November 1988 Terry, by now in situ at White Hart Lane, signed his protege on loan. So promisingly did he perform during a handful of outings that spring that, come June, the North Londoners opted to make the transfer permanent, securing the swarthy ball-artist for a bargain £400,000 as a makeweight in the Gary Lineker deal.

Thereafter he tended to drift in and out of the side - sometimes through injury and sometimes, presumably, because his Continental style was deemed too subtle for English demands - but it was a fact that Spurs looked far more inventive when Nayim was patrolling their left flank. His deft, penetrative passing, magnetic control and intelligent running carried a constant whiff of the unexpected, and no one at the club struck the ball more crisply. Against all that was an occasional tendency to loiter on the fringe of the action, and a penchant for extravagant penalty-area tumbles that did not endear him to opponents.

Arguably Nayim's most consistent senior sequences came in the first half of 1990/91 and after New Year in 1993, but perhaps his most dazzlingly memorable moment came in the League Cup at Southend in October 1989. Surrounded by defenders and facing away from goal, he flicked the ball over his head, eluded his markers and slotted the ball between the 'keeper's legs. More widely appreciated was a splendid FA Cup quarter-final hat-trick at Manchester City in 1993, at a time when rumours of his departure were rife. Sure enough, a few weeks later he joined Real Zaragoza for £500,000, leaving many fans to feel sad that the chant of 'Nayeeeeem' would no longer echo around White Hart Lane.

BORN: Ceuta, Morocco, 5.11.66.
GAMES: 118 (26). GOALS: 18.
HONOURS: FA Cup 90/1.
OTHER CLUBS: Barcelona, Real Zaragoza, both Spain.

1988/89 - 1992/93

PAUL MORAN

Paul Moran was a high-class schoolboy athlete who ran for Enfield Harriers; but what he always wanted was to run for Spurs. And so he did, making his debut at Everton in May 1987, then subsequently demonstrating speed, skill and fire in spasmodic outings as a utility forward over the next six seasons.

Sadly, though, 'Sparrow', so dubbed for his slight build and skinny legs, has found it impossible to rise in the pecking order above a succession of costly signings - he has endured the arrival of Walsh and Stewart, Lineker and Durie, Anderton and Sheringham - and has been further hindered by injuries.

Through it all, Paul - who has served four other clubs on loan - maintained commendable confidence, as he showed at home to Sheffield Wednesday in October 1989 when, put through on goal but with the unmarked Lineker lurking nearby, he opted coolly to find the net himself. In 1993, still only 25 but with regular promotion seemingly beyond him, Paul was an obvious subject for transfer speculation.

BORN: Enfield, London, 22.5.68.
GAMES: 18 (24). GOALS: 2.
OTHER CLUBS:
Portsmouth *on loan* 88/9 (3, 0);
Leicester City *on loan* 89/90 (10, 1);
Newcastle United *on loan* 90/1 (1, 0);
Southend United *on loan* 90/1 (1, 0).

1986/87 -

JOHN MONCUR

They called him 'The Loan Ranger' at White Hart Lane, so frequently did he temp with other clubs, but John Moncur deserves a reputation which better fits his undoubted skills. The blond schemer is a precise passer, a delightful manipulator of the ball and a persuasive dummy salesman. However, his presence could seem as lightweight as his build, and somehow the athleticism and stamina he displayed in training were not always evident in matches. It hardly helped the young Londoner that, after sampling senior action for the first time in May 1987, he was never given a settled run.

Of course, the major problem was the presence of Paul Gascoigne as chief play-maker, and by the time Gazza had gone, it was almost as if John had been hovering on the brink for *too* long. Those who championed the Moncur cause recall wistfully his creative performance at Derby in February 1990 and when he joined Swindon for £80,000 in March 1992, they wished him well. With Glenn Hoddle as his new boss, John could be assured, at last, that his subtle talent would have every chance to bloom.

BORN: Stepney, London, 22.9.66.
GAMES: 11 (13). GOALS: 1.
OTHER CLUBS: Doncaster Rovers *on loan* 86/7 (4, 0); Cambridge United *on loan* 86/7 (4, 0); Portsmouth *on loan* 88/9 (7, 0); Brentford *on loan* 89/90 (5, 1); Ipswich Town *on loan* 91/2 (6, 0); Swindon Town 91/2- (17, 1).

1986/87 - 1991/92

SCOTT HOUGHTON

The Tottenham crowd, not always the most tolerant of taskmasters where home-grown talent is concerned, cannot be faulted for their treatment of Scott Houghton. Indeed, in 1991/92 they clasped the chunky little midfield flankman to their collective bosom with a fervour that extended, in some sections, to mild outrage when his promising cameo displays as substitute were not rewarded with a first-choice sequence.

Standing only 5ft 5in, Scott radiates vigour and enthusiasm, and his readiness to run boldly at hulking defenders struck a chord with fans who felt, at times, that their side's engine-room was too passive. His contribution against Luton at the Lane in November was particularly dramatic as he enlivened proceedings with two goals, one of them a speculative long-shot from near the touchline.

But as more and more youngsters rose through the ranks, Scott was given no senior opportunity in 1992/93 and he was released on loan. Clearly, a return to first-team reckoning will require some exceptional form.

BORN: Hitchin, Hertfordshire, 22.10.71.
GAMES: 0 (14). GOALS: 2.
OTHER CLUBS:
Ipswich Town *on loan* 90/1 (8, 1);
Gillingham *on loan* 92/3 (3, 0);
Charlton Athletic *on loan* 92/3 (6, 0).

1991/92 -

GARY LINEKER

There is a theory that any team containing Gary Lineker was never quite as good as its results suggested, the inference being that he compensated for collective shortcomings by the well-nigh unparalleled efficiency with which he did his job. Naturally, the man himself would be far too modest to accept such a contention, but with all due respect to his Tottenham colleagues during three goal-laden seasons, it carries an unmistakable ring of truth. Like any marksman born of woman, Gary missed his share of opportunities, but his priceless art - for such it was, as sure as any schemer's most delicate touch - lay in spurning fewer than any of his peers.

So what elevated the personable Midlander to the uttermost peak of his profession? Searing pace is the answer most frequently trotted out but, as the plethora of fleet-footed under-achievers scattered around the divisions tends to suggest, that is a gross over-simplification. Certainly Gary's speed was central to his success, but it was the intelligent application of that prize asset which set him apart. He was a brilliant reader of the game whose timing of runs into the area behind defenders was superb. In tighter situations he would lead his marker astray with a sudden dart away from goal, only to spin off the hapless 'shadow' just as the ball was played into the space thus vacated.

Then, of course, there was that ultimate skill which gives meaning to all the others - the knack of putting the ball in the net. Gary could perform this notoriously difficult act clinically and repeatedly, evoking the deadliness and composure - if not the all-round ability - of one Jimmy Greaves. He took time when none seemed available, his instinct for stealing a yard in the most densely crowded goalmouth and his almost uncanny anticipation of a football's flight-path paying handsome dividends. He had a geometrician's feel for angles, an intuition for selecting the correct mode of shot - sidefoots and power-drives, chips and nudges, all were kept in their rightful place - and carried an aerial threat that was underrated at opponents' peril.

His critics would have it that he was useless without waiter-service, that only rarely would he fashion an opening himself, but as a specialist at the top level that was scarcely a weakness, witness his record. A further carp related to his lack of contribution outside the box, but that he was not always a passenger away from the front line was shown twice at Old Trafford in autumn 1989. First he dragged Gary Pallister out of position before setting up a League Cup goal for Vinny Samways, then three weeks later he cut in from the left flank to score with a 20-yard bender in a League encounter.

However, beyond all the analysis, the bare facts of Gary's Tottenham career speak for themselves. Arriving from Barcelona in June 1989 - at £1.2 million, the 28-year-old star was one of the bargains of the decade - he went six matches without scoring before hitting a hot streak that saw him finish the season as the First Division's leading scorer. His middle term at the Lane was disrupted by injury, but despite a lean spell he managed 19 in major competitions, including two crucial efforts in the FA Cup semi-final victory over Arsenal. Then in a 1991/92 campaign clouded by the serious illness of his baby son, he displayed remarkable resilience to strike no less than 35 times in 50 outings, probably saving Spurs from relegation and being rewarded with the writers' Footballer of the Year award. That summer the England captain failed narrowly to beat Bobby Charlton's scoring record for his country before retiring from the international scene and heading for Japan, his £900,000 move to Grampus Eight having been announced some months earlier. Thus Gary Lineker departed the English game held in a universal affection rivalled only by the aforementioned Mr Charlton himself.

BORN: Leicester, 30.11.60.
GAMES: 138. GOALS: 80.
HONOURS: FA Cup 90/1. 80 England caps (84-92).
OTHER CLUBS: Leicester City 78/9-74/5 (194, 95);
Everton 85/6 (41, 30);
Barcelona, Spain, 86/7-88/9 (99, 44);
Grampus Eight, Japan.

1989/90 - 1991/92

GARY MABBUTT

If money talks, and big money talks the loudest, then often during the eighties the noise from White Hart Lane was deafening as millions poured from the club coffers to recruit some of the game's finest and most flamboyant talent. By comparison, the £105,000 it took to persuade Bristol Rovers to part with Gary Mabbutt in August 1982 was little more than a muffled whisper; the reverberations, however, go on and on, and what a satisfying, reassuring, often uplifting sound it has been. Certainly, it would be difficult to overstate the importance of Gary to the Tottenham cause. His versatility alone - midfielder, central defender, full-back, even emergency striker, he's been the lot - made him well-nigh indispensable to a succession of managers; and that's without considering his loyalty, industry and a brand of single-minded dedication that, if it could be bottled for consumption by less disciplined individuals, would find an avid market among overwrought bosses everywhere.

In fact, but for that last-mentioned quality, Gary would never have become a leading player. Neither extravagantly gifted, nor particularly quick, he strove unstintingly from early boyhood - inspired by his father Ray, the former Bristol Rovers stalwart, and working in tandem with his brother Kevin, who played for Bristol City and Crystal Palace - to make the utmost of his natural athleticism, zest and will-power. Gary's desire to succeed in the game he loved was never shaken, not even by the shattering discovery as a 17-year-old that he was diabetic, a handicap he conquered to the extent that Bobby Robson dubbed him 'The Bionic Man'. Indeed, so impressed was the England manager with Gary's instant adaptation to the top flight that he awarded the young Bristolian his first full cap some two months after his move to North London, and it was to surprise many observers when future international appearances proved so intermittent.

Early seasons at the Lane were spent mostly in midfield - his first yielded ten League goals, just one short of top-scoring Steve Archibald - and despite finding himself out of the side for part of Peter Shreeves' first term at the helm, Gary remained a valuable asset who was improving with experience. Even so, it took a switch to the centre of defence in 1985/86 to bring out the best in a performer who, in more forward positions, was not always at home with Spurs' traditional flowing movement. Now, though, he was majestic, employing his fastidiously honed abilities to full effect and radiating the unfussy composure that became a trademark.

Though standing only 5ft 9in, Gary was brilliant in the air, the timing of his spring-heeled leaps winning duel after duel with giant opponents, while his strong, clean tackling was a joy and his shrewd anticipation defused countless threats on goal. In 1986/87, Richard Gough and he were the fans' 'dream ticket' at the rearguard's core, and it was supremely galling to end an exhilarating season with no honours, especially so for Gary, who against Coventry at Wembley became only the second man to score for both teams in an FA Cup Final. Soon after, having spurned reported advances from Liverpool, he replaced the departed Scot as skipper and in the years that followed no one did more to keep his club ticking over on the pitch while turmoil reigned in the boardroom.

Thus it was gratifying in 1991 when Gary's smile, such a constant part of the Spurs scene, appeared - wider than ever - between two arms that were holding aloft the FA Cup. Thereafter his playing standard remained high and when he came back from injury in autumn 1992, he transformed a hitherto porous defence, helping new partner Neil Ruddock look twice the player he had been. Perhaps outsiders do not appreciate his full worth, but at White Hart Lane, Gary Mabbutt will be remembered always as the most consistent and best-loved player of a supremely difficult era.

BORN: Bristol, 23.8.61.
GAMES: 461 (20). GOALS: 37.
HONOURS: UEFA Cup 83/4; FA Cup 90/1.
16 England caps (82-).
OTHER CLUBS: Bristol Rovers 78/9-81/2 (131, 10).

1982/83 -

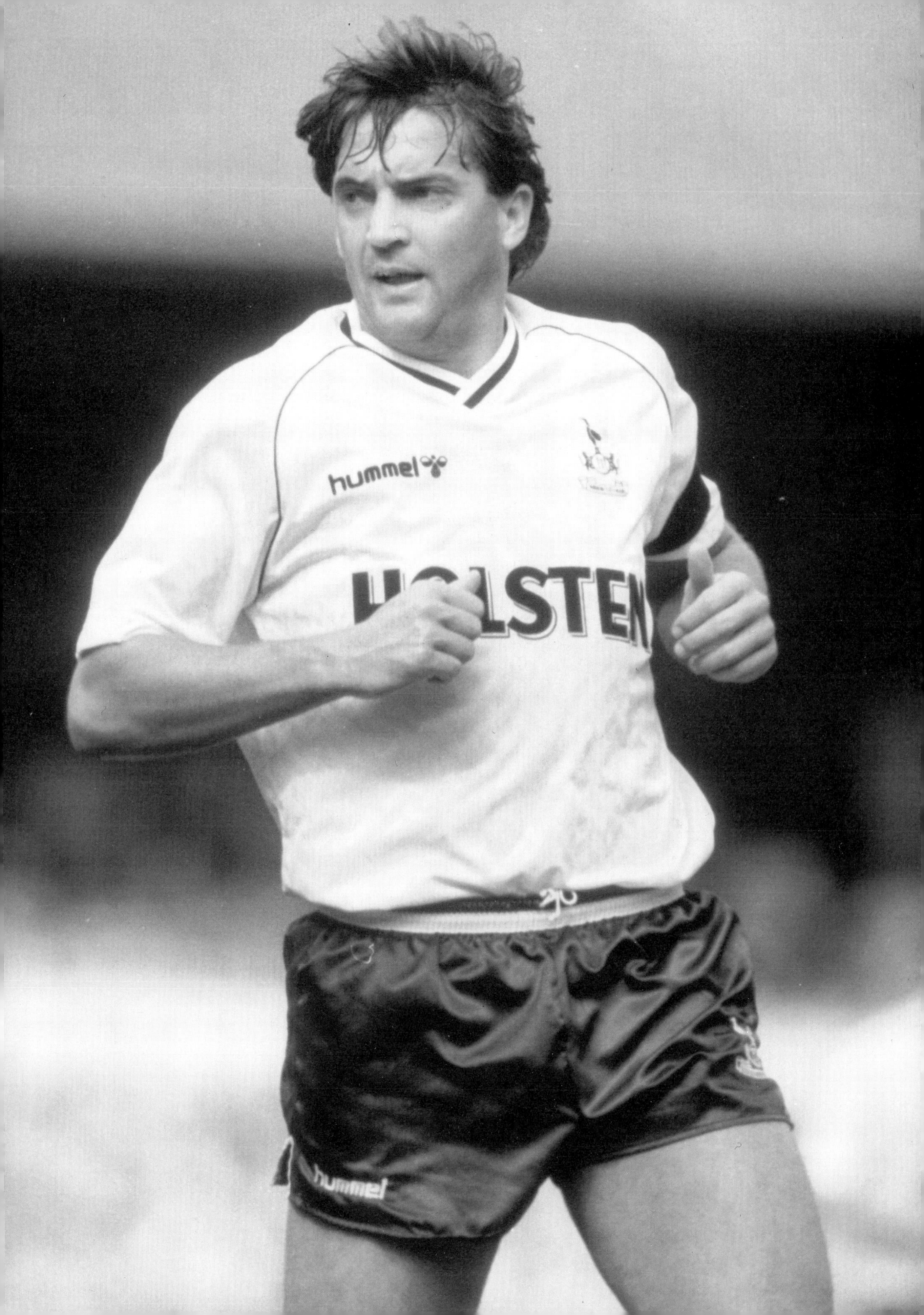
hummel
hummel

GUDNI BERGSSON	JOHN HENDRY	DAVID TUTTLE

Gudni Bergsson has made himself useful at White Hart Lane without ever managing to suggest that he would become indispensable. The slim, blond utility man, who can play at full-back and in midfield but is at his best sweeping alongside the centre-half, is quick, tackles briskly and relishes the chance to get forward, but his control and distribution have tended to detract from the overall effect.

Gudni, rejected by Aston Villa after a 1985 trial, stepped out of his native Icelandic league for a midwinter loan with Spurs in 1988 and found himself at right-back in a home encounter with Luton on Boxing Day. He gave the first of a commendable series of displays and in February was awarded a full contract. Thereafter he has enjoyed sporadic senior sequences - his most settled spell being in 1991/92 under Peter Shreeves - but the signings of Neil Ruddock, Dean Austin and Jason Cundy that summer dented his aspirations considerably and it would be surprising now if Gudni won a regular first-team berth.

BORN: Iceland, 21.7.65.
GAMES: 62 (25). GOALS: 2.
HONOURS: Iceland caps.
OTHER CLUBS: Valur, Iceland.

Promising striker John Hendry has been accorded few senior opportunities in the Tottenham attack, despite making a favourable impression in his limited outings. The slim, wiry Glaswegian had failed to make an early breakthrough at Dundee but had attracted attention with a prolific spell on loan with Forfar Athletic when Terry Venables hazarded £50,000 on an essentially unknown quantity in July 1990.

John's initial progress at White Hart Lane was hampered by injuries, but when his chance came in the spring of 1991, he took it. After scoring a debut goal at Norwich, he netted with a looping header at Old Trafford on his second full appearance, and at that stage looked a fine prospect. Adept at loping inconspicuously into dangerous positions, capable of turning sharply and possessing a neat first touch, John is the type who can be expected to steal a goal from nothing. But he was condemned to languish during the next two terms and, with competition for places hotting up, he might need a move to fulfil his potential.

BORN: Glasgow, 6.1.70.
GAMES: 5 (10). GOALS: 5.
OTHER CLUBS: Dundee 88/9 (2, 0); Forfar Athletic *on loan* 89/90 (10, 6); Charlton Athletic *on loan* 91/2 (5, 1).

Whatever doubts Tottenham fans may have about central defender David Tuttle, they need have none about his character. Making his League debut at Stamford Bridge in December 1990, the 18-year-old six-footer was handed the task of shackling Kerry Dixon. Within five minutes, the experienced marksman had put Chelsea ahead and proceeded to give David such a roasting that manager Terry Venables withdrew his rookie stopper from the action at half-time.

In the face of such trauma, the confidence of many players might have withered, but David was made of sterner stuff. Come the spring he was back in the side, tackling solidly and eager to learn, and in September 1991 sampled the smoother side of the soccer coin, scoring with a fierce drive at home to Hadjuk Split. However, the England youth international then suffered an injury that ruled him out for the season, enduring similar ill fortune while on loan to Peterborough the following term. The path to Spurs' first team will not be easy, but David is too young and too determined to be discounted lightly.

BORN: Reading, 6.2.72.
GAMES: 14 (4). GOALS: 1.
OTHER CLUBS:
Peterborough United *on loan* 92/3 (7, 0).

1988/89 -	1990/91 -	1990/91 -

STEVE SEDGLEY

When Steve Sedgley headed for White Hart Lane as a £750,000 recruit from Coventry City in July 1989, there was one telling factor in favour of the spindly North Londoner's chances of success - his heart was already there. Having cheered Spurs from the terraces as a boy and actually played for them at junior level - before being rejected and taking his talents to Highfield Road - he must have felt he was going home. However, the path that lay ahead was by no means smooth. Steve was bought as a midfield anchorman, his doughty defensive qualities seen as the ideal counterbalance to the ebullient skills of Paul Gascoigne. It was a role he had filled regularly for England under-21 but in which he now failed to impress. Though staunchly determined and capable of passing well with his left foot if given the time, he appeared sluggish and awkward, a considerable disappointment.

But during his first campaign as a Spur, Steve was switched to central defence in an emergency and displayed instant poise, linking effectively with Gary Mabbutt in a composed, generally solid partnership. Though prone to occasional bloomers - a rash pass here, a missed tackle there - suddenly at 21 he was a bright prospect again, remaining first choice until the end of 1990/91 and pocketing an FA Cup winner's medal in the process. Then a ponderous display at Southampton on the opening day of the new term signalled a period of uncertainty that saw him flitting in and out of the side, and come 1992/93 - with Neil Ruddock and Jason Cundy fresh on the scene - there was an inescapable feeling that he would become one of the club's many 'nearly men'.

Steve, however, had not read that particular script and, benefiting from injuries to others, he enjoyed two competent spells in his old midfield niche, the second marked by a smartly taken goal in the FA Cup quarter-final win over Manchester City at Maine Road. Still only 25 and now experienced, Steve Sedgley may yet prove an invaluable long-term acquisition.

BORN: Enfield, London, 26.5.68.
GAMES: 137 (24). GOALS: 5.
HONOURS: FA Cup 90/1.
OTHER CLUBS: Coventry City 86/7-88/9 (84, 3).

1989/90 -

PAUL STEWART

The old saying that you can't make a silk purse from a sow's ear held little credence for Spurs fans of the early nineties; after all, in the case of Paul Stewart, they had seen the evidence with their own eyes. The burly centre-forward cost £1.5 million from Manchester City in the summer of 1988, and early indications were not encouraging. After missing the first four games through suspension for earlier misdemeanours, he endured a traumatic debut at home to Manchester United. Coming on as a substitute palpably consumed with urgency to impress, he charged around like a man possessed until - near the end and with the scores level - he won a penalty. Terry Fenwick shaped to take the kick but Paul, on a high, pressed his own claim, was given precedence - and slammed the ball against the crossbar. Further ignominy awaited as six games passed without a goal; even worse, he didn't look the part, appearing crude, ponderous and out of his depth.

Paul's situation barely improved in the first six months of 1989/90 when, with new partner Gary Lineker garnering the glory, his blunt bludgeoning was exposed mercilessly by the gleaming rapier alongside. However, to his eternal credit, the bustling Mancunian tried ceaselessly, never hiding from the ball and refusing to make excuses as he endured a run of appalling luck in front of goal. Inevitably though, for a player to whom confidence was everything, the strain began to tell and his bearing on the pitch began to reflect the frustration and depression he must have been feeling.

A turning point of sorts arrived in March when, after being demoted to the reserves in favour of Paul Walsh, he was called off the bench and sealed a home victory over Liverpool with a marvellous, soaring header in front of the TV cameras. Suddenly self-belief was rediscovered and the goals began to flow, one in particular, against Coventry at the Lane in April, prompting his most caustic critics to goggle with amazement. Taking possession inside the penalty box with his back to goal, Paul flipped the ball up and over a marker's head before swivelling to lash an acute-angled volley into the net from ten yards. However, the following season had begun in ominous fashion, with just one strike in 17 League outings, when three days before Christmas, at home to Luton, the Stewart fortunes were transformed in the unlikeliest of circumstances. With Spurs reduced to nine men by the dismissals of Nayim and Van den Hauwe, Paul dropped back to midfield, where he was a revelation. The fact that he scored twice to win the match was the least of it; what transfixed the eye was his new assurance, the unimagined delicacy of his touch, the accuracy and perception of his passing, all underpinned by stamina, strength and the aggression of a natural ball-winner.

For a handful of matches he returned to the front line before settling in midfield, proving that with the extra time his new role allowed, and without the pressure of *having* to find the net, he could make a handsome contribution. Paul remained on song for the rest of the season, reserving the culmination of his rebirth for the grandest of settings, at Wembley in the FA Cup Final against Nottingham Forest. He played superbly throughout, capping his display with a ruthlessly executed equaliser, a low cross-shot from some 12 yards. Paul's form during the next term confirmed his progress - indeed, frequently he was the most impressive Spur on view - and he earned an England call-up, the very idea of which would have been risible only a year earlier. The fans, though, were not allowed to bask for long in their new hero's glory. Family reasons dictated a move north and in July 1992 Paul joined Liverpool for £2.3 million. It was a dream transfer for a wholehearted, and yes, gifted player who had experienced more than his share of nightmares.

BORN: Manchester, 7.10.64.
GAMES: 166 (5). GOALS: 37.
HONOURS: FA Cup 90/1. 3 England caps (91-).
OTHER CLUBS: Blackpool 81/2-86/7 (201, 56);
Manchester City 86/7-87/8 (51, 26).
Liverpool 92/3- (24, 1).

1988/89 - 1991/92

JASON CUNDY

The sight of Jason Cundy tackling mid-air on several occasions against Sheffield Wednesday in September 1992 highlighted vividly the major defect in the game of an otherwise promising central defender. Fast, fearless and ferocious he may be, but the enthusiastic stopper is prone to making rash challenges when prudence dictates a little restraint. That afternoon at Hillsborough, he looked out of his class against skipping, skilful opponents, and not long afterwards he lost his place to Gary Mabbutt, whose method it would profit him to study in depth. England under-21 international Jason arrived at White Hart Lane in spring 1992 on loan from Chelsea, where he had been accorded rabid terrace popularity. Bristling with aggression, aerially powerful and bitingly strong in the tackle, he did enough during the rest of the season to persuade Spurs to strike an £800,000 deal that summer, and as the new term began he formed a daunting partnership with Neil Ruddock.

Jason played well at times and enjoyed one moment of undiluted bliss, when his lusty 50-yard punt caught the wind and sailed into the Ipswich net for a freak goal at Portman Road. But faulty positioning and impetuosity marred his defensive work and the axe fell. Later he was tried briefly as a holding midfielder before injury halted his progress, though Jason is young enough, and probably good enough, to come again.

BORN: Wimbledon, 12.11.69.
GAMES: 25 (2). GOALS: 1.
OTHER CLUBS: Chelsea 90/1-91/2 (41, 1).

1991/92 -

ANDY GRAY

As a driving-force in the Crystal Palace midfield, Andy Gray could be guaranteed to impose himself on his Spurs counterparts. Hence when the combative, accomplished Londoner moved to White Hart Lane on loan in February 1992, his ineffective form was a sore letdown to expectant fans. In retrospect, however, that was inevitable. Andy, not always the easiest character to handle, had been at odds with Palace boss Steve Coppell and had put on weight after ceasing to train.

Nevertheless, that summer Tottenham parted with £900,000 to acquire his services on a permanent basis and in subsequent outings - mostly in his familiar central slot rather than the right-flank role of the previous campaign - he looked more like the player who had won an England cap in 1991. At his best Andy can inspire a team, both with an appetite for the fray that ensures he is near the heart of any rumpus and good all-round technique that encompasses a fierce shot, aerial power, underrated creativity and a havoc-inducing long throw. But he remained unpredictable and - troubled by injuries and brisk competition for places - he was never more than a useful squad member, at one point being released on loan to Swindon. Andy Gray's ability is unquestioned; whether he can harness it consistently is another matter.

BORN: Lambeth, London, 22.2.64.
GAMES: 23 (8). GOALS: 2. HONOURS: 1 England cap (91).
OTHER CLUBS: Crystal Palace 84/5-87/8 (98, 27);
Aston Villa 87/8-88/9 (37, 4); Queen's Park Rangers 88/9 (11, 2);
Crystal Palace 88/9-91/2 (90, 12). Swindon Town *on loan* (3, 0).

1991/92 -

PAT VAN DEN HAUWE

Pat Van den Hauwe is a Jekyll-and-Hyde footballer. One minute the Welsh international left-back might control the ball beautifully before clipping a precise pass to a colleague, his technique earning approbation from the most demanding of judges. But the next he would plough into an opponent with all the subtlety of a runaway warhead, demonstrating luridly why a baleful element among supporters of his previous club, Everton, gloried in christening him 'Psycho-Pat'. Undeniably the versatile defender - so combative in the air and an able stopper at need - has done little throughout his stormy career to defuse his image as an archetypal 'heavy'. The dead-eyed stare, the designer stubble, his very demeanour during a game, they all serve to emphasise and perpetuate the menacing persona that has become his trademark.

Having helped take two League titles and the Cup Winners' Cup to Goodison, 28-year-old Pat moved to White Hart Lane for £575,000 in August 1989. He marked his arrival with two bookings in his first three games, then settled capably into the side, going on to become popular with the fans in a jokey, anti-hero type of way. True, unnecessary fouls put the side under pressure at times, and moments of excess like the waist-high tackle on Luton's Iain Dowie which earned him a sending-off at the Lane in December 1990 were clearly reprehensible, but in general the good - which included crossing accurately and delivering a devastating long throw - outweighed the bad.

Pat, whose hopes of playing for his native Belgium disappeared when he opted out of National Service, must surely have won more caps for Wales, his adopted country, but for a tiff with the management. Nevertheless, his ambition remained undiminished and he assisted in Spurs' FA Cup triumph of 1991. After one more season as a first-team regular, younger men reduced him to the role of occasional substitute, but by then Pat Van den Hauwe had given ample value for money.

BORN: Dendermonde, Belgium, 16.12.60.
GAMES: 139 (6). GOALS: 0.
HONOURS: FA Cup 90/1.
13 Wales caps (85-).
OTHER CLUBS: Birmingham City 78/9-84/5 (123, 1);
Everton 84/5-89/90 (135, 2).

1989/90 -

DEAN AUSTIN

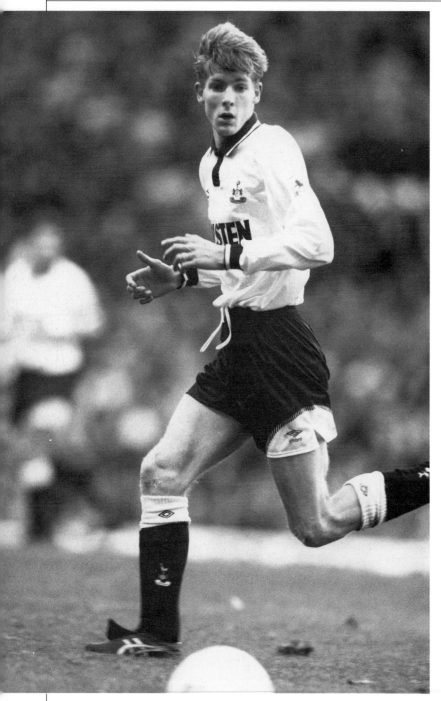

To paraphrase the words of the song, you've either got or you haven't got class - and Dean Austin has it in abundance. Indeed, that most elusive of qualities positively oozes from the slim six-footer, who lines up at right-back but could be more accurately described as a wing-back.

Dean arrived at White Hart Lane in June 1992, following in Justin Edinburgh's footsteps rom Southend United, who were not happy at being used as purveyors of full-backs to the footballing aristocracy. Indeed, when a transfer tribunal set the Austin fee at £375,000, rising to £525,000 after a certain number of games, the Shrimpers' outraged chairman announced a ban on future transfers to Tottenham.

Rapidly it became apparent that the North Londoners had secured a rare bargain. Having been consigned to the reserves at first, Dean made his senior bow in August as a substitute at home to Crystal Palace, marking the occasion by advancing smoothly down the right flank and crossing for Steve Sedgley to snatch a late and unexpected equaliser. The manoeuvre was typical of the stylish newcomer, whose close control enabled him to dribble past opponents and whose precise delivery meant that he rarely wasted the advantage thus gained.

Though the defensive side of his game needed some early attention, the rudiments were all in place, and as he gained in top-flight experience his solidity in the tackle, intelligence and speed became welcome features of a previously fragile Spurs rearguard. Dean's composed temperament, too, marked him out for an illustrious future, as illustrated on his full debut, in which he remained admirably steady on a night of communal Tottenham woe at Elland Road, Leeds annihilating their visitors 5-0. Clearly, if Dean Austin continued at his initial rate of progress, then not only his club, but also his country, would have reason for rejoicing.

BORN: Hemel Hempstead, Hertfordshire, 26.4.70.
GAMES: 40 (2). GOALS: 0.
OTHER CLUBS: Southend United 89/90-91/2 (96, 2).

1992/93 -

JUSTIN EDINBURGH

Justin Edinburgh is an ambitious young left-back with no shortage of technical qualifications for laying long-term claim to the number-three shirt at White Hart Lane. Yet perhaps his premier attraction to fans, certainly the younger element behind the goal, is more emotional. It's as plain as the navy-blue cockerel emblazoned on his chest: more than anything else, Justin *wants* to play for Tottenham Hotspur.

He was spotted by the North Londoners as a precocious teenager with Southend United, and he spent the opening months of 1990 on loan at the Lane. Though there were no senior opportunities, and he rejoined the Shrimpers to help clinch promotion to the Third Division, Justin had shown enough potential for Tottenham to secure his services on a permanent basis for £150,000 that summer. Though undeniably green, he won an unexpectedly early breakthrough as the squad was depleted by injuries, impressing with his incisiveness in the tackle and all-round eagerness. Against that was a tendency towards impetuous challenges in dangerous situations and the patent need to curb a quick temper, but the initial verdict was overwhelmingly favourable.

Justin completed his first season as a Spur with splendidly efficient displays in the FA Cup semi-final clash with Arsenal and the final victory over Nottingham Forest, and he appeared to be in the team to stay. However, the next term his rate of progress slowed, perhaps an inevitable hiatus for one so young. Reassuringly he soldiered through the lean patch, and by spring 1993 was noticeably more poised and mature. Justin's defensive work was sound and precise, and he made valuable attacking contributions, more by offering astute support to the man on the ball than as a conventional overlapper. His distribution was improving all the time - as evidenced by his cute pass to set up Steve Sedgley's FA Cup quarter-final strike against Manchester City - and it would take a good man, indeed, to remove that beloved shirt from his back.

BORN: Brentwood, Essex, 18.12.69.
GAMES: 89 (7). GOALS: 1.
HONOURS: FA Cup 90/1.
OTHER CLUBS: Southend United 88/9-89/90 (37, 0).

1990/91 -

NEIL RUDDOCK

One day, when season 1992/93 can be viewed in proper perspective, the renaissance of Neil Ruddock may be seen as one of the most significant events in Spurs' post-Nicholson era. The inevitable 'Bad Boy Makes Good' headlines were a nod in the right direction, but they did scant justice to the massive influence wielded by the glowering man-mountain who brought steel, confidence and something less definable - sheer presence, perhaps, begins to describe it - to the core of Tottenham's rearguard. But before enlarging on the merits of 'Razor', so dubbed in reference to the cutting edge of his game as much as to the heavyweight boxer who shares his surname, a spot of history is in order. He arrived at White Hart Lane for the first time in March 1986, an exceedingly raw 17-year-old recruit from Millwall who, costing £50,000 and without a senior outing to his name, represented a distinct gamble. It was a year before he made his full debut, as a substitute in an FA Cup quarter-final victory at Wimbledon. There followed sporadic chances over the next year - he scored Spurs' goal in the FA Cup disaster at Port Vale in January 1987 - and though Neil didn't claim a regular place, he did enough to suggest that former manager Peter Shreeves had made a shrewd investment.

However, with cash at a premium, new boss Terry Venables accepted a £300,000 offer in June 1988 and the 20-year-old stopper returned to The Den, only to be consigned once more to the 'stiffs'. Before long he switched to Southampton, where finally he was given the extended opportunity his potential deserved and made giant strides, soon earning an England under-21 call-up. Unfortunately, the Ruddock file reveals that his progress was marred by an appalling disciplinary record that, at one time, threatened his very future in the game. Nevertheless, in May 1992 when Spurs were casting around for the dominant centre-half they needed so desperately, they could find no more suitable target than the rugged Londoner, whose £750,000 fee was settled by a tribunal.

Events have proved that Venables could hardly have been wiser in shrugging off any embarrassment involved in re-signing a player with whom he had once dispensed, and in running the risk of Neil's well-publicised attempts to curb his temper ending in failure. The 'second coming' began auspiciously with a superb defensive performance - at The Dell, ironically enough - but in his third League outing, 'Razor' was sent off for two bookable offences. He professed himself mortified, took his punishment on that stubbly square chin and vowed not to let the side down again - and at the time of writing he had been as good as his word. More gratifying still was Neil's form and his effect on team morale. Paired with Jason Cundy in the term's opening months, he played extremely well, but in a defence that continued to ship goals wholesale, he did not always receive due personal credit. However, when Cundy was replaced by the immaculate Gary Mabbutt, results improved and Neil was thrown into stark relief as the high-quality bulwark he had become. Aggression personified, he was a towering authority in the air at either end of the pitch and tackled like a torpedo, though almost invariably within the laws of the game. In addition, he revealed a hitherto untrumpeted delicate left-foot touch, which was highlighted in the FA Cup fifth-round clash with Wimbledon. Several times he broke free on the flank and delivered some telling crosses, one of which resulted in a goal for Darren Anderton; of course, there was still time to confront and vanquish that ultimate warrior centre-forward, John Fashanu.

Having impressed when deputising as skipper, Neil is the prime long-term captaincy candidate and as spring arrived he became an increasingly talismanic figure to the fans, the slightest prospect of losing him through injury causing a communal shudder around the Lane. If he never played another game for Spurs, Neil Ruddock would go down as the 'wild' youngster who grew up late but in a hurry, becoming an instant folk hero in the process. If he keeps his head, and there is every indication that he will, his prospects are immense.

BORN: Wandsworth, London, 9.5.68.
GAMES: 55 (3). GOALS: 4.
OTHER CLUBS: Millwall 88/9 (2, 1);
Southampton 88/9-91/2 (107, 9).

1986/87 - 1987/88 & 1992/93 -

PAUL WALSH

That Paul Walsh never emerged as one of England's premier stars of the late eighties is a cause for considerable bafflement, tinged with sadness. Here was a footballer with scintillating talent who worked hard and played for two great clubs; yet as he entered his thirties, all he had to look back on was a tantalising collage of cameo achievements.

Paul joined Spurs from Liverpool in February 1988, ending an Anfield stint which could not be classed a flop but, mainly through injuries and bad luck, had failed to ignite. For his £500,000, Terry Venables had enlisted a quicksilver entertainer capable of thrilling crowds with his speed and control, his knack of riding tackles and selling dummies matched by slick distribution and, on his day, a waspish finish.

However, as the hirsute Londoner partnered first Clive Allen, then Paul Stewart and Chris Waddle, he never attained sufficient consistency, and Gary Lineker's arrival in 1989 was a chronic blow to his aspirations. Thus for his last three years at the Lane, Paul found himself cast repeatedly as a substitute or as Gary's deputy. In the latter role he could be sure that no matter how well he played - his splendid three-goal display at home to Sheffield United in October 1990 is a perfect example - he would be back on the bench for the next game, a woeful situation for a man who had won England caps as a 20-year-old.

Paul received a certain sympathy from the terraces - especially in 1989 and 1990 when many fans preferred him to Stewart - but though he had his chances, he never made it impossible for Venables to drop him. Of course from a manager's viewpoint, Paul was ideal number-12 material, a performer whose late introduction could invest urgency into the most sterile of encounters, yet it must be admitted that he threatened to turn more matches than he actually did. Paul and Spurs parted company in May 1992 when he switched to Portsmouth in a £400,000 deal, going on to play an integral role in Pompey's spirited bid for promotion to the Premier League

BORN: Plumstead, London, 1.10.62.
GAMES: 98 (58). GOALS: 21.
HONOURS: FA Cup 90/1. 3 England caps (83-84).
OTHER CLUBS: Charlton Athletic 79/80-81/2 (87, 24);
Luton Town 82/3-83/4 (80, 24);
Liverpool 84/5-87/8 (77, 25); Queen's Park Rangers *on loan* 91/2 (2, 0);
Portsmouth 92/3- (44, 9).

1987/88 - 1991/92

DAVID HOWELLS

A little more luck, a lot more credit; David Howells has deserved them both during an unobtrusive but enormously worthy career to date. He has let no one down, either when leading the attack or shoring up the centre of defence, but it has been as a midfield anchor man, prowling in front of the back four, that the affable all-rounder has been most effective. Never was this more evident than in 1989/90 and 1990/91 when David's blend of reliability and intelligence - spiced, it should be said, with occasional flashes of imagination - allowed Paul Gascoigne the freedom his genius demanded.

The teenage Howells arrived at the Lane as a striker good enough to win England youth and under-19 caps. He burst on to the senior scene with the winning goal against Sheffield Wednesday at Hillsborough in February 1986 and his cocktail of skill, industry and aerial prowess - he showed an enterprising knack of arriving late in front of goal - hinted at riches in store. But competition for a marksman's role was intense, and soon his comprehensive abilities were deployed in midfield, with the occasional stint as an emergency defender underlining his versatility.

Though perhaps lacking half a yard of pace, that matters little in his 'holding' job, in which the slim but wirily resilient David tackles firmly and passes constructively. He possesses a sure eye for goal, too, equally capable of striking with spectacular precision or battling for the messy tap-in. Unfortunately, he has suffered frequent injuries - as in February 1993, when a foot problem ruled him out for the duration - but, still only 25, he will surely come again, maybe even adding further representative honours to his 1990 Football League call-up.

And for those who call him 'anonymous', what about his display at Nottingham Forest in October 1990? That afternoon, David equalised with a delightful 20-yard curler, made a dramatic clearance from his own line, then immediately strode forward to nod a late winner. If that was anonymity, just wait till David finds his true identity!

BORN: Guildford, Surrey, 15.12.67.
GAMES: 153 (37). GOALS: 18.
HONOURS: FA Cup 90/1.

1985/86 -

IAN WALKER

When the chant of 'Ian the Saxon' took its place in the Shelf repertoire during the autumn of 1991, Tottenham's rookie goal-keeper knew he had arrived. The label, of course, referred to the nickname of regular custodian Erik 'The Viking' Thorstvedt, beloved of the fans but out of whose giant shadow his young rival looked increasingly likely to step.

Ian has a natural all-round aptitude for his chosen craft, together with one further asset, the absence of which has deprived many a fine technical 'keeper of a top-level career - the priceless gift of confidence. The England under-21 international - he was called up before making his League debut for Spurs - positively oozes self-belief, his style flamboyant without being foolhardy, his evident enjoyment of the game communicating itself to the fans.

Standing 6ft 1in, he is an agile and brave shot-stopper, quicker to get down than the even-taller Norwegian but not yet consistently dominant in the air, a situation that should be remedied by experience, a little extra weight and the expert tuition of Ray Clemence. Already Ian, the son of Norwich City boss Mike Walker, has earned several lengthy first-team sequences on merit, most impressively in early 1992/93, after which he lost his place only through injury. Barring mishaps, a glittering future awaits.

BORN: Watford, Hertfordshire, 31.10.71.
GAMES: 41. GOALS: 0.
OTHER CLUBS: Oxford United *on loan* 90/1 (2, 0);

1990/91 -

ANDY TURNER

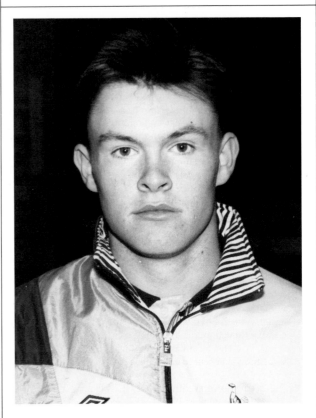

The presence of Andy Turner's name in the Spurs line-up on the opening Saturday of 1992/93 produced quizzical frowns among all but that coterie of dedicated enthusiasts who follow their club at junior levels. They were *not* surprised at the 17-year-old's inclusion on the left side of midfield; they knew what he could do. In snatches, that day at The Dell and in subsequent senior outings, it became apparent to a wider audience that Andy is one to watch. Though it was too much to expect him to command a regular place at such an early stage of his development, his combination of skill and grit quickly made him a crowd favourite.

A former England schoolboy whose dual nationality enabled him to switch allegiance to the Republic of Ireland (he was rewarded with an early under-21 call-up), Andy impressed with his neat passing, tenacity in chasing back and the sort of savage left-foot finish that brought a late winner at home to Everton in September. He showed admirable coolness, too, but above all it was his speed that took the eye - as Manchester City defender Keith Curle, no slowcoach himself, can testify. In the FA Cup quarter-final at Maine Road, the youngster - brought on as a deputy striker - accelerated blindingly past Curle, winning a penalty which Teddy Sheringham missed. In the years ahead, it will be a major surprise if the talent of Andy Turner does not yield far more bountiful results.

BORN: Woolwich, London, 23.3.75.
GAMES: 7 (14). GOALS: 4.

1992/93 -

Nick Barmby is one of . . . no, let's say exactly what we think. Surveying the national scene in the spring of 1993, and without wishing to inflict a destructively burdensome tag on an unspoilt young man, it was impossible not to conclude that Nick Barmby was *the* outstanding English talent of his generation.

The chunky 5ft 6in Humbersider's game is a bounteous, bubbling bundle of delights, but by far its most astonishing feature is maturity. Though just 19, he wields the influence of a footballer in his prime, bringing others into play with his vision and awareness - invariably making the appropriate pass at the optimum moment, a knack even Welsh prodigy Ryan Giggs has yet to master - and lubricating team movement by his perceptive running off the ball. Whether operating up front, in midfield or somewhere in between, Nick scampers eagerly, all bustling pace and perky audacity. Adhesive of touch, combative of tackle and strong enough to shield the ball under severe challenge, he carries a constant and varied threat to even the most experienced and mobile opponents.

After making his competitive debut at Sheffield Wednesday in September 1992, Nick gave notice of his special ability with a series of precocious displays that autumn and early winter, but it was a televised FA Cup tie at Norwich in January that underlined the Barmby phenomenon in the national consciousness. That day he sparkled, being showered with praise for a deft backheel to set up a chance for Gordon Durie, but it was his all-round prowess that really impressed. In the fifth round, at home to Wimbledon, he was at it again, this time stooping to dispatch a precision header into 'keeper Hans Segers' top corner from 12 yards. Messrs Venables and Livermore and some 26,000 fans positively purred.

An honours graduate from the FA School of Excellence, Nick Barmby was once the most sought-after schoolboy star in the country, having his pick of top clubs and plumping for Spurs. Over the coming seasons at White Hart Lane, the joy at his decision is likely to be unrestrained.

BORN: Hull, Humberside, 11.2.74.
GAMES: 22 (7). GOALS: 9.

GORDON DURIE

Gordon Durie remains, at the time of writing, Tottenham's most expensive acquisition - and one of their most frustrating. The Scottish international forward, a £2.2 million signing from Chelsea in August 1991, is potentially a fabulous player. Fast and strong, skilful and intelligent, he is willing to run himself into the ground and numbers a ferocious shot, delightful distribution and aerial power among his talents. Yet after two injury-marred seasons at White Hart Lane, that ostensibly captivating cocktail had produced less heady intoxication than flat disillusionment.

In retrospect, it was ominous that a cynical section of Stamford Bridge fans had seen fit to rechristen their striker 'Groin Strain'. However, this was far from the minds of his new followers as he made a sprightly start as a Spur, scoring on his debut at Southampton and contributing several more early-season strikes. But there followed a chronic, six-month goal drought, during which Gordon's industry could not be faulted but his confidence and fitness level suffered, and by summer there were disturbing rumours that he was on the point of joining Rangers. However, he stayed to begin his second term in fine fettle, and when Teddy Sheringham arrived to share his front-running burden, Gordon started to justify his fee with some brilliant all-round displays.

Then came disaster: he was charged by the FA with feigning injury, effectively branded a cheat, and until his name was cleared late in the year the slur combined with fitness worries to produce an understandably debilitating effect. At one point Gordon was dropped because the management felt he was mentally unfit to play, which upset many fans, and reportedly he came close to the much-trumpeted Ibrox move. Then, in the spring, injury ruled him out for the rest of the campaign. With the side increasingly buoyant in his absence, and with some supporters questioning whether his heart was in the club, the Tottenham future of Gordon Durie was in some doubt.

BORN: Paisley, Renfrewshire, 6.12.55.
GAMES: 66. GOALS: 16.
HONOURS: 23 Scotland caps (87-).
OTHER CLUBS: East Fife 81/2-84/5 (81, 26);
Hibernian 84/5-85/6 (47, 14);
Chelsea 85/6-90/1 (123, 51).

1991/92 -

ERIK THORSTVEDT

Entertainer, cult hero, larger-than-life character, Erik Thorstvedt became much more than a mere goalkeeper to Tottenham loyalists during the Venables era, a colourful and flamboyant but occasionally uncertain period that, curiously enough, reflected his own personal contribution. The blond, 6ft 4in Norwegian international - how naturally he wears his nickname of 'Erik the Viking' - had long harboured ambitions to play in England, having impressed in trials with QPR, Spurs and Arsenal, but it was not until December 1988 that he was able to obtain a work permit, allowing Venables to complete his £400,000 purchase from IFK Gothenburg.

Drafted in to replace the troubled Bobby Mimms, Erik suffered a traumatic debut at home to Nottingham Forest in January when, in front of a huge TV audience, he gifted the winner to Nigel Clough and looked generally uneasy. As he sought to adjust to English football, in which 'keepers are called to exert more physical presence than elsewhere, there were further scares and another clanger against Charlton before the turning point came at Southanpton. Having brought down Alan Shearer at the edge of the box, he faced the possibility of a red card; but the referee showed mercy, Erik grew in confidence and made a series of fine saves. At the final whistle, to mark his first clean sheet, he threw his gloves to the travelling Spurs fans; both a custom and a rapport were born.

Subsequently, though his style appears disconcertingly casual at times, Erik proved himself a high-class performer. Though he can be a little slow to reach low shots and is occasionally fallible on crosses - who isn't? - not many balls elude his spidery reach, which also makes him an effective smotherer of close-range threats. Though facing a growing challenge from young Ian Walker, who has unseated him for two lengthy spells and will surely come again, Erik fought back nobly to reclaim his place and in 1992/93 remained at the peak of his powers until a fractured finger ended his season in April.

BORN: Stavanger, Norway, 28.10.62. GAMES: 177 (2). GOALS: 0. HONOURS: FA Cup 90/1. Norway caps.
OTHER CLUBS: EIK, Viking Stavanger, both Norway; Borussia Moenchengladbach, West Germany; IFK Gothenburg, Sweden.

1988/89 -

TEDDY SHERINGHAM

Teddy Sheringham has sampled, and mastered, two distinct brands of attacking football - and in 1993, Spurs were reaping a rich harvest from the consequent blend. At Millwall, the blond striker became a flourishing practitioner of the frequently maligned but undeniably effective long-ball approach; then at Nottingham Forest, he garnered experience of the sophisticated precision-passing style as preached by Brian Clough. The result, following his £2.1 million switch to White Hart Lane in August 1992, was a strike-rate better than a goal every two games for the next nine months - with the promise of many more to come.

Unselfish and brave, Teddy is ever available ahead of the play, and so much did his touch improve on Trentside that, though he remains inelegant, there is little fear of moves breaking down around him. His shot is fierce, he is both powerful and subtle in the air, and his knack of peeling away from defenders at the last moment buys him crucial time and space. What he lacks is outright pace, but with plenty of greyhounds hunting alongside him that is scarcely a damning deficiency.

Furthermore, and importantly to many fans, Teddy seems happy in his work. Despite arriving when Spurs were struggling, and shouldering the pressure of being cast as some sort of saviour, there has been no shortage of smiles. Indeed, after netting on his home debut against Sheffield United in September, he cavorted to the corner flag, leant on it nonchalantly and milked the applause shamelessly.

Understandably, when the 'Sheri' move was first mooted, the Forest boss was reluctant to part with such a proven goal-scorer, prevaricating lengthily even when the player made it clear his dearest wish was to be a Spur. Come the second half of the season, not long after a purple patch in which Teddy netted 12 times in eight games for Tottenham, Mr Clough was asked by a courageous journalist why his team was wallowing punchlessly at the foot of the table, and he ventured a revealing reply: 'I should have kept Edward Sheringham.' As if further proof of his worth were needed, Teddy was called into the England squad in the spring.

BORN: Highams Park, London, 2.4.66.
GAMES: 47. GOALS: 28.
OTHER CLUBS: Millwall 83/4-90/1 (220, 93);
Aldershot *on loan* 84/5 (5, 0);
Nottingham Forest 91/2-92/3 (42, 14).

1992/93 -

DARREN ANDERTON

Like fellow flankman Cliff Jones more than 30 years earlier, Darren Anderton made a false start at Tottenham, then recovered from injury to show vastly improved form. The next stage for Welsh wonder Cliff was to emblazon his name across the football world as he grew into one of the most illustrious figures in Spurs history. Whether the coltish six-footer from the south coast can emulate such glory only time will tell, but initial indications were distinctly encouraging.

Darren cost £2 million from Portsmouth in the summer of 1992, fresh from starring in Pompey's marvellous FA Cup run, and was confronted with the spectre of Chris Waddle. Unproductive comparisons were made, partly because of a vague physical resemblance - the deceptively casual posture, the rather awkward gait, even the modest demeanour - but also prompted by the rookie's similarly penetrative dribble and deadly finish.

With the club's major stars all gone, pressure mounted on the expensive but inexperienced 20-year-old to fill the vacuum. Almost inevitably, Darren began poorly, not helped by being part of a lack-lustre side at that time, but mainly because - unknown to fans - his previously devastating acceleration was hampered by nagging groin pain. However, although the spark that had marked his rise at Fratton Park was missing, there was no shortage of toil and it was reassuring to know that whatever else was wrong, his attitude was right.

In late autumn his problem was diagnosed and by the New Year, after a hernia operation, the real Darren Anderton stood up. Suddenly there was confidence where there had been doubt; the harassed expression that had habitually disfigured the clean-cut features had lifted. Now, at last, he was flowing past defenders, then either whipping in the sort of wickedly curving crosses that Teddy Sheringham had met previously only in his dreams, or shooting for goal on his own account. Better on the right than the left, but at his best roaming free, Darren was a major reason for the turnaround in Tottenham's fortunes in early 1993. His prospects for the rest of the century and beyond are enticing, indeed.

BORN: Southampton, 3.3.72.
GAMES: 38 (3). GOALS: 8.
OTHER CLUBS: Portsmouth 90/1-91/2 (62, 7).

1992/93 -

MARK STIMSON

MARK ROBSON

PHIL GRAY

ANDY POLSTON

PETER GARLAND

MARK STIMSON   1986/87-1988/89

Defender. BORN: Hinckley, Leicestershire, 20.1.64.
GAMES: 2 (1). GOALS: 0.
OTHER CLUBS: Leyton Orient *on loan* 87/8 (10, 0);
Gillingham *on loan* 88/9 (18, 0); Newcastle United 89/90- (86, 2);
Portsmouth *on loan* 92/3 (4, 0).

PHIL GRAY   1986/87-1990/91

Forward. BORN: Belfast, 2.10.68.
GAMES: 4 (6). GOALS: 0.
HONOURS: 4 Northern Ireland caps (92-).
OTHER CLUBS: Barnsley *on loan* 89/90 (3, 0);
Fulham *on loan* 90/1 (3, 0); Luton Town 91/2- (58, 22).

MARK ROBSON   1988/89-1989/90

Forward. BORN: Newham, Northumberland, 22.5.69.
GAMES: 4 (5). GOALS: 0.
OTHER CLUBS: Exeter City 86/7 (26, 7);
Reading *on loan* 87/8 (7, 0); Watford *on loan* 89/90 (1, 0);
Plymouth Argyle *on loan* 89/90 (7, 0); Exeter City *on loan* 91/2 (8, 1);
West Ham United 92/3- (44, 8).

ANDY POLSTON   1989/90

Defender. BORN: Walthamstow, London, 26.7.70.
GAMES: 0 (1). GOALS: 0.
OTHER CLUBS: Cambridge United *on loan* 89/90 (3, 0);
Gillingham *on loan* 91/2 (2, 0).

PETER GARLAND   1990/91

Midfielder. BORN: Croydon, Surrey, 20.1.71.
GAMES: 0 (1). GOALS: 0.
OTHER CLUBS: Newcastle United 91/2 (2, 0);
Charlton Athletic 92/3- (13, 1).

IAN HENDON   1990/91 -

Defender/Midfielder. BORN: Ilford, Essex, 5.12.71.
GAMES: 1 (6). GOALS: 0.
OTHER CLUBS: Portsmouth *on loan* 91/2 (4, 0);
Leyton Orient *on loan* 91/2 (6, 0); Barnsley *on loan* 92/3 (6, 0).

JEFF MINTON   1991/92 -

Forward. BORN: Hackney, London, 28.12.73.
GAMES: 2 (1). GOALS: 1.

IAN HENDON

JEFF MINTON

KEVIN WATSON

SOL CAMPBELL

DANNY HILL

LEE HODGES

KEVIN DEARDEN 1990/91 -

Goalkeeper. BORN: Luton, Bedfordshire, 8.3.90.
GAMES: 1 (1). GOALS: 0.
OTHER CLUBS: Cambridge United *on loan* 88/9 (15, 0);
Hartlepool United *on loan* 89/90 (10, 0);
Swindon Town *on loan* 89/90 (1, 0);
Peterborough United *on loan* 90/1 (7, 0);
Hull City *on loan* 90/1 (3, 0);
Rochdale *on loan* 91/2 (2, 0);
Birmingham City *on loan* 91/2 (12, 0).

STUART NETHERCOTT 1992/93 -

Defender. BORN: Chadwell Heath, Essex, 21.3.73.
GAMES: 3 (2). GOALS: 0.
OTHER CLUBS: Maidstone United *on loan* 91/2 (13, 1);
Barnet *on loan* 91/2 (3, 0).

KEVIN WATSON 1992/93 -

Midfielder. BORN: Hackney, London, 3.1.74.
GAMES: 5 (3). GOALS: 2.

DANNY HILL 1992/93 -

Midfielder. BORN: Edmonton, London, 1.10.74.
GAMES: 2 (2). GOALS: 0.

SOL CAMPBELL 1992/93 -

Forward. BORN: Newham, London, 18.9.74.
GAMES: 0 (1). GOALS: 1.

LEE HODGES 1992/93 -

Forward. BORN: Epping, Essex, 4.9.73.
GAMES: 0 (4). GOALS: 0.

DAVID McDONALD 1992/93 -

Defender. BORN: Dublin, 2.1.71.
GAMES: 2. GOALS: 0.
OTHER CLUBS: Gillingham *on loan* 90/1 (10, 0).

KEVIN DEARDEN

STUART NETHERCOTT

DAVID McDONALD

BILL NICHOLSON - MANAGER OCTOBER 1958 - SEPTEMBER 1974

Bill Nicholson created one great team, then another very good one, a sequence of achievement that must have been supremely frustrating for a perfectionist whose pursuit of excellence was relentless. Yet none could dispute that the honest, inscrutable Yorkshireman ranks among the finest managers in British soccer history.

As his players will testify, Bill was not a comfortable man for whom to work. Praise was so rare that if they got any at all, they knew they'd been outstanding. More often, even after famous victories, Bill would grumble that they should have done *better*, an approach that some individuals could accept, but which grated with others. Never, though, did he demand greater dedication than he gave: as a magnificently imaginative coach and astute tactician he threw himself into the playing side, then tackled his paperwork with a tireless efficiency that made burning the midnight oil the rule rather than the exception. After a not-to-be underrated playing career - he was an industrious right-half in Arthur Rowe's title side - Bill joined Spurs' coaching staff in 1954, becoming assistant to boss Jimmy Anderson three years later. In October 1958, he was appointed manager, and his first match in charge ended in a 10-4 win over Everton.

But Bill's head was not for turning; he realised there was much work to be done, and suffered early setbacks as Spurs came close to relegation in 1958/59. Soon, of course, he got it right. An impeccable judge of ability and character, he bought brilliantly, got the best out of players already at his disposal and blended disparate talents into a wonderful whole. Thus he built the unforgettable League and FA Cup double-winners of 1960/61, a peak from which, alas, it was possible only to descend. Though more stars were acquired - including some all-time Spurs favourites - and there were cup successes in 1962, 1967, 1971, 1972 and 1973, never again did Bill attain that sublime level.

Though his exterior was dour, close associates maintain it masked deep emotions, which moved to the surface after dismal results in autumn 1974, when - disillusioned by functional modern tactics and increasingly out of tune with the new, precocious breed of player - he resigned. Though the board tried to change his mind, in the end his departure was handled clumsily. Upset that he couldn't nominate his successor - his choice was Blanchflower - he took a brief rest before spending a year as adviser to West Ham. Come 1976, Bill was back at the Lane as a consultant, and in the early nineties was still serving the club whose name he had made one of the most revered in the football world.

TERRY NEILL - MANAGER SEPTEMBER 1974 - JUNE 1976

Managing Spurs is a demanding proposition in any circumstances; for Terry Neill in autumn 1974 it was a task of particularly awesome magnitude. Though he arrived at the Lane fresh from guiding the fortunes of Hull City, and had been player-boss of Northern Ireland, he had spent the bulk of his career as an Arsenal player. Thus in the fans' eyes, he was a Highbury man to the core, a stigma which he never overcame.

Articulate, bubbly and easy-going, Terry offered a striking contrast in style to his illustrious predecessor. However, at 32 he found himself in charge of footballers of his own generation, some of whom had achieved far more than he, and the Irishman found it difficult to command universal respect. Having taken over a side in decline, and unable to compete at the top end of the transfer market - he was thwarted in efforts to sign Johan Cruyff and Charlie George - he struggled. Relegation was narrowly avoided in his first season, and though 1975/76 saw an improvement to ninth position in the League and a run to the League Cup semi-final, his relationship with the board deteriorated. That summer he resigned, following a dispute over players' bonuses, and two weeks later Terry Neill was back in his spiritual home as the new manager of Arsenal.

KEITH BURKINSHAW - MANAGER JULY 1976 - MAY 1984

Let there be no doubt: Keith Burkinshaw can be proud of his record at White Hart Lane. After stepping up from the position of coach under Terry Neill to inherit a lacklustre side, he couldn't prevent Spurs dropping into Division Two at the end of his first term in charge, but the board, to their enormous credit, retained faith in the honest, downbeat Yorkshireman.

Promotion in 1977/78 justified that decision, then the bold acquisition of Argentinians Ardiles and Villa caught the imagination of the soccer world and raised the curtain on one of the most stirring periods in Tottenham's post-War history.

Other high-quality performers were acquired as Keith assembled an attractive squad which, though never consistent enough to take the Championship, was to lift the FA Cup in 1981 and 1982 and the UEFA Cup in 1984. However, he became unhappy with boardroom politics and announced during 1983/84 that he would resign at season's end, thus departing on the wings of European triumph. Essentially a player's man - despite his much-publicised tiff with Steve Archibald - he had earnt widespread respect in the game, and went on to coach in the Middle East before becoming Ardiles' number-two at West Bromwich Albion.

DAVID PLEAT   MANAGER MAY 1986 - OCTOBER 1987

David Pleat, it seemed, was on the right track. In his first season at White Hart Lane, the former Luton boss lifted Tottenham to third place in the First Division (admittedly they never looked likely to win it), and took them to the FA Cup Final and a League Cup semi-final, both of which they lost after holding the upper hand. He had bought boldly (notably new club captain Richard Gough), boosted the confidence and performance of Chris Waddle, demonstrated tactical flair - the five-man midfield that so ably supported prolific goal-scorer Clive Allen was but one example of his innovative thinking - and, a factor not to be underestimated, he picked well-balanced sides that made sense to the supporters.

Many believed David was the man to make Spurs great again; sadly their theory was never to be tested. That summer he was the subject of lurid newspaper allegations about his private life, but appeared to have survived them, and Spurs made a promising start to 1987/88 with six wins and only two defeats in their first ten League games. But a second wave of scandal in the autumn proved too much and David resigned, later serving Leicester unsuccessfully before returning to Luton. When he had gone Spurs nosedived, begging the question: were they already on the verge of decline or did his departure precipitate the slide?

PETER SHREEVES - TEAM MANAGER JUNE 1984 - MAY 1986 & 1991/92

Peter Shreeves is the most underrated manager in Spurs' modern history. Quiet, uncharismatic and an almost shadowy figure in the public eye, he tends to be brushed aside as a twice-sacked failure, yet that is far too harsh. After contributing hugely to Tottenham's early-eighties success as coach under Keith Burkinshaw, Peter landed the top job in 1984/85 and that term led the club's most (only) meaningful title challenge since the prime of Bill Nicholson. Indeed, but for injuries in the spring the Championship pennant might have been fluttering over White Hart Lane, and Peter would have been placed on a pedestal. Instead there followed a disappointing campaign, and though he remained in high esteem among the players - who approved of his emphasis on skill and imaginative training routines - he was axed.

After coaching stints elsewhere, he had another chance in 1991/92, when Terry Venables opted to concentrate on business affairs. Not surprisingly with the club still reeling from recent turmoil, the side slumped and - as cynics had predicted - Peter it was who paid the price. True, some of his selections mystified the fans; possibly he was 'too nice'; but Spurs knew their man well when they appointed him, and it's hard to see his second coming as anything other than a hiding to nothing.

TERRY VENABLES - TEAM MANAGER DECEMBER 1987 - MAY 1991;
CHIEF EXECUTIVE MAY 1991 -.

Terry Venables is a unique figure in British football. An inspiringly innovative coach who became a successful manager, he went on to sink his life savings - and then some - into the club he had loved since childhood, claiming as his reward the total top-to-bottom control he had craved for so long. His management career had begun at Crystal Palace and QPR, then he led Barcelona to untold glory before his love affair with the Catalans ended in late 1987. Next the man who had twice refused the boss's chair at Highbury accepted the Tottenham job, taking over an unhappy club heading for the foot of Division One. Terry led Spurs to a mid-table finish, then invested boldly for the future, buying Gascoigne and Stewart. Now his side looked attractive but as Waddle was sold and Lineker bought against a background of mounting cash problems, it was amazing that he was able to juggle his attention between business and football. Terry deserves monumental credit for the FA Cup triumph of 1991, and the combination of courage and acumen he displayed under intense pressure during the club takeover that same year is a source of pure wonder. Invariably approachable and chirpily streetwise, he was adept at handling the media and it's a tribute to that Cockney nous that he never got a *really* bad press, no matter how low Tottenham's fortunes dipped on or off the field. Having taken a season off from coaching in 1991/92, he climbed back into his tracksuit thereafter to considerable effect. His ambitions to run the club off the pitch as well as on it were challenged by chairman Alan Sugar in the summer of 1993, a distraction that made it more difficult than ever to pass unclouded judgement on the White Hart Lane reign of Terry Venables.

DOUG LIVERMORE - CHIEF COACH MAY 1992 -.

It would be an unreasonably demanding Tottenham fan who did not own himself or herself more than satisfied with Doug Livermore's first season in charge of team affairs. After a sticky opening as new players settled in, his side entertained royally, at times looking the equal of any in the land, and with so many youngsters involved the future seems buoyant.

Of course, he did not shoulder responsibility alone, working in harness with his assistant, former Liverpool team-mate Ray Clemence, and chief executive Terry Venables, still active as a coach. With two such media-friendly colleagues, Doug - whose lugubrious features bely a typically keen Scouse wit - was content to adopt a relatively low public profile, but supporters perceived him as a sound, wise man and, certainly, his selections met with wider approval than those of Messrs Venables and Shreeves before him.

A former assistant boss of Wales and a coach for several clubs, Doug arrived at the Lane to run the reserves in 1984, rising to become assistant manager in 1989, then chief coach in 1992. Beginning with eighth place in the Premier League and an FA Cup semi-final was fine; the acid test, of course, was yet to come.

PLAYERS' STATISTICS

Player	Season	LEAGUE App	Sub	Gl	FA CUP App	Sub	Gl	LEAGUE CUP App	Sub	Gl	EUROPE App	Sub	Gl	TOTAL App	Sub	Gl
Aleksic M	78-81	25		0	7		0	0		0	0		0	32		0
Allen C	84-87	97	(8)	60	11	(1)	9	13	(1)	13	3	(1)	2	124	(11)	84
Allen L	59-64	119		47	15		13	0		0	3		1	137		61
Allen P	85-	276	(15)	23	26	(1)	1	42	(2)	4	6	(1)	0	350	(19)	28
Anderton D	92-	32	(2)	6	4	(1)	1	2		1	0		0	38	(3)	8
Archibald S	80-83	128	(3)	58	17	(1)	5	18		7	22		8	185	(4)	78
Ardiles O	78-87	222	(16)	16	32		4	31	(1)	3	8	(1)	2	293	(18)	25
Armstrong G	76-80	65	(19)	10	6	(4)	3	3	(1)	3	0		0	74	(24)	16
Austin D	92-	33	(1)	0	5		0	2	(1)	0	0		0	40	(2)	0
Baker P	52-64	299		3	27		0	0		0	16		0	342		3
Barmby N	92-	17	(5)	6	3	(1)	3	2	(1)	0	0		0	22	(7)	9
Barton K	60-63	4		0	0		0	0		0	0		0	4		0
Beal P	63-74	330	(3)	1	30		0	27		0	30		0	417	(3)	1
Beavon S	78-79	3	(1)	0	0		0	0	(1)	0	0		0	3	(2)	0
Bergsson G	88-	51	(20)	2	2	(2)	0	4	(2)	0	5	(1)	0	62	(25)	2
Blanchflower D	54-63	337		15	33		4	0		0	12		2	382		21
Bond D	66-70	20	(3)	1	0		0	2	(1)	0	1		0	23	(4)	1
Bowen M	83-86	14	(3)	2	3		0	0		0	0		0	17	(3)	2
Brace R	1983	0	(1)	0	0		0	0		0	0		0	0	(1)	0
Brazil A	82-83	29	(2)	9	1		0	0	(1)	0	3	(2)	4	33	(5)	13
Brooke G	80-84	49	(24)	15	4	(8)	1	4	(1)	1	6	(5)	1	63	(38)	18
Brooks J	52-59	166		46	13		5	0		0	0		0	179		51
Brotherston N	1975	1		0	0		0	0		0	0		0	1		0
Brown L	63-65	62		3	3		0	0		0	0		0	65		3
Brown R	1966	1		0	0		0	0		0	0		0	1		0
Brown W	59-65	222		0	23		0	0		0	17		0	262		0
Butters G	88-89	34	(1)	1	1		0	2	(1)	0	0		0	37	(2)	1
Campbell S	92-	0	(1)	1	0		0	0		0	0		0	0	(1)	1
Chiedozie J	84-86	45	(8)	12	5	(3)	2	7		0	7		0	64	(11)	14
Chivers M	67-75	268	(10)	118	22	(2)	11	33		23	32		22	355	(12)	174
Claesen N	86-87	37	(13)	18	1	(5)	2	7		3	0		0	45	(18)	23
Clarke R	1972	0	(1)	0	0		0	0		0	0		0	0	(1)	0
Clayton E	57-67	88	(4)	20	9		0	1		0	1		0	99	(4)	20
Clemence R	81-87	240		0	25		0	38		0	27		0	330		0
Close S	86-87	3	(6)	0	0		0	3		2	0		0	6	(6)	2
Coates R	71-77	173	(15)	14	11	(1)	0	19	(3)	1	26		9	229	(19)	24
Cockram A	1983	2		0	0		0	0		0	0		0	2		0
Collins Jim	1961	2		0	0		0	0		0	0		0	2		0
Collins John	65-67	2		0	0		0	0		0	0		0	2		0
Collins P	68-72	77	(6)	4	8	(1)	0	5	(2)	1	1	(1)	0	91	(10)	5
Conn A	74-76	35	(3)	6	2		0	1	(2)	1	0		0	38	(5)	7
Cooke R	82-85	9	(2)	2	1		0	1	(1)	0	1	(2)	0	12	(5)	2
Corbett P	81-82	3	(2)	1	0		0	0		0	0		0	3	(2)	1
Crook I	81-85	10	(10)	1	0	(1)	0	1		0	0	(2)	0	11	(13)	1
Crooks G	80-84	121	(4)	48	21		9	19	(1)	9	15	(1)	9	176	(6)	75
Culverhouse I	1983	1	(1)	0	0		0	0		0	0		0	1	(1)	0
Cundy J	91-	23	(2)	1	0		0	2		0	0		0	25	(2)	1
Daines B	71-80	146		0	11		0	14		0	2		0	173		0
Dearden K	90-	0	(1)	0	0		0	1		0	0		0	1	(1)	0
Dick A	81-85	16	(1)	2	2		0	0		0	3	(3)	0	21	(4)	2
Dillon M	72-73	21	(3)	1	1		0	1		0	2	(1)	0	25	(4)	1
Ditchburn E	46-58	418		0	34		0	0		0	0		0	452		0
Dodge W	58-59	6		0	4		0	0		0	0		0	10		0
Duncan J	74-78	101	(2)	53	7		2	10		7	0		0	118	(2)	62
Dunmore D	53-59	75		23	6		3	0		0	0		0	81		26
Durie G	91-	48		10	2		0	8		3	8		3	66		16
Dyson T	54-64	184		41	16		6	0		0	9		8	209		55
Edinburgh J	90-	67	(4)	1	10		0	9	(3)	0	3		0	89	(7)	1
England M	66-74	300		14	32		2	30		0	35		3	397		19
Evans R	68-74	132	(4)	2	7		0	13		0	22	(3)	2	174	(7)	4
Fairclough C	87-88	60		5	3		0	7		0	0		0	70		5
Falco M	78-86	162	(12)	68	15		5	19	(3)	3	21	(4)	14	217	(19)	90
Fenwick T	87-	90	(3)	8	7		0	14		2	4		0	115	(3)	10
Galvin T	78-86	194	(7)	20	23	(1)	2	20	(3)	3	25		6	262	(11)	31
Garland P	1990	0	(1)	0	0		0	0		0	0		0	0	(1)	0
Gascoigne P	88-90	91	(1)	19	6		6	13	(1)	8	0		0	110	(2)	33
Gibson T	79-82	16	(2)	4	5		1	1		1	0	(2)	1	22	(4)	7
Gilzean A	64-73	335	(8)	93	40		21	27	(1)	6	27	(1)	13	429	(10)	133
Gorman J	76-78	30		0	2		0	0		0	0		0	32		0
Gough R	86-87	49		2	6		0	10		0	0		0	65		2
Gray A	91-	23	(8)	2	0		0	0		0	0		0	23	(8)	2
Gray P	86-90	4	(5)	0	0	(1)	0	0		0	0		0	4	(6)	0
Greaves J	61-69	321		220	36		32	8		5	14		9	379		266
Hancock K	69-70	3		0	0		0	1		0	0		0	4		0
Harmer T	51-59	205		47	17		4	0		0	0		0	222		51
Hazard M	79-85	73	(18)	13	7	(3)	2	11	(3)	5	22	(1)	3	113	(25)	23

Player	Season	LEAGUE App	Sub	Gl	FA CUP App	Sub	Gl	LEAGUE CUP App	Sub	Gl	EUROPE App	Sub	Gl	TOTAL App	Sub	Gl
Hendon I	90-	0	(4)	0	0		0	1		0	0	(2)	0	1	(6)	0
Hendry J	90-	5	(9)	5	0		0	0	(1)	0	0		0	5	(10)	5
Henry R	54-65	247		1	23		0	0		0	17		0	287		1
Hill D	92-	2	(2)	0	0		0	0	.	0	0		0	2	(2)	0
Hills J	57-59	29		0	3		0	0		0	0		0	32		0
Hoddle G	75-86	370	(7)	88	47	(1)	11	44		10	17	(4)	1	478	(12)	110
Hodge S	86-87	44	(1)	7	7		2	2		0	0		0	53	(1)	9
Hodges L	92-	0	(4)	0	0		0	0		0	0		0	0	(4)	0
Holder P	71-73	9	(4)	1	0		0	0		0	0	(6)	1	9	(10)	2
Hollowbread J	58-63	67		0	6		0	0		0	0		0	73		0
Holmes J	76-78	81		2	9		0	2		0	0		0	92		2
Hopkins M	52-63	219		0	20		0	0		0	1		0	240		0
Houghton S	91-	0	(10)	2	0		0	0	(2)	0	0	(2)	0	0	(14)	2
Howells D	85-	122	(30)	15	8	(4)	1	17	(3)	2	6		0	153	(37)	18
Hoy R	65-67	10		0	0		0	0		0	2		0	12		0
Hughton C	79-89	293	(4)	12	34	(2)	1	33	(2)	2	29	(1)	4	389	(9)	19
Iley J	57-58	53		1	4		0	0		0	0		0	57		1
Ireland J	57-58	3		0	0		0	0		0	0		0	3		0
Jenkins D	68-69	11	(3)	2	2	(1)	0	0		0	0		0	13	(4)	2
Jennings P	64-76	472		0	43		0	39		0	36		0	590		0
Johnson N	65-70	27	(7)	5	4		1	0		0	0		0	31	(7)	6
Jones Chris	74-81	149	(15)	37	10	(2)	4	7	(1)	1	0	(1)	0	166	(19)	42
Jones Cliff	57-68	314	(4)	135	35	(4)	16	2		1	19		7	370	(8)	159
Keeley A	1976	5	(1)	0	0		0	0		0	0		0	5	(1)	0
Kendall M	78-80	29		0	6		0	1		0	0		0	36		0
Kinnear J	65-75	189	(7)	2	24		0	20		0	18		0	251	(7)	2
Knowles C	64-75	400	(1)	15	42		1	32	(1)	0	30		1	504	(2)	17
Lacy J	78-82	99	(5)	2	12		0	11		1	4	(1)	0	126	(6)	3
Lee C	77-79	57	(5)	18	6	(1)	3	2		0	0		0	65	(6)	21
Lee T	1973	1		0	0		0	0		0	0		0	1		0
Leworthy D	84-85	8	(3)	3	0		0	0	(1)	1	0		0	8	(4)	4
Lineker G	89-91	105		67	9		3	16		8	8		2	138		80
Low R	64-66	6	(2)	1	0		0	0		0	0		0	6	(2)	1
Mabbutt G	82-	355	(13)	27	33	(2)	4	51	(2)	2	22	(3)	4	461	(20)	37
McAllister D	74-80	168	(4)	9	16	(1)	0	13		1	0		0	197	(5)	10
McGrath C	73-75	30	(8)	5	0		0	1		0	7	(1)	5	38	(9)	10
Mackay D	58-67	268		42	33		4	0		0	17		5	318		51
McNab N	73-78	63	(9)	3	2		0	5	(1)	0	0		0	70	(10)	3
Marchi A	49-56 & 59-64	232		7	16		0	0		0	12		0	260		7
Mazzon G	80-82	3	(1)	0	1		0	0	(2)	0	0		0	4	(3)	0
Medwin T	56-62	197		65	13		7	0		0	5		0	215		72
Metgod J	1987	5	(7)	0	0		0	2		0	0		0	7	(7)	0
Miller P	78-86	206	(2)	7	30	(1)	1	22	(1)	0	23		2	281	(4)	10
Mimms R	87-89	37		0	2		0	5		0	0		0	44		0
Minton J	91-	2		1	0		0	0	(1)	0	0		0	2	(1)	1
Moncur J	86-91	10	(11)	1	0		0	1	(2)	0	0		0	11	(13)	1
Moores I	76-78	25	(4)	6	0		0	3		2	0		0	28	(4)	8
Moran P	86-	14	(17)	2	3	(1)	0	1	(5)	0	0	(1)	0	18	(24)	2
Morgan R	68-71	66	(2)	8	6		2	3		1	2	(1)	1	77	(3)	12
Mullery A	63-71	312		25	33		1	18		0	10		4	373		30
Nayim	88-92	95	(17)	11	6	(3)	4	11	(6)	3	6		0	118	(26)	18
Naylor T	69-79	237	(6)	0	17	(1)	0	23	(1)	1	13	(6)	0	290	(14)	1
Neighbour J	70-76	104	(15)	8	10	(1)	1	14	(3)	1	6	(3)	1	134	(22)	11
Nethercott S	92-	3	(2)	0	0		0	0		0	0		0	3	(2)	0
Norman M	55-65	357		16	37		2	0		0	17		1	411		19
O'Reilly G	80-83	39	(6)	0	2		0	4		0	2	(2)	0	47	(8)	0
Osgood K	73-77	112	(1)	13	3		0	11		1	0		0	126	(1)	14
O'Shea T	86-87	1	(2)	0	0		0	0		0	0		0	1	(2)	0
Parks A	81-87	37		0	5		0	1		0	5	(1)	0	48	(1)	0
Pearce J	68-72	108	(33)	21	4	(6)	3	21	(6)	7	8	(7)	4	141	(52)	35
Perryman S	69-85	653	(2)	31	69		2	66		3	63	(1)	3	851	(3)	39
Peters M	69-74	189		46	16		5	23		12	32		13	260		76
Piper R	1962	1		0	0		0	0		0	0		0	1		0
Pitt S	1965	1		0	0		0	0		0	0		0	1		0
Polston A	1989	0	(1)	0	0		0	0		0	0		0	0	(1)	0
Polston J	86-89	17	(7)	1	0		0	3	(1)	0	0		0	20	(8)	1
Possee D	63-65	19		4	0		0	0		0	0		0	19		4
Pratt J	68-79	307	(24)	39	23	(5)	2	27	(4)	7	24	(1)	1	381	(34)	49
Price P	81-83	35	(4)	0	6		0	7		0	10		0	58	(4)	0
Robb G	51-58	182		53	18		5	0		0	0		0	200		58
Roberts G	80-86	200	(9)	23	27		2	24	(1)	5	25	(1)	6	276	(11)	36
Robertson J	63-68	153	(4)	25	18		3	2		0	4		3	177	(4)	31
Robinson M	75-77	5	(1)	2	0		0	0		0	0		0	5	(1)	2
Robson M	88-89	3	(5)	0	0		0	1		0	0		0	4	(5)	0
Ruddock N	86-87 & 92-	45	(2)	3	6	(1)	1	4		0	0		0	55	(3)	4
Ryden J	55-58	63		2	5		0	0		0	0		0	68		2
Samways V	86-	126	(28)	8	12	(1)	2	22	(4)	4	6		1	166	(33)	15
Saul F	60-67	112	(4)	37	7		6	1		0	5		2	125	(4)	45
Sedgley S	89-	105	(17)	3	9	(1)	1	19	(3)	1	4	(3)	0	137	(24)	5
Sharpe F	1958	2		1	0		0	0		0	0		0	2		1
Sheringham T	92-	38		21	5		4	4		3	0		0	47		28

Player	Season	LEAGUE			FA CUP			LEAGUE CUP			EUROPE			TOTAL		
		App	Sub	Gl	App	Sub	Gl	App	Sub	Gl	App	Sub	Gl	App	Sub	Gl
Smith G	78-81	34	(4)	1	0		0	6		0	0	(1)	0	40	(5)	1
Smith I	1975	2		0	0		0	0		0	0		0	2		0
Smith J	59-63	21		1	2		0	0		0	1		0	24		1
Smith R	55-63	271		176	32		22	0		0	14		10	317		208
Souness G	1971	0		0	0		0	0		0	0	(1)	0	0	(1)	0
Southey P	1979	1		0	0		0	0		0	0		0	1		0
Statham B	87-88	20	(4)	0	0	(1)	0	2		0	0		0	22	(5)	0
Stead M	75-77	14	(1)	0	0		0	0		0	0		0	14	(1)	0
Stevens G	83-89	140	(7)	6	13	(4)	0	19	(2)	0	15		3	187	(13)	9
Stewart P	88-91	126	(5)	28	9		2	23		7	8		0	166	(5)	37
Stimson M	86-88	1	(1)	0	0		0	0		0	0		0	1	(1)	0
Stokes A	52-58	65		40	4		2	0		0	0		0	69		42
Taylor P	76-80	116	(7)	31	8	(3)	2	4	(2)	0	0		0	128	(12)	33
Thomas D	83-86	80	(7)	1	4		0	11	(2)	0	8	(4)	0	103	(13)	1
Thomas M	86-90	136	(21)	6	12		1	28	(1)	1	0		0	176	(22)	8
Thorstvedt E	88-	138	(2)	0	13		0	20		0	6		0	177	(2)	0
Turner A	92-	7	(11)	3	0	(1)	0	0	(2)	1	0		0	7	(14)	4
Tuttle D	90-	10	(3)	0	0		0	3	(1)	0	1		1	14	(4)	1
Van Den Hauwe P	89-	110	(6)	0	7		0	16		0	6		0	139	(6)	0
Venables T	65-68	114	(1)	5	15	(1)	2	6		1	4		1	139	(2)	9
Villa R	78-82	124	(9)	18	21		3	15	(1)	3	8	(1)	1	168	(11)	25
Waddle C	85-88	137	(1)	33	14		5	21		4	0		0	172	(1)	42
Walford S	1975	1	(1)	0	0		0	0		0	0		0	1	(1)	0
Walker I	90-	36		0	0		0	3		0	2		0	41		0
Walsh P	87-91	84	(44)	19	4	(4)	0	9	(7)	2	1	(3)	0	98	(58)	21
Want A	67-71	46	(4)	0	3		0	3		0	0		0	52	(4)	0
Watson K	92-	4	(1)	1	0	(1)	0	1	(1)	1	0		0	5	(3)	2
Webster S	82-83	2	(1)	0	0		0	0		0	0		0	2	(1)	0
Weller K	64-66	19	(2)	1	0		0	0		0	0		0	19	(2)	1
White J	59-63	183		40	19		1	0		0	17		6	219		47
Woolcott R	1969	1		0	0		0	0		0	0		0	1		0
Worley L	1959	1		0	0		0	0		0	0		0	1		0
Yorath T	79-80	44	(4)	1	7		0	7		0	0		0	58	(4)	1
Young W	75-76	54		3	2		0	8		1	0		0	64		4

Dates shown indicate first years of each season. Thus 70-77 means 1970/71 to 1977/78. A single entry indicates one season only, eg 1964 refers to 1964/65.